THE VIRTUAL REPRESENTATION OF THE PAST

Digital Research in the Arts and Humanities

Series Editors
Marilyn Deegan, Lorna Hughes and Harold Short

Digital technologies are becoming more and more important to arts and humanities research and are expanding the horizons of research methods in all aspects of capture, investigation, analysis, modelling, presentation and dissemination. This important series will cover a wide range of arts and humanities disciplines with each volume focusing on a particular area, identifying the ways in which technology impacts specific disciplines. The aim is to provide an authoritative reflection of the 'state of the art' in the application of computing and technology to arts and humanities disciplines. The series will be essential reading for experts in digital humanities and technology issues but will also be of wide interest to all scholars working in humanities and arts research.

Forthcoming titles in the series

Text Editing, Print and the Digital World
Edited by Marilyn Deegan and Kathryn Sutherland
ISBN 978 0 7546 7307 1

Modern Methods for Musicology
Prospects, Proposals and Realities
Edited by Tim Crawford and Lorna Gibson
ISBN 978 0 7546 7302 6

The Virtual Representation of the Past

Edited by

MARK GREENGRASS
University of Sheffield, UK

LORNA HUGHES
King's College London, UK

ASHGATE

Published by
Ashgate Publishing Limited
Wey Court East
Union Road
Farnham
Surrey GU9 7PT
England

Ashgate Publishing Company
Suite 420
101 Cherry Street
Burlington, VT 05401-4405
USA

www.ashgate.com

British Library Cataloguing in Publication Data
Expert Seminar (2006 : Sheffield, England)
    The virtual representation of the past. - (Digital research
    in the arts and humanities)
    1. History - Methodology - Data processing - Congresses
    2. Archaeology - Methodology - Data processing - Congresses
    I. Title II. Greengrass, Mark, 1949- III. Hughes, Lorna M.
    907.2'0285

Library of Congress Cataloging-in-Publication Data
The virtual representation of the past / edited by Mark Greengrass and Lorna Hughes.
        p. cm. -- (Digital research in the arts and humanities)
    These papers were presented at The Expert Seminar, held in Sheffield, England, on 19-21 April 2006.
    Includes bibliographical references and index.
    ISBN 978-0-7546-7288-3
    1. History--Data processing. 2. History--Methodology. I. Greengrass, Mark, 1949- II. Hughes, Lorna M.

    D16.12.V48 2008
    901--dc22

Reprinted 2010   2008014375

ISBN 978 0 7546 7288 3

Mixed Sources
Product group from well-managed
forests and other controlled sources
www.fsc.org Cert no. SA-COC-1565
© 1996 Forest Stewardship Council
FSC

Printed and bound in Great Britain by
MPG Books Ltd, Bodmin, Cornwall.

Contents

List of Figures

List of Tables

List of Plates

Notes on Contributors

David Arnold is the Dean of the Faculty of Management and Information Sciences, and Professor of Computing Science at the University of Brighton. He has worked for over thirty years in the field of Computer Graphics and its applications to Architecture, Engineering, GIS and in recent years Cultural Heritage reconstruction. That has been the focus of his major research and publishing activities, helping to organize about thirty international conferences and workshops, both in the UK and elsewhere. Most recently he was co-chair for VAST2003 (Virtual Reality Archaeology and Cultural Heritage) which was held in November 2003 in Brighton.

Ravish Bhagdev is a member of the Natural Processing Language Research Group at the University of Sheffield. He is currently working on the creation of integrated products and services (IPAS) to bring together different knowledge management systems and applications to build a 'Designer Knowledge Desktop'(see <http://www.3worlds.org/>).

Richard Beacham heads the Visualisation Lab, King's College London. Together with Professor James Packer he directs the 'Pompey Project', a comprehensive investigation of Rome's earliest theatre, with major sponsorship from the AHRC and the US NEH, currently excavating at the site. He leads an AHRC project 'The Body and Masks in Ancient Performance Space' and with Hugh Denard, the 'Making Space' Project, documenting the creation of 3D computer models, which has convened two international symposia and the drafts of 'The London Charter', governing use of 3D visualization in cultural heritage research. Together with Hugh Denard he directs THEATRON 3, an extensive programme of research and development in the Second Life virtual world, sponsored by the Eduserve Foundation. He has been visiting professor at Yale and the University of California, and a Resident Scholar at the Getty Museum, where he oversaw productions of ancient comedy based upon his research. In addition to over fifty scholarly articles, he has published *The Roman Theatre and Its Audience* (Harvard), *Spectacle Entertainments of Early Imperial Rome* (Yale) and translations of Roman Comedies (Methuen). With Hugh Denard he recently completed *Performing Culture: Theatre and Theatricality in Roman Pictorial Arts* (Yale). He is the leading authority on the theatre designer and theoretician, Adolphe Appia, on whom he has published five books, and numerous articles. He is a founding member of the International Workshop for Art and Culture, Hellerau Germany, securing major Getty sponsorship for a programme of architectural restoration of the Appia/Dalcroze Festspielhaus. His German-language book on Appia, *Adolphe Appia: Kunstler und Visionär des Modernen Theaters* (Alexander Verlag) appeared this year.

Anna Bentkowska-Kafel is Associate Director of the Corpus of Romanesque Sculpture in Britain and Ireland (<http://www.crsbi.ac.uk>) and is responsible for the creation and long-term preservation of the project's digital archive. She is also a Research Fellow for the JISC 3D Visualisation in the Arts Network hosted by the Centre for Computing in the Humanities, King's College London. Her research, teaching and publications have been mainly on Early-modern visual culture in Western Europe, with special interest in cosmological and anthropomorphic representations of nature, as well as the use of digital imaging in iconographical analysis and interpretation of paintings. She has an MA in the History of Art (Warsaw), an MA in Computing Applications for the History of Art (London) and a PhD in Digital Media Studies (Southampton).

Caroline Bowden was Research Fellow for the 'Health of the Cecils c1550–c1660' Project at Royal Holloway, University of London. She is now Research Fellow and Project Manager at Queen Mary, University of London on the AHRC funded project 'Who were the Nuns?', a prosographical study of the English convents in exile. She has published a number of papers on women religious and on women's education.

Sam Chapman is a member of the Natural Processing Language Research Group at the University of Sheffield. He is currently working on Web Intelligence Technologies, providing knowledge applications and management (see <http://nlp.shef.ac.uk/wig/>).

Fabio Ciravegna is Professor of Language and Knowledge Technologies at the University of Sheffield and coordinator of the Web Intelligence Technology Laboratory, which brings together text-mining, Human Computer Interaction researchers and Semantic Web specialists. He directs X-Media, a major project addressing the issues of knowledge management across media in complex distributed environments (<http://www.x-media-project.org>). One of the direct outcomes of the expert workshop, from which this volume derives, is his collaboration with Julian Richards on the eArchaeology Project, a major data-mining application, funded by the AHRC and EPSRC.

Paul Cripps is a Teaching Fellow in the department of archaeology at Southampton University, where he teaches the Core Computing and Spatial Technologies modules of the MSc Archaeological Computing courses. He has worked for English Heritage Archaeological Projects, formerly the Centre for Archaeology based at Fort Cumberland, Portsmouth, and has also worked on the Stonehenge and Avebury World Heritage Site GIS and the World Heritage Site GIS User Group.

Vince Gaffney holds the Chair in Landscape Archaeology and Geomatics at the University of Birmingham (UK) and is the Director of the Visual and Spatial Technology Centre (VISTA). His wide-ranging research has included projects in Croatia, Italy, Zimbabwe and the USA, as well as at Stonehenge in Britain. More recent projects include the mapping of the inundated Mesolithic landscapes of the Southern North Sea, internet mapping of the Mundo Maya region to support sustainable tourism and agent-based modelling of the battle of Manzikert. Professor

Gaffney is a member of the Cyrene Archaeological Project and leads the UK team creating 3D and virtual imaging of the remains at Cyrene as well as an extensive programme of geophysical survey exploring the unexcavated and largely unknown areas of the city. Further information at <http://www.iaa.bham.ac.uk/staff/gaffney.htm>.

Ian Gregory is a Senior Lecturer in Digital Humanities at Lancaster University. His PhD was on creating the Great Britain Historical GIS, a system that he designed. Since then he has worked extensively on using GIS in historical research and in the humanities more generally. Since 2000 he has written around a dozen journal articles and two books on this subject, *A Place In History: A Guide to Using GIS in Historical Research* (Oxbow), and *Historical GIS: Technologies, Methodologies and Scholarship* (CUP, co-authored with P.S. Ell). He has been actively raising the profile of GIS in the humanities through his roles in international organizations such as the Social Science History Association, the Electronic Cultural Atlas Initiative and the Royal Geographical Society.

Mark Greengrass is Professor of Early-modern History at the University of Sheffield and an Associate Director of the AHRC ICT Methods Network Programme. His interests in ICT applications to the Humanities began in 1987 when he co-directed the first major project in the UK to produce an electronic facsimile and transcription of a historic archive – resulting in the *Hartlib Papers on CD-ROM* (1994). He currently directs the British Academy John Foxe Project, which is producing a complete 'variorum edition' online of Foxe's Book of Martyrs, a huge and complex text of central importance for understanding the English Reformation.

Catherine Hardman is the Collections Development Manager for the Archaeology Data Service and Project Manager for the OASIS Project in the UK. After leaving the Central Government Civil Service in the 1990s, she studied Archaeology and Heritage Management at postgraduate level before embarking on her archaeological career. She worked for an English Heritage funded project before joining the ADS in 2001. She manages collection services for the ADS, negotiating with depositors and acquiring access to collections.

Tim Hitchcock is Professor of Eighteenth-century History at the University of Hertfordshire. He has published widely on the histories of poverty, gender and sexuality. With Professor Robert Shoemaker of the University of Sheffield he has also helped to create an online and entirely searchable edition of the Old Bailey Sessions Proceedings, 1674 to 1834 (<http://www.oldbaileyonline.org>). With Professor Shoemaker and Clive Emsley of the Open University (and an extensive team of collaborators and researchers), and with support from both the AHRC and the ESRC, he is currently digitizing a further billion words of eighteenth and nineteenth-century manuscript sources, and records of the history of crime. This work will form the basis for a series of projects designed to demonstrate the role of 'pauper agency' in the evolution of modern social institutions.

Lorna Hughes is the Deputy Director of the Centre for e-Research, King's College London. From 2005–2008, she was the Manager of the AHRC ICT Methods Network, also based at King's College London. Before joining the Methods Network, she was Assistant Director for Humanities Computing at New York University. Lorna has written extensively on humanities computing topics, including the book *Digitizing Collections: Strategic Issues for the Information Manager.* She was President of the Association for Computers in Humanities (ACH) from 2004–2008.

Jamie McLaughlin is currently working on a number of web applications in his capacity as Technical Officer at the University of Sheffield's Humanities Research Institute (HRI). These include the successor to the Old Bailey Proceedings Online website. Since joining the HRI in 2002, Jamie has developed online components for around twenty projects including Foxe's Book of Martyrs Variorum Edition and the Armadillo project.

Andrew Prescott was formerly a curator of manuscripts at the British Library, where he was the lead curator in the 'Electronic Beowulf' project and edited the book documenting the British Library's Initiatives for Access programme. After leaving the British Library, he joined the Humanities Research Institute at the University of Sheffield, where he was Director of the pioneering Centre for Research into Freemasonry. He is currently Librarian of the University of Wales Lampeter. His publications include studies of the Peasants' Revolt of 1381 and of the history of the manuscript collections of the British Library.

Julian D. Richards is Professor of Archaeology in the Department of Archaeology, University of York, where he is Director of the Archaeology Data Service and Co-Director of the e-journal Internet Archaeology. His research interests are in the early medieval archaeology of north-western Europe, particularly Anglo-Saxon and Anglo-Scandinavian settlement patterns and funerary rites, and in computer applications in archaeology. He undertook a PhD using computer processing to study the significance of Anglo-Saxon mortuary behaviour and went on to co-author *Data Processing in Archaeology* in 1985, the first textbook dedicated to the use of computers in archaeology. He has gone on to publish widely on computer applications and early medieval archaeology. He has excavated in England at early medieval sites at Wharram Percy, Cottam and Heath Wood, Ingleby.

Donald Spaeth is Senior Lecturer in Historical Computing at the University of Glasgow. He has a long-standing interest in using database software to support historical research and teaching, and has served as Convenor of the Association for History and Computing (UK), Director of the History Courseware Consortium, and Convenor of Glasgow University's M.Litt/Sc in History and Computing. His chapter came out of a project exploring what the physical organization of sources such as early modern English probate records reveals about the thinking of those who prepared them. The project was supported by research leave from the AHRB in 2002.

Manfred Thaller received his PhD (1975) in Modern History from the University in Graz, Austria as well as a Sociology postdoctorate at the Institute for Advanced Studies, Vienna, Austria. Since 1978 he has been a fellow at the Max-Planck-Institut for History, Göttingen. He founded the working group on historical computer science there, and in recent years has been active in all aspects of digital repositories of cultural heritage material. In 1995, he became professor at the University of Bergen, Norway and, from 1997 to 2000, he was founding director of its 'Humanities Information Technology Research Center'. In March 2000, he became the holder of the very first dedicated chair in Humanities Computer Science at the University of Cologne, Germany.

Meg Twycross is Emeritus Professor of English Medieval Studies at Lancaster University. She is Executive Editor of the journal *Medieval English Theatre*, and has published widely on medieval theatre in all its aspects. Her recent work on high-resolution digital manuscript images is casting new light on the origins of the York Mystery Cycle.

Series Preface

The Virtual Representation of the Past is volume 1 of the series *Digital Research in the Arts and Humanities.*

Each of the titles in this series comprises a critical examination of the application of advanced ICT methods in the arts and humanities. That is, the application of formal computationally based methods, in discrete but often interlinked areas of arts and humanities research. Usually developed from Expert Seminars, one of the key activities supported by the Methods Network, these volumes focus on the impact of new technologies in academic research and address issues of fundamental importance to researchers employing advanced methods.

Although generally concerned with particular discipline areas, tools or methods, each title in the series is intended to be broadly accessible to the arts and humanities community as a whole. Individual volumes not only stand alone as guides but collectively form a suite of textbooks reflecting the 'state of the art' in the application of advanced ICT methods within and across arts and humanities disciplines. Each is an important statement of current research at the time of publication, an authoritative voice in the field of digital arts and humanities scholarship.

These publications are the legacy of the AHRC ICT Methods Network and will serve to promote and support the ongoing and increasing recognition of the impact on and vital significance to research of advanced arts and humanities computing methods. The volumes will provide clear evidence of the value of such methods, illustrate methodologies of use and highlight current communities of practice.

Marilyn Deegan, Lorna Hughes, Harold Short
Series Editors
AHRC ICT Methods Network
Centre for Computing in the Humanities
King's College London
February 2008

About the AHRC ICT Methods Network

The aims of the AHRC ICT Methods Network were to promote, support and develop the use of advanced ICT methods in arts and humanities research and to support the cross-disciplinary network of practitioners from institutions around the UK. It was a multi-disciplinary partnership providing a national forum for the exchange and dissemination of expertise in the use of ICT for arts and humanities research. The Methods Network was funded under the AHRC ICT Programme from 2005 to 2008.

The Methods Network Administrative Centre was based at the Centre for Computing in the Humanities (CCH), King's College London. It coordinated and supported all Methods Network activities and publications, as well as developing outreach to, and collaboration with, other centres of excellence in the UK. The Methods Network was co-directed by Harold Short, Director of CCH, and Marilyn Deegan, Director of Research Development, at CCH, in partnership with Associate Directors: Mark Greengrass, University of Sheffield; Sandra Kemp, Royal College of Art; Andrew Wathey, Royal Holloway, University of London; Sheila Anderson, Arts and Humanities Data Service (AHDS) (2006–2008); and Tony McEnery, University of Lancaster (2005–2006).

The project website (<http://www.methodsnetwork.ac.uk>) provides access to all Methods Network materials and outputs. In the final year of the project a community site, 'Digital Arts & Humanities' (http://www.arts-humanities.net>) was initiated as a means to sustain community building and outreach in the field of digital arts and humanities scholarship beyond the Methods Network's funding period.

Acknowledgements

This volume was prepared under the auspices of the AHRC ICT Methods Network. In 2005–2006, a series of Expert Seminars brought together individuals who shared an agenda in the use of advanced ICT methods in research in the arts and humanities. This volume is the result of the Seminar on 'Virtual History and Archaeology' that was held at the Humanities Research Institute, University of Sheffield, on 19–21 April 2006. The success of the Seminar as an event was, in large measure, the result of the willingness of all the 30 participants to cross their disciplinary boundaries and consider the broader issues raised by the representation of the past in digital media. The dialogue that was established was assisted substantially by the reflections of the *rapporteurs* for each of the sessions. The editors therefore owe a particular debt of gratitude to Seamus Ross, Matthew Woollard and Kate Devlin, whose remarks at the time of the Seminar served to enlarge its perspectives, and are incorporated into the introduction and conclusion to the volume. The Seminar would not have been possible without the organization and support of the staff of the Methods Network, in particular Hazel Gardiner, Lorna Gibson, Neil Grindley and Stuart Dunn. It was equally assisted locally by the Secretary to the HRI in Sheffield, Julie Banham, and its technical officer, Jamie McLaughlin. The editors are grateful to the following organizations and individuals for permission to reproduce the images included in the text: British Library, Kevin Kiernan, Oxford University, Duderstadt Municipal Archive, The National Archives, Newport Libraries and Information Service, York City Archives, DIAMM, Historical Methods, Heldref Publications, the Institute of Archaeology and Antiquity, Oxfordshire Records Office, University of Birmingham, Meg Twycross, Her Majesty's Stationery Office, R. Baxter, K. Morrison, Annals of the Association of American Geographers, Taylor and Francis, A.C. Addison, Franco Niccolucci, Archaeolinga and to the European Commission under the EPOCH project (FP6 Network of Excellence). Finally, the editors are grateful to Lydia Horstman, King's College London for her assistance in preparing the volume.

Mark Greengrass and Lorna Hughes
February 2008

Note on the Text

All publications in English are presumed as published in London unless otherwise stated. A glossary of acronyms and terms in capital letters is provided as an appendix.

List of Abbreviations

ACLS	American Council of Learned Societies
ADL	Alexandria Digital Library
ADS	Archaeology Data Service
AHDS	Arts and Humanities Data Service
AHRC	Arts and Humanities Research Council
CAD	Computer-Aided Design
CAQDAS	Computer-Assisted Qualitative Data Analysis Software
CEU	Central Excavation Unit of English Heritage
CIDOC	International Committee for Documentation of the International Council of Museums
CRM	Conceptual Reference Model
CRSBI	*Corpus of Romanesque Sculpture in Britain and Ireland*
dpi	dots per inch
DCMI	Dublin Core Metadata Initiative
DIAMM	Digital Image Archive of Medieval Music
DUA	Department of Urban Archaeology at the Museum of London
ECCO	Eighteenth Century Collections Online
EEBO	Early English Books Online
EPOCH	European Research Network of Excellence in Processing Open Cultural Heritage
EPPT	Edition Production and Presentation Technology
EPSRC	Engineering and Physical Sciences Research Council
ESRI	Environmental Systems Research Institute
GIFF	Graphical Interchange File Format
GIS	Geographic/Geospatial Information System
HER	Historic Environment Record
HLC	Historic Landscape Characterization
HTTP	Hypertext Transfer Protocol
ICOM	International Council of Museums
ICT	Information and Communication Technologies
IR	InfraRed
JPEG	Joint Photographic Experts Group
LEADERS	Linking EAD to Electronically Retrievable Sources
LiDAR	Light Detection and Ranging
MARC	Machine Readable Catalogue
MDA	Museum Documentation Association
METS	Metadata Encoding and Transmission Standard
MICHAEL	Multilingual Inventory of Cultural Heritage in Europe

MIDAS	Monument Inventory Data Standard
NERC	Natural Environment Research Council
OHCO	Ordered Hierarchy of Content Objects
OAI	Open Archives Initiative
ODNB	*Oxford Dictionary of National Biography*
OWL	Web Ontology Language
PDA	Personal Digital Assistant
PDF	Portable Document Format
PGS	Petroleum Geo-Services
QDA	Qualitative Data Analysis
RAE	Research Assessment Exercise
RDF	Resource Description Framework
SLR	Single Lens Reflex
SOAP	Simple Object Access Protocol
SPARQL	SPARQL Protocol and RDF Query Language
SQL	Structured/Query Language
SMR	Sites and Monuments Record
SRIF	Science Research Infrastructure Fund
SVG	Scalable Vector Graphics
TEI	Text Encoding Initiative
TIFF	Tagged Image File Format
TNA	The National Archives
TMT	Thesaurus of Monument Types
UV	UltraViolet
URI	Uniform Resource Identifier
VICODI	Visual Contextualization of Digital Content
VRE	Virtual Research Environment
VSC	Video-Spectral Comparator
W3C	World Wide Web Consortium
WKT	Well Known Text
WSDL	Web Service Description Language
XML	eXtensible Markup Language
XPath	XML Path
XQuery	XML Query
XSLT	eXtensible Stylesheet Language Transformation

Chapter 1

Introduction

Mark Greengrass

This volume is a comparative exercise in representation. The Expert Seminar, from which its papers derive, was held in Sheffield on 19–21 April 2006. It brought together two communities of research practitioners in the humanities – archaeologists and historians. Both are engaged in interpreting the past. Yet, partly because they have traditionally concentrated on different kinds of evidence, they do not often sit round the same table. One of the advantages of applying the advanced methodologies of computer science and informatics to the humanities is that it helps to break down disciplinary boundaries. The two-dozen expert practitioners who came to Sheffield in April 2006 found that they had much to discuss, and to compare.

Computational science and informatics is concerned essentially with representation. Machines can only undertake calculations, handle data, search text or form analogue images if they are represented for them in (ultimately) numeric form. That process of representation involves language and selection – implying culture, thought and choice. Both archaeologists and historians are also confronted by the issue of representation: that of the past. And, when it comes to doing so in computer terms, the distinctiveness of their disciplinary approaches and documentation diminishes before the common problem of how we represent the historic Cartesian coordinates of space, time and place, or (in documentary terms), the material cultural remains of the past, its objects and traces, its texts and images.

For computer scientists, the dominant concern is: can we 'represent' problems sufficiently realistically to provide computational solutions to them? For archaeologists and historians, however, the issue of 'representation' and 'realism' is essentially problematic, as appears throughout this volume. Many historians now understand the past as a rich, confusing and ultimately unknowable landscape.[1] The historical accounts through which we try to reconstruct it are representations, framed by the window and obscured by the glass through which we try to view it. Both the window and the glass stand in the way of any realistic, let alone objective, picture that we are able to make of it. But the picture is, nevertheless, structured, capable of being understood, and full of meaning. And it is constrained in every pixel by the evidential remains of the past. Archaeologists equally see themselves as reconstructing the past into a believable story, necessarily partial and always subject to revision. They had to confront much sooner than historians (over two decades ago) the reality that realistic graphical representations of the past are as

---

1 K. Jenkins, *Re-thinking History* (Routledge, 1991); cf. Richard J. Evans, *In Defence of History* (Granta, 1997).

problematic and conjectural as any other claims to objectivity.[2] In this volume, the issue is not the 'realism' or the 'objectivity' of the representation in question – it is the methodologies, tools and applications of advanced computing to assist us to make sense of the incomplete, contradictory or doctored evidence of the past. They can help us to see the patterns, and put together the pieces of the jigsaw, from the chaotic plethora of information that confronts us about parts of the past. By enabling us to represent (and document) more clearly our own preconceptions to ourselves and others, they help us the better to compare and to understand one another's frames of reference. This volume documents the potential and the challenges, the frustrations and the achievements of trying to do just that.

So the objective of this volume is to evaluate critically the virtual representation of the past through digital media. The challenges that we face are philosophical (how much we can ever represent from the past?), methodological (what are the best ways of representing different perspectives of historic and pre-historic space, time and place?) and technical (how can we apply the latest tools and approaches – often developed in other disciplines – to bear on these problems?). This volume therefore is not just about digital *representation* of spatial and temporal analysis in historical and archaeological data, it is also about the digital *interrogation* of cultural objects, how best to record the various assumptions and circumstances that go into any virtual representation, and about the digital *reinterpretation* of the past through such cultural objects.

These are essentially interdisciplinary questions, something that was emphasized by Kate Devlin, Lorna Hughes, Seamus Ross, and Matthew Woollard, the *rapporteurs* for each of the workshop sessions. It was also a common theme for two of the papers that were presented to the workshop but did not find their way into this volume. In 'Shared Spaces: Library and Archive Metadata, Encoded Documents and Research Needs', Professor Susan Hockey reminded us that both archaeologists and historians rely upon library and archival repositories for a good deal of their structured knowledge of the past, and that their electronic forms of representing that knowledge (notably, the MAchine Readable Catalogue record (or MARC) for librarians, and the Encoded Archival Description (EAD) for archivists) are fundamental. She demonstrated through her analysis of the LEADERS project how these records could be integrated with the sources themselves.[3] Similarly, in 'Encoding and the Scholarly Community', Professor Harold Short underlined the fact that digital editions of historical documents (and, by extension, cultural artefacts)

---

2 D. Spicer, 'Computer Graphics and the Perception of Archaeological Information: Lies, Damned Statistics and … Graphics!', in C.L.N. Ruggles and S.P.Q. Rahtz (eds), *Computer Applications and Quantitative Methods in Archaeology 1987*, BAR International Series 393 (Oxford: Archaeopress, 1988), pp. 187–200; P. Reilly, 'Towards a Virtual Archaeology', in K. Lockyear and S. Rahtz (eds), *Computer Applications and Quantitative Methods in Archaeology 1990*, BAR International Series 565 (Oxford: Archaeopress, 1991), pp. 133–40; and P. Reilly, 'Three-dimensional Modelling and Primary Archaeological Data', in P. Reilly and S. Rahtz (eds), *Archaeology and the Information Age* (Routledge, 1992). The debate about realistic graphics, and attempts to define graphics continues for a further decade in the archaeological literature about ICT applications.

3 <http://www.ucl.ac.uk/leaders-project/> (accessed 8 January 2008).

are fundamentally collaborative, dependent upon a shared understanding and use of encoding systems. It would, indeed, be difficult to find a longer, larger, more internationally based and collaborative humanities project than the Text Encoding Initative (TEI).[4] It celebrated its twentieth anniversary as this volume went to press. Its achievement has been to bring many hundreds of scholars together from across the globe, providing a continuing forum for scholarly debate about the ways in which text is to be 'represented'. A similar initiative for representing the implicit and explicit concepts and relationships used in cultural heritage documentation (the CIDOM-CRM) is now beyond its infancy.[5] These are two fundamental points of departure for this volume. They point us towards how archaeologists and historians need to work more closely to develop digital resources whose functional representation of the past can be shared in the context of more 'global' libraries.

One of the documents circulated to seminar participants was a list of ongoing research projects in history and archaeology that are using advanced ICT Methods. As this information, like much on the internet, quickly dates, the editors have decided that the list not be included in the printed volume, but should instead live on a dedicated website, which will be updated regularly. The reader is therefore encouraged to view the list of projects available at <http://www.arts-humanities.net/publications/virtual_representation_past> as a companion website to the volume. Material on this site will be checked, updated and modified regularly.

4 <http://www.tei-c.org/index.xml> (accessed 8 January 2008).
5 <http://cidoc.ics.forth.gr/> (accessed 29 January 2008).

PART I
THE VIRTUAL REPRESENTATION
OF TEXT

Chapter 2

The Imaging of Historical Documents

Andrew Prescott

'If we look back at what "history and computing" has accomplished, the results are slightly disappointing. They are not disappointing because "computing" failed to do what was expected of it, which was to provide "history" with computerized tools and methodologies that historians could use to expand the possibilities and to improve the quality of their research, but because "historians" failed to acknowledge many of the tools "computing" had come up with'. That is the pessimistic conclusion of Onna Boonstra, Leon Breure and Peter Doorn in an important review of 'historical information science' in 2004.[1] Let us begin by examining it in closer detail in the context of several recent and important projects on the surviving papers of giants in the history of science: Charles Darwin (1809–82), Isaac Newton (1643–1727) and Robert Boyle (1627–91)

Charles Darwin's field notebooks, and particularly those from his epoch-making voyage as naturalist on *HMS Beagle*, provide the fundamental evidence for understanding and tracing the development of his scientific thought. Darwin was insistent on the importance of keeping detailed records of his observations, declaring 'Let the collector's motto be, "Trust nothing to the memory;" for the memory becomes a fickle guardian when one interesting object is succeeded by another still more interesting.'[2] The importance attached by Darwin to his notebooks is evident from the meticulous way in which he kept them, using a sharp pencil to prevent water damage to the text and buying the finest quality notebooks. One of Darwin's notebooks was described by its first editor, Nora Barlow:

> The paper is excellent; and on the inside of the cover is a beautifully engraved little plate, surmounted by an engraved lion and unicorn – 'Velvet Paper Memorandum Book, so prepared as effectually to secure the writing from erasure; with a Metallic Pencil the point of which is not liable to break. The point of the pencil should be kept smoothly scraped flat and in writing it should be held in the manner of a common Pen'.[3]

---

1 Onna Boonstra, Leon Breure and Peter Doorn, *Past, Present and Future of Historical Information Science* (Amsterdam: Netherlands Institute for Scientific Information, Royal Netherlands Academy of Arts and Sciences, 2004), p. 9.

2 Charles Darwin, *Narrative of the Surveying Voyages of His Majesty's Ships Adventure and Beagle between the Years 1826 and 1836 . . .* (Henry Colburn, 1839), p. 598.

3 Cited in the description of Darwin's Beagle Field Notebooks at: <http://darwin-online.org.uk/EditorialIntroductions/Chancellor_fieldNotebooks.html> (all cited URLs were accessed in February 2007 unless otherwise stated).

Apart from their significance as artefacts, the physical make-up of Darwin's notebooks is an important clue to the chronology of Darwin's thought. The use of both pencil and ink, and the different types of ink, are vital evidence for the chronology of the entries in the 'Red Notebook' kept by Darwin after he returned from his voyage on the *Beagle*.[4]

In 2006, to a considerable fanfare in the UK press, the complete works of Darwin, including new transcriptions of his notebooks, were made freely available online by the University of Cambridge.[5] The BBC report on the new resource declared that '[t]he project run by Cambridge University has digitized some 50,000 pages of text and 40,000 images of original publications – all of it searchable. Surfers can even access downloadable audio files to use on MP3 players.'[6] Darwin's great-great-great-grandson was quoted as saying that '[i]t is astonishing to see the notebook that Darwin had in his pocket as he walked around the Galapagos – the scribbled notes that he took as he clambered over the lava'.[7] However, users of Darwin Online wishing to share in this excitement will perhaps be disappointed to find that images of only *one* of the Galapagos notebooks are available. Moreover, they are poor-quality greyscale scans from microfilm, which convey little of the physical character of the original notebook. So it is impossible, for example, to determine from the web image whether the notebook was written in pencil or ink. The directors of Darwin Online explain that the cost of providing high-quality colour scans of the manuscripts was prohibitive. What, however, does this mean? The cost of re-editing the notebooks must have been much greater than that of scanning them, yet these editorial costs were found to be tolerable, unlike those for high-quality facsimiles. In other words, the editors of Darwin Online decided that the provision of an edited text was more important than good-quality images of the original notebooks.

A similar outlook is evident from another large collection of the writings of a major scientist being made available online – the project based at Imperial College London, currently producing an online edition of the works of Sir Isaac Newton.[8] Like the Darwin project, the Newton Archive seeks to assemble all the known writings of Newton in order 'to grasp the organic unity of Newton's writing by garnering all his astonishingly diverse productions into a single, freely accessible electronic edition'.[9] Like Darwin Online, the Newton Archive has given priority to the preparation of new transcripts. While the Newton project aspires eventually also to make available digital images of the manuscripts, at present only a very limited selection of images is accessible.[10] By contrast, the Boyle Project based at Birkbeck

---

4 Discussed in S. Herbert, 'The Red Notebook of Charles Darwin', *Bulletin of the British Museum (Natural History) Historical Series,* 7/24 (1980): 5–19.

5 <http://darwin-online.org.uk/>.

6 <http://news.bbc.co.uk/1/hi/sci/tech/6064364.stm>.

7 Ibid.

8 <http://www.newtonproject.ic.ac.uk/>.

9 <http://www.newtonproject.ic.ac.uk/prism.php?id=26>.

10 At the time of writing (February 2007), the only images of Newton manuscripts unique to the Newton Archive are of the following manuscripts: ASC MS. N47 HER in the James White Library, Andrews University, Berrien Springs, Michigan and Kings College Cambridge, Keynes MSS. 3, 6, 7, 9, 10 and 11 (all accessible from <http://www.newtonproject.ic.ac.uk/

College London offers a complete set of high-quality colour images of the most important papers relating to Robert Boyle in the archives of the Royal Society.[11] Moreover, the related Boyle Work Diaries Project at the Centre for Editing Lives and Letters at Queen Mary University of London has produced a complete edition of British Library, Additional MS. 4293 with a facing colour digital facsimile of the manuscript.[12] However, in both these instances, the web version of the images has unfortunately been scaled down in such a way that, while the text can be read in the manuscript, any closer examination of complex or difficult readings is impossible, even when the image is saved and viewed separately. This suggests that, for the editors of these projects, the images of the manuscripts are seen primarily as didactic tools. Their underlying assumption appears to be that researchers will chiefly be interested in the searchable, edited text. This is apparently confirmed by the way in which the search facility for the Boyle work diaries links not to a view of the text and image, but rather to the edited text only.

These projects are part of a more widespread phenomenon. The most common treatment of images of manuscripts within electronic editions of historical papers has been as an 'added extra' rather than as an 'integral component' of the research resource provided by the edition. We find it reflected elsewhere. So, while the Thomas Jefferson Digital Archive at the University of Virginia contains transcripts of over 1,500 letters by Jefferson, digital images are provided for only a small selection of them.[13] The enormous electronic edition of the *Proceedings of the Old Bailey London* from 1674 to 1834 includes images of each of the contemporary printed reports of these trials, but again these are low-quality black and white scans, generated from microfilm and in PDF format. They are inherently subsidiary to the main edited text.[14] Even archives providing commercial copies of images of historical documents tend to assume that users will be satisfied with greyscale scans from microfilm. So, for example, the Documents Online service of The National Archives (TNA) is designed to provide images of probate copies of wills in greyscale PDF format apparently taken from microfilm.[15] Collections of high-quality colour images of historical records tend mostly to be provided not as part of online scholarly editions but rather as part of packages provided by libraries and archives chiefly for educational and

---

prism.php?id=44>). The site also holds images of Keynes's correspondence about the purchase of his Newton manuscripts: <http://www.newtonproject.ic.ac.uk/prism.php?id=19>. There are links to images of Newton manuscripts in the related Chymistry of Isaac Newton project: <http://webapp1.dlib.indiana.edu/newton/index.jsp>. It should be noted that images on the Chymistry of Isaac Newton website are also greyscale scans, apparently from microfilm. Links are also provided to images of material in the Burndy Library, but at the time of writing these are temporarily unavailable. I am grateful to Dr John Young of the Newton project for providing information on the extent of manuscript images within the archive.

11 <http://www.bbk.ac.uk/boyle/>.
12 <http://www.livesandletters.ac.uk/wd/>.
13 <http://etext.virginia.edu/jefferson/>.
14 <http://www.oldbaileyonline.org/>.
15 <http://www.nationalarchives.gov.uk/documentsonline/>. Other material provided by this service, such as the indexes of campaign medals in World War I and World War II, is also made available only in greyscale scan from microfilm.

general public use, such as the British Library's Collect Britain website[16] or the Staffordshire Past Track website of the Staffordshire Archives Service.[17] Valuable though these sites are, material is rarely presented in such a form as to be useful for research purposes.

By contrast with historians, literary scholars preparing electronic editions have placed great emphasis on the provision of high-quality colour digital images of key manuscripts. Kevin Kiernan's Electronic Beowulf, for example, includes large colour images of the early eleventh-century manuscript of *Beowulf*, together with an enormous number of scans taken under special lighting conditions and images of early transcripts and collations made before the restoration of the original manuscript (see Plate 1).[18]

An edition of *Beowulf* by Kiernan is included, but this is just one element in a complex digital archive, and the formal edition is by no means the most prominent component. The CD of the Hengwrt Manuscript of Chaucer's *Canterbury Tales* edited by Estelle Stubbs likewise includes colour images of the manuscript which, when magnified, reveal details which cannot easily be seen with the naked eye.[19] The various CDs produced by the Piers Plowman Electronic Archive also provide full-colour digital facsimiles of key manuscripts of Langland's poem.[20] The need for access to high-quality digital facsimiles of literary manuscripts is not restricted to medieval texts. Emily Dickinson never formally published her poems, and for this reason the way in which she laid out her poetry in her notebooks is of great significance. The Emily Dickinson Archive therefore includes digital images of one of her notebooks, and aspires to create a complete image archive of Dickinson manuscripts.[21] Similarly, the Wilfred Owen Archive includes many very high-quality colour images of the poet's manuscripts, which vividly illustrate the process of composition (see Plate 2).[22]

In these early stages of the development of digitally aided scholarship, this disparity of practice between historians and literary scholars is striking. It apparently reflects a profoundly different view as to how texts should be used and explored. Historians seem to be chiefly interested in making available large quantities of text and in quickly recovering particular pieces of information. Literary scholars are more concerned with the detailed exploration of the genesis of texts and in assembling all the available evidence for this. However, these approaches need not be mutually exclusive. Manfred Thaller, who for nearly thirty years has been the outstanding visionary in historical information science, and who has made some of the most penetrating analyses of the ways in which historians might use digital images, pointed out a decade ago that:

---

16 <http://www.collectbritain.co.uk/>.
17 <http://www.staffspasttrack.org.uk/>.
18 <http://www.uky.edu/~kiernan/eBeowulf/guide.htm>.
19 <http://www.llgc.org.uk/drych/drych_s007.htm>.
20 <http://jefferson.village.virginia.edu/seenet/piers/>.
21 <http://www.emilydickinson.org/>.
22 <http://www.hcu.ox.ac.uk/jtap/>.

A change in the colour of the ink a given person uses in an official correspondence of the nineteenth century could be an indication of the original supply of ink having dried up; or of a considerable rise of the author within the bureaucratic ranks. Let us just emphasize for non-historians, that the second example is all but artificial: indeed the different colours of comments to drafts for diplomatic documents are in the nineteenth century quite often the only identifying mark of which diplomatic agent added which opinion.[23]

Likewise, J. Burt and T.B. James have described how the appearance and alteration of entries in a census enumerator's book can provide important historical information:[24]

The refusal of a young woman to reply to the question on occupation in the 1881 census for Winchester, coupled with the comments of the enumerator, whose definition of her occupation as 'on the town' (implying prostitution) provides an important glimpse behind the curtain of the surviving sources – the enumerators' book, and towards an understanding of the process through which the original census schedules (which have not survived) were transformed into the documents we have today. Conversely, a two-line entry in the census which reads 'Assistant Classical Master/BA Trinity College Dublin' which is reduced by the editorial pen to 'Prof' helps the researcher to grasp some of the smoothing out process of categorisation which went to contribute to census statistics overall.

Despite these salutary examples, historians remain reluctant, when it comes to constructing digital editions, to give priority to the provision of images of the original documents. The recent CD-ROM of the medieval Parliament Rolls, for example, surprisingly only includes sample images of the records, despite the fact that scribal practice in compiling the original document was considered sufficiently important for the details to be carefully noted in the edition itself.[25] A contrasting approach is that of the *Calendar of Fine Rolls Project* at King's College London, where digital images of the original record are provided and the only searchable component is a summary English calendar.[26] The difference between these two publications suggests that there is still considerable uncertainty as to how digital images can most effectively be used in editions of historical documents.

The cost of making available the large quantities of information demanded by historians has always been an important factor in determining the form of publication of historical records. In his guide to *Editing Records for Publication* published (before electronic techniques were widely available) in 1977,[27] Roy Hunnisett, one of the most distinguished British records scholars, argued that in view of the great cost of printing full transcripts of modern historical documents, most post-1200 records should be published only in calendar form unless there are exceptional reasons otherwise.

---

23 Manfred Thaller, 'Text as a Data Type', paper presented at ALLC-ACH 1996. Available online at <http://gandalf.aksis.uib.no/allc-ach96/Panels/Thaller/thaller2.html>.

24 J. Burt and T.B. James, 'Source-oriented Data Processing: The Triumph of the Micro over the Macro?', *History and Computing*, 8/3 (1996): 160–68.

25 <http://www.sd-editions.com/PROME/>.

26 <http://www.finerollshenry3.org.uk/home.html>.

27 R.F. Hunnisett, *Editing Records for Publication*, Archive and the User, 4 (British Records Association, 1977).

Hunnisett's advice reflected the limitations of print technology and is arguably no longer valid in a digital environment. However, the cost of providing digital images of full runs of administrative records is also likewise often cited as a reason for preferring edited texts. Manfred Thaller has argued that this is a false position and in his Duderstadt Project demonstrated how, by very precise control of production techniques, it is possible to digitize the entire archive of a city before 1600 at a very low unit cost.[28] The Duderstadt electronic archive comprises over 80,000 images (see Plate 3). These are mostly greyscale images, but Thaller has gone on to show how similar methods can be used cost effectively to produce colour images of decorated medieval manuscripts in the *Codices Electronici Ecclesiae Colonensis*, which already contains complete digital facsimiles of over 300 medieval manuscripts. When completed, it will present the entire manuscript library of a medieval cathedral.[29] In 2001, Thaller commented on the issues of cost that:[30]

> The creation of digital collections does not *have* to be particularly expensive anymore. One of the more spectacular technical developments in recent years has been the drop in the pricing of digital cameras, where the resolution achievable by a $1,000 camera has been climbing sharply. At the other end, cameras like the 4096 x 4096 pixel camera offered by Kodak, with an observed workflow of ca. 5–10 seconds per exposure, are today still in the six-digit price range. With an emerging mass market of digital hobby photographers, it seems to be a safe bet that high-speed digital cameras at a professional resolution will become achievable for routine projects in less than ten, presumably within the next five years. This means that with 2,000 exposures per campaign day – being a serious barrier for quite some time – 1,000,000 page digitization projects will be possible with a limited budget and over a two-year or 500-day time frame.

Thaller's predictions as to the cost of digital cameras proved very accurate, but the large-scale digitization projects he anticipated are still not very commonplace. This suggests that the barriers to the more widespread use of high-quality digital images in historical editions are not simply those of cost, copyright or the issues associated with access to and handling of original materials. The difficulties are more profound, and are perhaps connected with the way in which historians make use of documentary materials. This leads us back to other issues which were identified as 'problematic' in 'historical information science' in Boonstra et al.'s 2004 article.[31]

The authors delineate a situation in which digital technologies have had a limited impact on historical practice because historians see their primary function as identifying, analysing and debating changes in society over periods of time. In this context, the exploration of archival materials is seen to a large extent as an activity which is ancillary and preparatory to the true business of the historian, namely debating the nature of past societies. Since much work on the use of digital technologies in history is concerned with representing and improving access to

---

28 <http://www.archive.geschichte.mpg.de/duderstadt/dud-e.htm>.

29 <http://www.ceec.uni-koeln.de/>.

30 Manfred Thaller, 'From Digitized to the Digital Library', *D-Lib Magazine*, 7/2 (February 2001). Available online at <http://www.dlib.org/dlib/february01/thaller/02thaller.html>.

31 Boonstra et al., *Past, Present and Future of Historical Information Science*.

source materials, historical computing is consequently also seen as an ancillary skill. Charles Harvey has argued, similarly, that a form of historical computing which focuses on how textual sources were represented in electronic form would always be marginal to the main historical profession.[32] In Harvey's view, true historical computing should address wider questions in the methodology of the reconstruction of societies in time, a vision which is only just beginning to become a realistic prospect. Harvey's underlying concern – that historical computing as it has been most commonly defined in the past thirty years risks becoming marginalized from mainstream historical research – seems to have been largely realized.

The way in which electronic resources for the study of history have been developed and used suggests that historians are primarily interested in rapidly assembling large quantities of factual (and increasingly statistical) information to test the validity of preconceptions of the nature of past societies. The way in which these historical texts operate and were put together is of concern only insofar as it challenges these preconceptions. This concern rapidly to assemble information doubtless explains the preoccupation of historians with databases and their more limited interest in automated text handling although, as other essays in this volume describe, this is shifting as the use of XML becomes more widespread. Historians too often view their textual sources in a positivistic fashion, as quarries of raw factual material.

Such a view of historical research can be seen as representing a paradigm particularly appropriate to the study of more modern periods of history. It overlooks the fact that there is a long and distinguished tradition of historical research in Britain which has been less concerned with the reconstruction of past societies and more interested in how we know about the past, and in exploring the limitations, failures and deceptions of the documentary sources on which historians rely. This is a tradition closely associated with medieval studies, and is represented by such distinguished scholars of the historical record as V.H. Galbraith, Charles Johnson and Roy Hunnisett himself. The distinction can perhaps be seen by comparing the work of Barbara Hanawalt and Hunnisett on medieval coroners' records. Hanawalt uses information in coroners' inquests to undertake direct reconstructions of many aspects of everyday life in the medieval period.[33] By contrast, Hunnisett exposes the complex processes by which the information in returns by coroners' juries was assembled and emphasizes that much of the detail in it is fictitious. Hunnisett engages profoundly with the textuality of the archive and ultimately leaves one uncertain how far archival materials can be used with any confidence to reconstruct the past.[34] For a scholar such as Hunnisett, the interest is more in how the archive operates and less in pursuing the chimera of past societies.

---

32 See, for example, Charles Harvey and John Press, *Databases in Historical Research: Theory, Methods and Application* (Macmillan, 1996), esp. ch. 1.

33 B. Hanawalt, 'Violent Death in Fourteenth- and Early Fifteenth-century England', *Comparative Studies in Society and History*, 18 (1976): 297–320, or, more recently, 'The Voices and Audiences of Social History Records', *Social Science History*, 15 (1991): 159–75.

34 Apart from Hunnisett's indispensable monograph, *The Medieval Coroner* (Cambridge: Cambridge University Press, 1961), see also 'The Reliability of Inquisitions as Historical Evidence', in D.A. Bullough and R.L. Storey (eds), *The Study of Medieval Records: Essays in Honour of Kathleen Major* (Oxford: Oxford University Press, 1971), pp. 206–35.

The way in which many historical records are presented in electronic form, with the assumption that geographical and statistical presentations can readily be generated from the electronic resource, suggests that many historians have still not broken away from the complacent assumptions of their Victorian forebears that administrative records are somehow more inherently trustworthy than other texts, no matter how many warnings we have recently been given by 'dodgy dossiers' and fabricated police evidence. Yet for a historian in the tradition of Galbraith or Hunnisett, the way in which a 'dodgy dossier' might be compiled and the influence it might have are fascinating issues, connecting to themes which reach back through the archives to Domesday Book and beyond. As Galbraith, whose work epitomizes this tradition, puts it: 'administrative records, no less than the literary sources, are generally compiled from other documents, often unknown to us, and they rarely tell the whole truth'.[35] In Galbraith's view, administrative documents are as much artificial constructs as literary texts and are as prone to the same inherent deceptions as all textual communication. Galbraith's vision of a history in which our concern is not to pursue the reconstruction of the past but rather to engage in an open-ended dialogue with the textuality of the past is inherently a relativistic one: 'The past itself is dead, and the books we write tombs of learning, except insofar as they live in the consciousness of their readers. So conceived, we travel pleasantly, but by the nature of things we never arrive.'[36]

In a world where knowledge is becoming increasingly 'google-ized', there is a serious risk that information simply becomes a commodity which is consumed, and that many of the critical skills in handling information which underpin much of humanities scholarship will vanish. It would be ironical if historians, by constructing electronic resources in which textual sources are treated as relatively unproblematic in structure, actually hastened this process of 'google-ization'. One way in which the complexity of texts can be effectively conveyed in electronic editions is through the inclusion wherever possible of digital images of the records, scanned in colour and at a sufficiently high resolution to allow issues connected with the genesis of the text to be explored by the user. Galbraith dreamed of a new type of history, which would be an archivist's history:[37]

> To him [the archivist], the past presents itself as a vast collection of 'original documents'
> . . . . To name a century to him is to call up a mental picture of the relevant records,
> the progress of history appearing to him as a slow pageant of slowly changing records,
> marked from time to time by the occasional disappearance of one class and the gradual
> emergence of another.

This is a vision of a history which is less concerned with the incestuous and self-serving study of historiography, is far more focused on text and closer in its intellectual approach to the study of literature. To quote Galbraith once more:

---

35 V.H. Galbraith, *Introduction to the Study of History* (C.A. Watts, 1964), p. 13.

36 *The Historian's Workshop*, ed. L.P. Curtius (New York: Knopf, 1970), p. 7; reprinted in *Kings and Chroniclers: Essays in English Medieval History* (Hambledon Press, 1982)

37 *Studies in the Public Records* (Thomas Nelson, 1948), p. 7.

History is once more consciously, almost self-consciously, allying itself with literature . .
. .What matters in the long run is not so much what we write about history now, or what
others have written, as the original sources themselves. They are an inexhaustible and an
invaluable inheritance.[38]

Digital editions which incorporate digital images of historical records have the
potential to create something akin to Galbraith's vision of an archivist's history.
Images of documents, for example, can convey a sense of the process by which the
information in the record was assembled in a way that it is impossible to do in a
transcribed edition. As Galbraith emphasized, historical documents of all kinds are
complex montages of different types of information, with many different layers.
Domesday Book, for example, is no original document, but a condensed summary
of a complicated series of semi-judicial proceedings, and, moreover, full of errors.
Most records – from Acts of Parliament to balance sheets of public companies – have
some sort of bias of their own, and seek to conceal the truth or part of it.[39]

Disentangling these levels of information within the record is a difficult process and
one in which visual clues are often very important. For this reason, digital images are
an indispensable tool in investigating further the genesis and structure of the record.
To illustrate this fundamental point further, we turn to some extended examples from
the records of the judicial proceedings arising from the Peasants' Revolt in England
of 1381 and, in order to do so, some brief historical contextualization is necessary.
Following the slaying of the rebel leader Wat Tyler at Smithfield and the collapse
of the rebellion which had overwhelmed much of southern England in June 1381, a
series of commissions were issued to 'chastise and punish' the insurgents.[40] These
form part of a series of legal records relating to the revolt which enumerate thousands
of insurgents and provide details of local disturbances throughout the affected
areas. On the face of it, the Peasants' Revolt is one of the best documented events
of its kind in the Middle Ages. But the legal proceedings against the rebels were
extensively affected by false litigation, as claimants took advantage of the disturbed
situation and the extra-judicial proceedings against the rebels to settle a variety of
old scores. Men described in indictments as leaders of the revolt submitted petitions
to the crown protesting their innocence, insisting that the allegations against them
were brought by their enemies, claims which were accepted by the crown.[41] In such
a context, it is vital to know how the accusations against individuals in the judicial
proceedings were pieced together.

---

38 Galbraith, *Introduction to the Study of History*, pp. 75, 79–80.

39 Ibid., p. 13.

40 For general background on the following, see A.J. Prescott, 'The Judicial Records of
the Rising of 1381', unpublished Ph.D. thesis, University of London (1984); 'Writing about
Rebellion: Using the Records of the Peasants' Revolt of 1381', *History Workshop Journal*, 45
(1998): 1–27; and '"The Hand of God": the Suppression of the Peasants' Revolt of 1381', in
N. Morgan (ed.), *Prophecy, Apocalypse and the Day of Doom*, Harlaxton Medieval Studies,
12 (Donington: Shaun Tyas, 2004), pp. 317–41.

41 E.g., The National Archives (henceforth, TNA), SC 8/262/13099, a petition by John
Creek al. Bettes of Wymondham, protesting that the allegations of insurgency against him were
false. On the accusations against Creek, see further Prescott, '"The Hand of God"', n. 6.

Much of our information about local incidents in Kent during the revolt comes from the records of a commission comprising the Earl of Kent, John Middleton and Thomas Trevet which heard cases against participants in the rising at sessions in the county during July 1381. Some of the accusations collected by this commission are preserved in two files in The National Archives, one containing indictments relating to East Kent[42] and the other covering West Kent.[43] Digital images of the West Kent file reveal aspects of the commission's procedure which are not apparent from the printed edition of this record published by Powell and Trevelyan in 1899. The way in which the material is presented in Powell and Trevelyan's edition might lead the unwary user to suppose that the accusations were fairly straightforward reports of information presented by local juries. The records of the commission's work were kept by at least two clerks, one of whom apparently had a supervisory role. These clerks shaped and manipulated the information presented in the indictments, apparently undertaking (presumably with the commissioners) detailed investigations into what had gone on in Kent during the revolt.

The active character of the inquiries undertaken by the commission is apparent from odd working notes preserved in the records, such as a small scrap of vellum on which one of the clerks has noted that 'Robertus Man cognovit quod cepit episcopum per totam Cantuariam apud la Tour in Schep' ['Robert Man [who] confessed that he held captive the [arch]bishop of [all] Canterbury in the Tower in Sheppey']. (See Plate 4).[44]

This is apparently an aide-mémoire that Robert Man, who confessed to taking part in the seizure of the Archbishop of Canterbury at the Tower of London, was in Sheppey. The words 'totam Cantuariam' are obscured by an accidental inkblot but, as Powell pointed out, they were apparently struck through by the clerk, presumably because this was not the correct version of the archbishop's title. The interlineation of the word 'la' also suggests that the clerk was struggling to get a correct verbal form for the note of the offence, presumably with a view to eventually working up the final indictment. The informal character of this note is confirmed by the dorse on which is a reminder to investigate John Gylot of Dartford and another incomplete note (see Plate 5).[45] This scrap of vellum was apparently one of many such rough notes made in the course of the work of the commission as it sought out rebels in Kent

Other evidence of the process by which the information in this file was pieced together is a list headed 'Tenentes abbatissae de Mallyng' ['Tenants of the Abbess of Malling] (see Plate 6).[46] The list comprises more than thirty names. The majority have been struck through. The men whose names were not deleted were afterwards

---

42 TNA, JUST 1/400, printed in translation by W. Flaherty, 'The Great Rebellion in Kent of 1381 illustrated from the Public Records', *Archaeologia Cantiana*, 3 (1890): 71–96.

43 TNA, KB 9/43, printed in an abridged version in E. Powell and G. M. Trevelyan, *The Peasants' Rising and the Lollards* (Cambridge: Cambridge University Press, 1899), pp. 3–12.

44 TNA, KB 9/43 m. 9.

45 TNA, KB 9/43 m. 9d. This note is omitted in Powell and Trevelyan's edition.

46 TNA, KB 9/43 m. 14. This membrane is noted by Powell and Trevelyan, but the list of names is not printed by them.

indicted by a presenting jury from the Hundred of Larkfield for coercing the abbess into giving them a charter releasing them from labour services. Moreover, the last five names in the list were added separately by the supervising clerk. This suggests that the tenants of the Abbess of Malling were systematically interrogated by the commissioners or their clerks as to which of them had been involved in the revolt. The addition of the last five names indicates that there may have been more than one such examination. The preparation of this list of names was evidently only a first stage in assembling information about the insurgents. The indictment from Larkfield Hundred bears clear traces that information was still being gathered while the indictment was being compiled (see Plate 7).[47] For example, details of goods seized by insurgents were inserted as an interlineation, presumably as additional information came to hand. The names of some of the tenants accused of attacking the Abbess of Malling were also inserted later, presumably as a result of the second interrogation of the tenants. The final indictment against John Leg of Birling also seems only to have been squeezed in at a late stage.

So the information in these indictments was compiled as the result of a complex iterative process in which the commissioners and their clerks took an active role. Much of the evidence for this process, and thus the status of the information in the indictments, depends on visual clues which are difficult adequately to convey through a conventional edited transcript. Further illustrations of this process can be found in another set of proceedings against the insurgents, this time from East Anglia.

The discovery and publication by André Reville and Edgar Powell of some records of proceedings against rebels in Norfolk and Suffolk by the commission of William Ufford, Earl of Suffolk and others helped make historians more aware of the great extent and violence of the disturbances in East Anglia in 1381.[48] However, the records of Ufford's commission are complex in structure. The earl died in 1382 and after his death a writ dated 13 May 1382 was sent to his executors summoning to chancery all records in their possession relating to the commission against the rebels.[49] The reason why the records were summoned to Westminster is not clear. Possibly it was related to process arising from pardons being granted to the rebels. It may also have reflected concern that the powerful commissions issued after the revolt were getting out of control. Whatever the reason, it is only thanks to the issue of this writ that this roll and file, the most detailed source of information about the rising in Norfolk and Suffolk, survives. Without it, the records would have vanished completely, as happened with the records of other commissions relating to the revolt in, say, the north of England. The commission to Ufford and the others was not recorded on the patent rolls, but is described in the writ requesting the records as a commission to 'chastise and punish' the rebels. We know from other surviving commissions that those authorized to chastise and punish the rebels had very sweeping powers. They could take proceedings against the rebels both according to the law of England and following their discretion. This could (and in places such as Essex did) include military action against the insurgents. Arguably, Ufford and his

47 TNA, KB 9/43 m. 15.

48 TNA, KB 9/166/1.

49 TNA, KB 9/166/1 m.1.

fellows were not obliged by the terms of their commission to keep records, but they evidently did, and very carefully so.

On the back of the writ requesting the commission records is a return made by a clerk on behalf of Sir Roger de Boys saying that he was sending all the documents relating to the commission, but that those relating to the liberty of St Edmund were held by Thomas Morreaux, another member of the commission. However, the clerk helpfully sent to chancery a list of those named in the indictments held by Morreaux.[50] The question arises how the clerk had access to this information. Did he check through the documents held by Morreaux, or did he have his own set of notes? In this list, the clerk pays particular attention to those who participated in one of the most notorious incidents in the revolt, the killing of John Cavendish, the Chief Justice, giving brief summaries of the allegations against each of these individuals (see Plate 8).

Those involved in Cavendish's death were excluded from the general pardon, which is presumably why this extra information was provided. Again the question arises of where the clerk compiling this list obtained this information. The corrections in the list suggest that the clerk was indeed working from some other form of documentation. For example, he noted that Katherine Gamen released a boat so that Cavendish could not escape death. He subsequently added the words 'from the land' after boat, as if he was uncertain whether his summary was clear and wished to make it more emphatic. The list of those named in the indictments held by Morreaux emphasizes again the point that records are often compilations of other records, now lost. Moreover, this list is mysterious because it could not have formed the basis for formal proceedings in a court like King's Bench.

As in West Kent, the indictments heard by Ufford's commission bear clear traces of their origin in an iterative process of interrogation of the presenting jurors. This can be seen, for example, in an indictment by the jurors of Hartismere Hundred in Suffolk (see Plate 9).[51]

The first item in this indictment states that 'The jurors of Hartismere say that James of Bedingfield was chief leader of a company of the commons which robbed Edmund of Lakingheath of his goods and chattels worth 40s. at Stoke, which goods were afterwards restored to Edmund.' As with the Kentish indictment, at first sight this seems to be highly circumstantial historical evidence, made by local men within a month of the rising, but its words are a long way from any ever uttered by any jurors. The forms used in an indictment followed strict legal formulae. For example, the value of the goods stolen was critical. Thefts were only punishable by death if the goods stolen were worth more than twelve pence. In the case of this indictment, an image shows clearly that the value of the goods stolen was only established at a late stage in the interrogation of the jury, and the value (40s) has been inserted by the clerk in a gap specially left for the purpose.

Nor were the juries the 'twelve good men and true' of popular imagination. Attached to each indictment is a *panellum* listing potential jurors. On the panel, one of the clerks associated with the commission has carefully selected who would

---

50 TNA, KB 9/166/1 m. 2.
51 TNA, KB 9/166/1 m. 5.

be a suitable juror, marking those who were sworn and striking through those who were apparently not suitable. In an empanelment of a jury from Mutford Hundred in Suffolk, one juror has been sworn and then his name struck through by the clerk who swore in the jurors (see Plate 10).[52]

Another name has been added late to the list of jurors, but nevertheless sworn, while a third was sworn, then removed from the jury and finally sworn again. In the case of Ufford's commission, it seems that particular care was taken to ensure that the jurors contained the best representatives of local society, by making them swear allegiance and even give a recognisance of forty pounds each for the faithful performance of their duties.[53]

The way in which the clerks attached to the commission were the key figures in determining the wording and final form of the indictments is particularly apparent from the way in which the issue of treason was treated. Curiously, it was not clear from existing legislation that popular rebellion of this kind was indeed treason, and in the indictments various textual strategies were used to try to establish the treasonable status of the rebels.[54] These included the highlighting of certain actions (such as the use of banners) or the use of phrases such as 'in a warlike manner and against the dignity of the crown of the lord king'. Particular clerks can be seen preferring particular phrases. In another example, uncertainty as to the treasonable status of the offence seems to have continued until the very last moment, and the word 'produciose' (treasonably) has been inserted by the clerk in a gap (see Plate 11).[55]

Evidence of the way in which the indictments were the result of an iterative process, in which judge or clerks interrogated the presenting jury can be found throughout this set of documents. In another example, which describes the murder of a justice of the peace near Ipswich during the revolt, the date in the indictment has been altered by another scribe.[56] When was this done and why? The answer is not immediately obvious, but clearly it has considerable importance in appraising the evidential value of this indictment. Moreover, the answer to this question will affect our view of the entire group of documents, since the correction is made to an indictment in the hand of the scribe responsible for most of the Suffolk indictments. All these features of these documents are not immediately evident from an edited transcript but are given immediate prominence by images.

One of the most widely discussed indictments relating to the revolt in East Anglia alleges that Thomas Sampson of Ipswich led 'the great society of Suffolk' (see Plate 12).[57] There has been extensive discussion as to whether this can be taken as an indication that there was a central organizing body controlling the insurgents. In all this discussion there has not been as far as I am aware any mention of the fact that this indictment again contains later amendments by another clerk. It looks as if this was done because the indictment was felt to be deficient in form – it lacked, for example,

---

52 TNA, KB 9/166/1 m. 40.
53 E.g. TNA, KB 9/166/1 m. 25.
54 Discussed further in Prescott, 'Judicial Records'.
55 TNA, KB 9/166/1 m. 27.
56 TNA, KB 9/166/1 m. 18.
57 TNA, KB 9/166/1 m. 31.

a verb and another clerk has duly added 'rose' at an appropriate point. The form of date given is also deficient. This tends to suggest that the clerk responsible for the original indictment, whose hand does not appear very much in the commission records, was struggling with the correct form of the indictment, which may perhaps explain why he plumped for the unusual reference to 'the great society'. If images of the indictment against Sampson had been available to historians, perhaps their lengthy discussion of whether or not 'the great society' actually existed would have been rendered otiose.

It is by no means surprising to find that the information about the revolt was gradually pieced together in this way. More surprising is that historians using these records have been so willing to accept this information at face value and have shown little interest in the sources of the information on which they rely. The gradual assembly by administrators of the complex layers of information in historical documents is a feature of many records from the time of Domesday Book onwards. To cite another example from the 1380s, Jan Gerchow has shown in a brilliant study how the various return of the regulations of local guilds made in 1389 are a mixture of oral declarations made in chancery at Westminster, returns written by officials of the guilds themselves and returns compiled by local writing offices, often using the same template for different guilds.[58] In attempting to differentiate these various records, images are essential for comparing the scribal practice in the hundreds of surviving returns.

Close examination of records such as these brings home forcefully how we still have very little information about how the documents on which so much of our history depends were put together. In better understanding the evidential character and textuality of our 'primary sources', digital images can make a fundamental contribution and should be regarded as an indispensable component of future online editions. This implies the development of an approach to electronic editing which puts the digital image more at the heart of the edition and gives less priority to the database or transcribed text. Here much can be learnt from literary scholars. A fascinating vision of an image-based edition is provided by the Edition Production and Presentation Technology (EPPT), which is being developed by Kevin Kiernan and Emil Iacob.[59] This suite of generic editing tools was developed from concepts first worked out in editing very badly damaged Old English manuscripts but its use with any documentary materials is currently being demonstrated in trials with many independent projects.[60] EPPT comprises a range of innovative editing tools, but here we shall briefly allude to features which are relevant to the particular issues discussed here in respect of the Peasants' Revolt records. Its potential for dealing with a wide range of other materials is, however, evident.

First, the relationship between the clerks who produced the various records in 1381 is mysterious, and we can only start to understand it if we can compare and

---

58 Jan Gerchow, 'Gilds and Fourteenth-century Bureaucracy: The Case of 1388–9', *Nottingham Medieval Studies*, 40 (1996): 109–48.

59 <http://www.eppt.org>; <http://beowulf.engl.uky.edu/~kiernan/eBoethius/edit.htm#remodelling>.

60 <http://www.eppt.org/eppt-trial/EPPT-TrialProjects.htm>.

manipulate images of the large number of membranes which constitute an individual record. In particular, we need to be able to link the transcribed texts, duly tagged to note changes in hand, directly to images of those hands. This is a concept at the heart of EPPT, in which the editor can map the position of particular portions of text on the image and automatically encode the coordinates in the XML underlying the text. In principle, this will enable all instances of the appearance of a particular hand to be drawn together and relevant patterns to be identified (see Plate 13). Were different scribes used for particular sessions of the commission or in different parts of the country? Was there an overall supervising scribe? How far did towns (for example) provide their own scribes? These are all questions fundamental to our understanding of the evidential value of these documents, and ones which we can start to answer through an image edition of the sort that EPPT facilitates.

In building image-based editions, we quickly reach the limitations of our current tools for the tagging of texts. In particular, where it is necessary to indicate not only the linguistic character of the text but also to mark up information about the physical medium on which the text is preserved, complex multiple hierarchies of markup are required. The editing tools within EPPT allow such complex XML hierarchies to be built up for individual documents using intuitive tools, all the time tied closely to images of the documents themselves. The answers to some of the questions raised here may be quite simple – but they can only be found if our digital edition incorporates all the relevant information about the structure and character of the manuscript and the procedures of the scribes who created them.[61]

In comparing different hands, it is clearly unsatisfactory to rely on the judgement of a trained (or otherwise) eye in the absence of any accompanying illustrative evidence. The 'DucType' tool in EPPT allows the editor to compare, define, encode and display the characteristics of individual letter forms and thus allows the scribes to be more precisely distinguished. The collection of such detailed, searchable information facilitates the identification of scribal (and thus administrative) procedures in the preparation of records such as the one we have been considering. Existing collation tools such as COLLATE tend to focus on individual variants, rather than identifying the scribal manipulation and transmission of larger blocks of text. Yet, in examining scribal practice in administrative documents, it is the way in which larger textual units move which is significant. We have noted how different clerks in 1381 struggled to find a form of indictment which established that insurgents were guilty of treason. An EPPT collation tool called SaMod (Old English for 'together'), under development for textual analysis, automates the detailed comparison of blocks of text as well as of individual words. The tool should therefore facilitate a detailed examination of the way in which legal forms were manipulated and enhanced by different clerks in 1381.

It may be argued that these techniques are chiefly relevant to medieval records and have limited application to more modern materials, but a digital image of the examination of a leader in another uprising nearly five hundred years later, the Chartist rising at Newport in 1839, shows that the same issues that we saw in examining the

---

61 A. Dekhtyar, I.E. Iacob, J.W. Jaromczyk et al., 'Support for XML Markup of Image-based Electronic Editions', *International Journal on Digital Libraries*, 6 (2006): 55–69.

records of the 1381 revolt are just as relevant for historians of Chartism (see Plate 14). As in 1381, the successive annotations reflect an iterative process of interrogation, with some key components of the examination being altered in pencil.

The examination of Morgan James could be taken as an emblem of the way in which we are increasingly beginning to appreciate that administrative records represent artificial textual constructions and are in a way literary genres. In examining the way in which these literary productions were put together, the tools developed to investigate literary texts such as EPPT are invaluable. Whether it is a Chartist trial record, *Beowulf* or an indictment against an insurgent in 1381, we cannot separate the text from the medium in which it is preserved and, to secure a full understanding of that text, a high-resolution digital image is indispensable. Digital images give us a new awareness of the physical character of the historical records which should be at the heart of our historical understanding. Image-based editions of historical documents offer the potential to move towards that archivists' history of which Galbraith dreamed.

Chapter 3

Virtual Restoration and Manuscript Archaeology

Meg Twycross

Digitization has ushered in a new age of manuscript studies. We can now view the image of a folio on a computer screen in colour in a detail which would have been unimaginable as little as 15 years ago. We can read it; compare it with other texts in other libraries; transcribe it; even, if it is faded or illegible, restore it. We need never see the document itself (though I would not recommend this). Remote-access scholarship is here to stay.

With processing power and storage capacity increasing virtually exponentially, digital images seem set to become a normally accepted research tool for amateurs as well as professional scholars. We now take it for granted, for example, that the general public can and will want to download pages from the National Archives' (TNA) *Domesday Book* website for a modest fee.[1] Driven by the boom in family and local history, repositories have scrambled to go online with digitized images of wills, indentures and records of births, deaths and marriages. Facsimiles of the National Census for England and Wales from 1841 to 1901 are now available via various genealogy websites licensed by TNA,[2] and users are encouraged to propose corrections to the official searchable transcription, on the very good grounds that they are the most likely to recognize any mis-spelling of the names of their own ancestors. Is it possible that the public is gradually being trained to rely on primary rather than secondary sources? For the scholar, there is a plethora of websites providing reasonable- to good-quality images of manuscripts, either in picture libraries or in electronic editions.

Looked at in close-up, flaws begin to appear in this optimistic picture. Much public-access material appears to be window-dressing. There is nothing wrong with advertising the attractions of our national treasures and making the general public and indeed students aware of and enthused about them; but one would like evidence that their audience is expected to proceed to the next stage of appreciation, which is to do something with them. The colour images of the Domesday Book are picture-postcard

---

1 At <http://www.nationalarchives.gov.uk/documentsonline/domesday.asp>. The images are delivered as PDF files in colour. They were made from the Alecto Publications facsimile (1987–92), published on CD in 2005 as *The Digital Domesday Book*.

2 E.g. <http://www.ancestry.com>. The Scottish census records are available on a pay-per-view basis from <http://www.scotlandspeople.gov.uk> together with facsimiles of government and parish birth, marriage, and death documents.

bright, but it is not clear how they are to be used except as souvenirs.[3] Customers of the National Archives are clearly not expected actually to (be able to?) read them, as they come provided not with a transcription but with a translation. (This is of course a major drawback about access to archives: the further back in time the documents originate, the more incomprehensible they become without proper training. TNA provides online palaeography lessons; it would be interesting to know how many users take advantage of them.) The engaging 'Turning the Pages' facility on the British Library's website is a technical marvel, and the image of the closed book on the first page of each example gives a sense not only of anticipation but also of a real physical object, but, presumably for delivery reasons, it is not large-scale or detailed enough to work from.[4] This would not matter if it were not for the suspicion that the emphasis on the just-good-enough for a mass audience is unintentionally creating a mind-set in which the serious scholar of manuscripts is going to be sold short.

Part of the problem is that we are now conditioned to expect online delivery. Most websites will allow the reader to download images for private study, either directly or through a pay-per-view checking system. But the resolution, and thus the size and quality of image provided can often be very low. There are two practical reasons for this: first, a lowest-common-denominator estimate of the size of file that can come down the available bandwidth.[5] It seems that we are in an interim period where our expectations have been raised but the technology cannot quite be trusted to deliver yet. Few web-providers have the courage to put up the size and quality of electronic facsimile offered on the Early Manuscripts at Oxford University website.[6] It is encouraging, however, that when I first started to access it an image took about five minutes to download: now it takes less than a second.

Second, and often unacknowledged, is copyright protection – the confidence that a very low-resolution file will not be suitable for pirated publication on paper.[7] But it is also an executive editorial decision: online images tend to be provided according to the perception of what the end-users are expected to do with them. The word 'overkill' is evoked. It then becomes an in-built concept in project management as a whole, even if the end-users are academics who are not envisaging downloading

---

3 They are delivered online as PDF files. The script is legible, but only just.

4 The display in the Library itself is of course life-size.

5 Possibly also the storage capacity of the server is a consideration.

6 At <http://image.ox.ac.uk>. This was a spin-off from the Oxford Celtic MSS Project, which set out to digitize Welsh and Irish materials at the highest possible achievable resolution, and went on to capture a sample of other Oxford manuscripts *in toto*. Apparently put online purely because the images were there, its very eclecticism and the size and detail of the images have made it an immensely useful resource.

Unfortunately, the site furnishes no technical metadata for the original scans – they are only referred to as 'high resolution digital images' – though some of the college MSS are stated to be 600 dpi. The online images are compressed as JPEGs to produce smaller files, and are therefore less detailed than the originals. A centimetre rule is included in the image, one of the few sites to do this, though sometimes in a way that suggests it has been added afterwards.

7 Pirated web publication is a different matter which has not really been solved, despite watermarking and other devices.

their work material from a website, and who could reasonably be expected to do more than just read the documents.[8]

From the providers' or project managers' point of view, there are practical and above all financial considerations. Best practice presupposes the existence of two sets of images: the original an archival-quality TIFF to be preserved and refreshed in a secure digital repository, and a reduced and compressed version for delivery, usually a JPEG. We might expect the archival image to be at the highest technically feasible resolution; and that we should be able to access it (not, at the moment, via the web) if we need that quality for our work.

But digitization takes time and money. The Phase One PowerPhase FX digital scanning back used by the Digital Image Archive of Medieval Music Project (DIAMM), and used in my case study, takes four to six minutes to capture a page of roughly A4 size.[9] In late 2005, Phase One introduced their one-shot P45 digital camera back. This was developed for the commercial market, not for manuscript copying. One-shot instantly opens up the possibility of a vastly increased workflow, and those repositories and projects that can afford it have leapt upon it enthusiastically.[10] But the camera is only 39 megapixels as opposed to the PowerPhase FX's 144 (currently a good-quality non-professional digital camera aspires to 10). Project managers must decide whether this is going to be adequate for any one particular manuscript by guessing at the uses to which the image might be put in the foreseeable future.

It is probably insufficiently realized that though a digital image can always be scaled down (losing information as you go), it cannot be scaled up to display more information. Popular perception equates them with 5" × 7" photographic prints, whereas the 100 per cent on-screen image is actually equivalent to the optimum possible print enlargement conditioned by the grain of the film – also assuming optimum focus. (Similarly the 'digital zoom' advertised on many cameras works by interpolation, and is just a good guess by the camera's software. This is also true of most flatbed scanners.)

The technical quality of the image is also crucial. Photography is, of course, a highly professional craft skill. An expert practitioner can make all the difference between a usable and an unusable image, though they may both look identical when reduced. This is cogently demonstrated on the DIAMM website, which also discusses

---

8 The Oxyrhynchus Papyri project (see below) made a decision about scale on grounds of fitness for purpose: 'the highest resolutions (thousands of dpi) are better than we need even for archiving. This makes them overkill for most useful purposes – even for quite detailed consultation. So we're following the APIS sites in archiving sharp 600dpi TIFF images, and putting lower resolution images online in JPEG format'. See <http://www.papyrology.ox.ac.uk/POxy/imaging/imaging.html>. It is not clear what the editors mean by 'sharp 600dpi images'. Have they been artificially sharpened post-production? The reference to 'thousands of dpi' presumably refers to the methods of capture, small items in close-up, or perhaps to scientific imaging: the scanning back used in the case study below cannot achieve much more than 1100 ppi.

9 See <http://www.diamm.ac.uk/content/description/capture.html#d0e165>.

10 E.g. the Cambridge Parker Library digitization project: see <http://parkerweb.stanford.edu/about/index.jsp>.

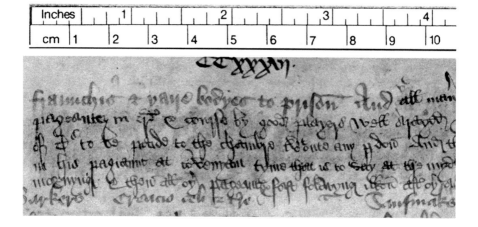

Figure 3.1 York City Archives, A/Y Memorandum Book, fol. 255r: the top of the 'mapping pen' folio, actual size

the drawbacks of scanning from surrogates, a common time-saving short-cut.[11] They also warn against depending on post-production 'quick fixes' to disguise the effects of bad photographic practice in the actual shoot.

The case study on which I want to concentrate for the rest of this chapter depends on having very good, very high resolution colour images of your subject. It is a form of manuscript restoration, which because it is done on screen is non-invasive, and far more effective than anything that was possible before digitization.

But while I was engaged in this, I found that I was embarked on a much more complex investigation: nothing less than the rediscovery of a historical sequence. Most of this account is however about practicalities: only when these had been successfully deployed could the implications begin to surface.

11 See <http://www.diamm.ac.uk/content/description/quality.html>. A common argument is that the use of existing surrogates is the only way to protect very fragile and precious manuscripts from the dangers of light and handing. In other cases, this is an interim exercise providing data without having to spend years on a re-photographing campaign. For example, the Corpus Vitrearum Medii Aevi project provides a splendid resource with over 13,000 images, but some have been digitized from ancient and faded surrogates in the National Monuments Record: see <http://www.cvma.ac.uk/>. Likewise the Bodleian Library's main image site does not pretend to be much more than an image-ordering service, with the originals scanned from existing 35 mm slides of very variable quality on a proprietary Nikon LS–2000 slide scanner. They were then batch-processed into JPEGs for the web. The website signals when the image is particularly poor. See <http://www.bodley.ox.ac.uk/dept/scwmss/wmss/medieval/browse.htm>.

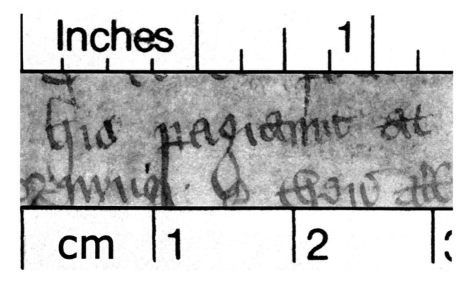

Figure 3.2   York City Archives, A/Y Memorandum Book, fol. 255r: detail enlarged

Manuscript study on-screen

The most obvious advantage of high-resolution digital photography is that it hands the scholar a virtual magnifying glass.[12] This has several immediate uses in manuscript study. Obviously, it helps you to read very small writing. For example, the fifteenth-century document I am working on at present is about 202–205 mm wide and 290–293 mm deep – slightly narrower than a piece of A4 (295 x 210 mm). The writing is correspondingly small – in one case minuscule (in size, not style), apparently written with a late medieval mapping pen (see Figure 3.1).

But with an 967 ppi scan at my current desktop screen resolution of 1024 x 768 pixels, the word *pagiaunt* in the fourth line, 14.7 mm in the manuscript, appears 'enlarged' to 172 mm on screen, with no loss of clarity (see Figure 3.2).

The letters are also large enough to show the turns of the pen and the flow of ink. This makes it an excellent tool in teaching palaeography[13] and, at a more advanced level, invaluable for the identification of hands. Examples of a known hand can be superimposed in a different colour over samples from the questioned hand (see Figure 3.3).

---

12 The scholars working on the Archimedes Palimpsest (see below) found that 300 dpi scans 'were insufficient to their needs. The scholars liked to "blow-up" individual characters to the size of their computer screens when they try to decipher the text, and to do this successfully, the images needed to be of a higher resolution': <http://www.archimedespalimpsest.org/imaging_initialtrials1.html>.

13 See M. Twycross, 'Teaching Palaeography on the Web', *Journal of Literary and Linguistic Computing* 14:2 (1999): 257–83.

Figure 3.3   Left: Hand X; right: Hand Y; centre: Hand X colour converted and superimposed on Hand Y

Overlay is still apparently the favourite technique of forensic document examination.[14] Though there are several on-going projects to establish an automatic digital method of hand recognition, so far they only really work on formal book-hand.[15] Cursive script is much more difficult, especially when written at speed. Besides this, fifteenth- and sixteenth-century clerical staff were trained to write in several different scripts, and only the highly experienced palaeographer can identify an individual's work across the board.[16]

The ability to zoom in and out on-screen is also an essential palaeographical tool. It allows for a range of types of perceptual word recognition, ranging from the slotting-together of individual letters (zoom in) to whole-word pattern recognition (zoom out). The latter is particularly useful with the restricted palette of ultraviolet images which in close-up disintegrate into a mosaic of blue (or black) and white.[17]

The fact that it is much easier to show this technique than to describe it also suggests that the proper forum for the presentation of this kind of work is the screen rather than the printed book. Images are not merely dispensable 'illustrations': they form part of the argument. The print medium is just inadequate. As I said above, the word *pagiaunt* in Figure 3.2 appears on screen as if it were 172 mm. It cannot be printed at this scale onto paper without giving a completely misleading impression of the sharpness of the image. I have currently no idea at what size or how sharp it will appear in the printed book. Also, the fact that images are in colour is not merely a cosmetic attraction, or only important to art historians. Greyscale commonly gives you 256 tones to work with and manipulate; 24-bit colour, 16,777,216, or, as the scanners say, 'millions of colours'.[18] In this kind of discipline it is essential to work with subtle distinctions of colour, but cost considerations make it highly unlikely that the results can be reproduced in the appropriate learned journal, where greyscale

---

14 I was delighted to find that all the techniques I had devised for my palaeography students to describe scripts: angles to the horizontal, closeness of minims, letter aspect – are also used by forgery-detection experts.

15 The Digital Atheneum is working on a form of OCR which will help to identify damaged and partial letters by probabilistic pattern matching, but this is not at a stage where it can help in identifying individual hands: see <http://beowulf.engl.uky.edu/~eft/digitalatheneum/>.

16 See for example M.B. Parkes, *English Cursive Book Hands 1250–1500* (Oxford: Clarendon Press, 1969) plates 22 and 23, and commentary.

17 See S. Coren, L.M. Ward and J.T. Enns, *Sensation and Perception*, 6th edn (Hoboken, NJ: Wiley, 2004), pp. 317–19, for an explanation of this effect, and chapter 10 in general for questions of object perception.

18 In practice the human eye can only see between 2,000,000 and 8,000,000, but the computer can locate them. See Coren, Ward, and Enns, *Sensation and Perception*, pp. 101–102.

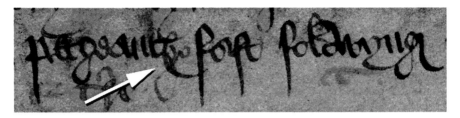

**Figure 3.4   York City Archives, A/Y Memorandum Book, fol. 255r, detail
from the bottom of the entry enlarged**

is the norm. Some of my images may not be meaningless, but in greyscale they will
not be communicating the full range of their information.

Altered and damaged manuscripts

Working with digital images thus makes one aware of detail. On screen you see things
which the naked eye can see, but does not notice.[19] For example, on the 'mapping-
pen' folio above (Figure 3.1), a tiny *go* has been inserted between *pageantes* and
fast folowyng in the text. It is not surprising that this has been completely missed by
previous editors of the manuscript (see Figure 3.4), though when you return to the
manuscript with hindsight, it is perfectly clear.

This may be something to do with having the light source behind the screen, so
that changes of colour are translucent rather than sinking into the generally matt
background provided by parchment or paper. It particularly draws one's attention to
small gradations in the colour of ink and to the change of texture created by erasures.

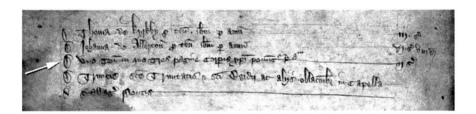

**Figure 3.5   York City Archive, A/Y Memorandum Book, fol. 4v, detail:
erasure and overwriting (see the middle line)**

For example, in an earlier folio (4v) from the same manuscript, there is a list of rents,
dated 1376, which contains what is generally accepted as the earliest reference to
pageants in York (see Figure 3.5).

---

19 'Seeing but not noticing' may be due to 'contour interference': see Coren, Ward, and
Enns, *Sensation and Perception*, pp. 231–6.

With a high-resolution digital image on screen, however, we can see quite clearly that in that one line the ink is a different colour from the surrounding items; that there is an erasure at the beginning of the line; and that the hand is different. So far, I have not been able positively to identify this hand elsewhere in the manuscript, but the style of script suggests that the entry may have to be post-dated by as much as 20 years. When we go back to the manuscript and look at it again, the fact of the alteration is perfectly clear; and theories about the prehistory of the York Corpus Christi Play will have to be at least reconsidered.

With advances in electronic image manipulation, scholars have been applying forensic techniques (so called because some versions of these are routinely applied by the police and immigration authorities to 'questioned documents' – altered cheques and doctored passports, for example) to the study of alterations and damage in ancient and, to a lesser extent, medieval manuscripts. New techniques and applications have been and are continually being established. The trail-blazing project here was the *Electronic Beowulf*, edited by Kevin Kiernan and published by the British Library in 1993.[20] It not only presented a domain in which scholars could study a facsimile of BL Cotton MS Vitellius A XV, the unique but damaged witness to the poem, alongside the eighteenth-century transcripts organized by the Danish scholar Thorkelin, two early nineteenth-century collations, and a purpose-made transcription and edition: in the process of making this edition it confirmed and presented new discoveries. It recorded readings using fibre-optic light which had been lost under the nineteenth-century paper guards protecting the friable fire-damaged edges, and which could only be photographed digitally.[21] The digital format enabled these, and ultraviolet readings of scribal erasures and corrections, to be displayed in a way impossible on paper. Digital imaging was firmly established as a major editorial tool. Editions like these have also created the obligation to display one's evidence: it is no longer sufficient to state that a reading is there because you have seen it.

Different techniques have been developed to address different problems. To date the impetus has largely come from the study of documents from the ancient world. The Vindolanda stylus tablets were Roman writing materials consisting of a wax writing-surface contained in a wooden case. The wax has perished, leaving only the marks of the stylus which had gone through the wax onto the backing wood. Often there are overlapping marks from several messages which had been written on the wax and then erased for reuse. *Shadow Stereo*, a delightfully simple concept but rather more difficult to implement in practice, is a technique apparently first developed for satellite espionage imaging ('stereo photography of denied areas').[22] It photographed a 3D object under a light source directed from a sequence of different angles – in the case of satellite imaging, the sun – and layered the results to create overlapping images. With the Vindolanda stylus tablets, these are images of the shadows in the indentations which are then manipulated to show the edge

---

20 See <http://www.uky.edu/~kiernan/eBeowulf/guide.htm>.

21 On fibre-optic backlighting, see K.S. Kiernan, 'The State of the Beowulf Manuscript 1882–1983', *Anglo-Saxon England*, 13 (1984): 23–42.

22 See <http://rst.gsfc.nasa.gov/AppA/Part1_7.html>.

of the stylus mark.[23] This technique has now been customized for documents by the Department of Engineering Science and the Centre for the Study of Ancient Documents at Oxford.[24] A simpler version using raking light can be used to pick up the indentations left by a quill pen on parchment when the ink has been washed away (see below).

The Oxyrhynchus Papyri, retrieved in fragments from the dusty rubbish dumps of a vanished desert city, are being read through *multi-spectral imaging.*[25] This is becoming the technique of choice. The popular scientific press inevitably refers to it as 'NASA imaging technology', and it is true that several of these techniques were first developed for use in space.[26] Electronic images are taken at graduated stages along the electro-magnetic spectrum of visible and 'invisible' light (the latter is a misnomer, but convenient – it refers to both the ultraviolet and infrared bands). At certain wavelengths the ink reflects the light being directed at it, and can be photographed, and the background material (papyrus, parchment, paper) does not; or more frequently, the background material reflects and the ink absorbs light, appearing as black on a white background. This even works with severely carbonized material such as the Herculaneum Papyri, which were incinerated in the Vesuvius eruption of 24 August AD 79.[27]

It is not however a matter of simply finding the magic wavelength which will reveal everything: different areas of ink will react to different wavelengths, and true multi-spectral imaging combines the results from several images, usually by layering them experimentally to retrieve the optimum amount of information.[28] (For other uses of the layering technique in Adobe Photoshop, see below.)

---

23 See Vindolanda Tablets Online <http://vindolanda.csad.ox.ac.uk/> and <http://www.csad.ox.ac.uk/Stilus/Stilus.html> (fullest description); also <http://www.classics.ox.ac.uk/research/projects/csad6.asp>. On the tablets as a whole, see <http://vindolanda.csad.ox.ac.uk/exhibition/docs.shtm>.

24 See the description furnished by Melissa Terras at <http://www.hb.se/bhs/ith/23-00/mt.htm>: 'camera position and the tablet are kept fixed; but a number of images are taken in which the tablet is illuminated by a strongly orientated light source. If the azimuthal direction of the light sources (that is, the direction to the light source if the light were projected directly down on to the table) is held fixed, but the light is alternated between two elevations, the shadows cast by incisions will move but stains on the surface of the tablet remain fixed.' They can then calculate the edge of the incisions. They have also developed an algorithm for removing the distracting grain in the wood.

25 See <http://www.papyrology.ox.ac.uk/POxy/multi/index.html> for an account of the process and its results. Technical assistance has been provided by Brigham Young University.

26 For example, 'NASA Imaging Technology Illuminates Ancient Egyptian Manuscripts' at <http://discovermagazine.com/2006/jan/archaeology-copy/>.

27 See <http://www.herculaneum.ox.ac.uk/papyri.html>; <http://www.herculaneum.ox.ac.uk/hercinfo.html>.

28 For a clear explanation of the process, see <http://www.archimedespalimpsest.org/imaging_production1.htm>. William Noel of the Archimedes Project points out (in a private communication) that the term 'multi-spectral' is often misused. 'Again and again we find people using it in the sense that they take an image at a particular wavelength, and then just run with the best one. This is not what we do. It did not work for us. We post-process our

The team working on the Archimedes Palimpsest, on the face of it a thirteenth-century Greek liturgical book, set themselves to recover the ancient Greek scientific texts which had been erased to provide the scribes in Constantinople with the recycled parchment. They have had spectacular success with multi-spectral imaging.[29] (Their website gives a comprehensive and comprehensible description of the various processes they attempted, usefully including those which did not work and why.) Some parts of the palimpsest, however, were particularly difficult as the original text was completely overlaid with full-page painted and gilded illuminations (incidentally twentieth-century forgeries). They recovered the Archimedes text from underneath these by subjecting these pages to *X-ray fluorescence imaging* by the Stanford Linear Accelerator Center's synchrotron. Under the X-rays, different metallic elements fluoresce at different wavelengths, so an individual element can be detected and then 'mapped' as an image. Here the iron in the ink was used to produce an elemental X-ray iron map. The procedure is immensely time-consuming because the X-ray beam is so narrow. Post-processing is complicated by the fact that data is picked up from both sides of the parchment (a problem which occurs on a much less advanced technological level with ordinary RGB photos made on a light box), and the investigators had to develop an algorithm allowing them to distinguish between the writing on the recto and verso through differences in contrast, and to display them in different false colours.[30]

One version or another of multi-spectral imaging has become the investigator's stock in trade, but there are other problems to be solved with other techniques. The team working on the Digital Atheneum at the University of Kentucky, also led by Kevin Kiernan, is particularly interested in *3D modelling* of the fragmentary and crumpled manuscripts damaged in the fire of the Cotton Library of 1731.[31] This will again have wider applications.

DIAMM[32] has evolved a method of *virtual restoration* which involves working on the very fine gradations of colour in a high-resolution RGB image to restore

---

images using more than one wavelength of light, and we have found this to be astonishingly successful.'

29 See <http://www.archimedespalimpsest.org/index.html>.

30 See <http://www.archimedespalimpsest.org/imaging_experimental4.html>; Uwe Bergmann *X-Ray Fluorescence Imaging of the Archimedes Palimpsest: A Technical Summary* at <http://www.slac.stanford.edu/gen/com/images/technical%20summary_final.pdf>: 'The crucial thing about these so called fluorescence X-rays is the fact that different elements generate X-rays with different wavelengths. A fluorescence X-ray sent out from an iron atom is different from an X-ray sent out by a calcium atom, or an atom of gold. These fluorescence X-rays could then be detected with a device that can recognize these different X-rays. The idea is simple: by mapping these X-rays, we could create "element maps" of individual pages of the Palimpsest.'

31 See <http://beowulf.engl.uky.edu/~eft/digitalatheneum/>, in particular, their work on the 'Boethius Manuscript', British Library, MS Cotton Otho A VI. For discussions, see <http://www.rlg.org/preserv/diginews/diginews3-6.html#technical1> and <http://www.infotoday.com/cilmag/feb00/seales.htm>.

32 See <http://www.diamm.ac.uk/index.html>.

the ghost of faded and erased ink.[33] Dr Craig-McFeely developed this technique to retrieve the musical notation under palimpsests. This is peculiarly useful to scholars like myself without a heavily funded technical team behind them. All the technology and the expense comes in acquiring the original images: after that the work can be done with Adobe Photoshop, probably the most familiar proprietary image-manipulation package,[34] on the kind of computer usually bought by gaming enthusiasts. At this stage the emphasis is thrown back on the specialist expertise of the manuscript scholar rather than on scientific advance; as indeed there would be no point in recovering the unknown works of Archimedes if nobody in the team could read Greek script. The best projects show a healthy collaboration between technicians and end-users, who should each know something about what the other is doing. I am particularly grateful to Dr Julia Craig-McFeely, the DIAMM Project Manager, for starting me off with a masterclass in her techniques of virtual restoration, and being generous with suggestions, advice and experiments with filters; and to Dr Lynda Sayce for deploying her photographic expertise on the various often horrendous problems of my case-history manuscript.

Case study: methods and techniques

The York City Archives document on which I am currently working is contained in six sides of parchment, folios 252v–255r of the York City Archives MS E 20, the A/Y Memorandum Book, in which from the 1370s the city recorded things that were 'to be remembered': council decisions, royal decrees, guild ordinances, certificates of denization, a *History of the Archbishops of York* ... – an interesting assortment revealing the preoccupations of a late medieval city and the people who ran it.

These six pages are crucial to the early history of the York Corpus Christi Play, now commonly called the York Mystery Cycle.[35] It is a list of the pageants in the Play as compiled in 1415 by the Common Clerk. (The individual items were called *pageants*; the whole Cycle was called the *Play*.) It is called the *Ordo paginarum*, the 'Order of the Pageants'. They were officially recorded both because they were the checklist for the civic administration as to which guilds were responsible for which 'pageant' at that particular time, and because they were also the copy text for the notifications sent out to each guild or group of guilds warning them to be ready to 'bring forth' (the English version of *produce*) their individual pageant on Corpus Christi Day.

It is a textbook case of two different kinds of illegibility. First, it is a fine example of a distressed manuscript. Almost everything that can happen to a manuscript has happened to it, except cremation, which it narrowly escaped in the Second World

---

33 For a detailed explanation of this technique see <http://www.diamm.ac.uk/content/ restoration/intro.htm>.

34 The TASI site puts it at the head of currently available imaging packages, saying: 'Photoshop has long been considered an industry standard among imaging professionals': <http://www.tasi.ac.uk/advice/creating/imgedsw.html>.

35 This was not a contemporary term.

War when the Guildhall in which it was stored was fire-bombed on 29 April 1942. Fortunately, as the Honorary Archivist Angelo Raine reported:[36]

> In the angle between [*the Common Hall and the old Council Chamber*] is the strong room containing the MSS., but it was not damaged in the slightest degree. Students of History everywhere will feel grateful to the Corporation for the precautions they adopted to make safe their historical treasures.

It was not so fortunate fifty years earlier. In the nineteenth century, it was stored in the basement of the Guildhall. The watermarks in the manuscript, which come two-thirds of the way up the page, are a souvenir of the 1892 Ouse flood (see Plate 15). The thin places in the parchment, many caused by the scraping away of erasures, sprang even larger holes, and the pages were not properly dried out, and so became distorted. In addition, some time before the late nineteenth century, an anti-Catholic zealot had attacked it with a knife. After the flood, this damage was mended by well-meaning archivists[37] with paper patches attached by 'various kinds of glue'.[38] Underlying ink has started to seep through in some places, which gives a blurred image of the text, but much is still invisible. Even in the upper third of the page, it is routinely rubbed and faded. It provides an interesting challenge.

The methods of recovery depend on using Adobe Photoshop, a proprietary tool which has become almost universal,[39] and the best digital scans one can get. Those that are illustrated here are from two stages of my campaign. The first were commissioned in August 2004 from DIAMM. The project photographer at that date was Peter Scott. He used a Phase One PowerPhase FX digital scanning back, mounted on a Fuji GX 680 III professional SLR camera body, with a medium format lens, taking images as RGB under daylight-balanced 'cold light'. Capture times were between four and six minutes.[40] DIAMM digitizes its images at the highest resolution the camera will

---

36 A. Raine (ed.), *York Civic Records, Vol III*, Yorkshire Archaeological Record Series 106 (1942), vii.

37 Much damage has been done to manuscripts by the well-meaning vandalism of archivists themselves. In the nineteenth and early twentieth centuries, a solution of oak-galls (tannic acid) painted on faded writing restored the intensity of the ink for a brief while, before it itself oxidized further and turned a deep brown. In the York City Archives, this was done to the Scriveners Pageant of *Doubting Thomas*, the only known copy of a York mystery play known to exist before 1844, when Sir Frederick Madden identified a mysterious manuscript (now BL Additional MS 35290) bought by the Rev. Thomas Russell as the full script of the surviving plays. In the early twentieth century, a favoured method of cleaning was 'vigorous scrubbing with hot soda-water' with predictable results (personal communication from Louise Hampson, York Minster Archivist).

38 Recent attempts to remove this have had to be suspended, as it turned out to be dangerously tenacious.

39 The Vindolanda website refers enthusiastically to Adobe Photoshop as a tool. <http://vindolanda.csad.ox.ac.uk/tablets/TVdigital-2.shtml>: excerpted from the Introduction to A.K. Bowman and J.D. Thomas, *The Vindolanda Writing Tablets Volume III* (British Museum Press, 2003) 14.

40 Information from the Project Manager. See also <http://www.diamm.ac.uk/content/description/capture.html>: 'The maximum capture resolution is 144 Megapixels and the dpi

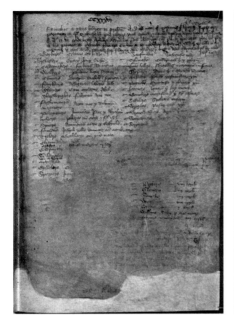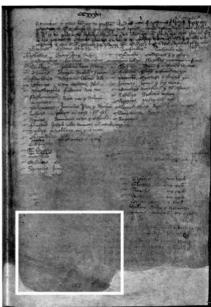

**Figure 3.6   York City Archives, A/Y Memorandum Book, fol. 255r, detail
showing severe water damage to the bottom half of the folio**

record, given the size of the object. These came out at 850 ppi, and they are each 238 MB in size. Originals are archived on the Oxford University Computing Services hierarchical file server and with the AHDS.

The second batch were taken by the current DIAMM photographer Dr Lynda Sayce in May 2006, with the same scanning back mounted on a custom built large-format camera with motor-driven focus designed by ICAM Archive Systems. Images this time came out at between 967 and 1097 ppi, and were between 310–335 MB each. Images were taken under daylight-balanced 'cold light'; on a cold-light lightbox; with raked lighting; and with UV lighting.

The Adobe tools which I have found most useful on RGB images are Levels Adjust, Replace Color and Color Select. Others, like High Pass, Threshold and Invert, are mainly useful to see if there is something that requires closer investigation.[41] It is vital to remember that all edits are destructive.[42] Even if the originals are safely archived, always work on copies of your copy 'original'.

---

obtainable depends on the size of the original source ... All images are captured at the highest possible resolution in the hope that there will be no necessity to revisit the manuscript for photography in the near future.'

41   See also the description on the DIAMM website at <http://www.diamm.ac.uk/content/restoration/process.html>.

42   See <http://www.adobe.com/designcenter/dialogbox/why_shoot_raw_print.html>: 'Edits in Photoshop are "destructive"—when you use a tool such as Levels, Curves, Hue/Saturation, or Color Balance, you change the actual pixel values, creating the potential for

Figure 3.7   York City Archives, A/Y Memorandum Book, fol. 255r, detail showing faded ink brought up using the Adobe 'Replace Color' procedure

Figure 3.6 shows a folio which has been badly water-damaged. The selection to be worked on is shown by the box. It has been washed out, but the ghost of writing is still visible.

On a copy of the original, use the Replace Color procedure (see Figure 3.7). This targets a range of colours and changes their values. With the eye-dropper tool, select a pixel with the shade of colour you want to enhance, and open the dialogue box. Decide how much tolerance (Fuzziness) you want: not much more than 20 and preferably less. The larger the tolerance, the more blunt-edged the results: too small, and the results will be virtually invisible. There is no optimum figure: each case has to be calibrated by eye. Push the Lightness slider so that the selected (faded) colour becomes darker. Sometimes it is useful to target the background and lighten it. It sometimes helps to increase the Saturation levels as well. Adjusting the colour using the Hue slider makes the script more distinctive from the background (blue is useful here); it also has the added virtue, recommended by the DIAMM website, of showing clearly that the colour has been faked. (One of the main worries by archivists about digital imaging is that images can potentially be cleaned up and sharpened to give a false impression of the original. We have an obligation not only to preserve the original archival scan, but to be aware, and to make others aware, of the provisional nature of our photographic adjustments.)

This is without altering the original brightness levels. Actually one of the most heavy-handed but effective procedures for a preliminary foray is merely to hit Image > Adjust > Auto Levels. Subtler and more effective procedures use Curves to adjust the three separate channels, R, G and B.

---

either or both of two problems' – posterization and detail loss, which occurs 'when you compress a tonal range. Where the levels were formerly different, they're now compressed into the same value, so the differences, which represent potential detail, are tossed irrevocably into the bit-bucket, never to return.'

Figure 3.8   York City Archives, A/Y Memorandum Book, fol. 255r, detail showing previous image clarified using the Adobe 'Color Range > Select and Copy' procedures

If there is a lot of background interference from the parchment or other blots and blotches, use the Select > Color Range procedure to pull out the colour you want, and then Copy it to a clean canvas (See Figure 3.8). However, because the writing is not made up of one colour, you will probably have to select and copy a whole range of shades, stacking them on top of one another in Layers, altering some colours, and possibly hiding others, until you arrive at an acceptably legible image (see Figure 3.9). The resulting layers should be saved as a PSD before flattening them to produce a composite TIFF.

This technique works particularly well with faded and even scraped-out inks if there is a vestige of colour remaining. This is why you need a very high-resolution TIFF image: very small distinctions in shade are picked out pixel by pixel and then built up into a final image. Compressed formats like JPEG have lost too much information and are not nearly flexible enough.

This kind of material cannot be subjected to batch processing: it is even impracticable to use one procedure for the entire page, because the colours of the ink and of the background material vary to such an extent. In this case (see Figure 3.7), the colours in the paper patch are identical to the faded ink on the rest of the page, so that area must be treated separately. The ink that has soaked through is a different colour from the ink on the parchment, and the lines in the weave of the paper can obliterate what is underneath. Restoration is a painstaking and detailed process in which revelations are few and far between.

Beyond the visible spectrum, there is the invisible, for practical purposes, ultraviolet and infrared. *Ultraviolet* images (taken as RGB)[43] were particularly

---

43 Film-based photography usually does this in black-and-white. This limits you to working in greyscale. A colour scan still has a very limited range, but each shade can be altered (e.g. blue to red) so as to emphasize the relevant script.

useful for erasures and areas where the ink had been washed away, though where the diluted ink is thinly spread across the surface it also shows up, and results can be blurred. Paper patches show up as opaque, again with the lines in the weave very obvious, but where the ink has soaked through from underneath, letters can be detected. It is also a rather blunt instrument. Because it only uses a narrow band of the spectrum, even after processing the image looks grainy, without the subtle gradations of an RGB image, and letter forms are more difficult to see in close-up (see above). So UV photography and Virtual Restoration of RGB files should be thought of as complementary techniques, bringing up different facets of the same subject (see Figure 3.9).

 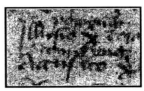 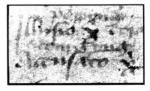

Figure 3.9   York City Archives, A/Y Memorandum Book, fol. 255r, details. Left, UV photograph; centre: UV photograph with darker shade selected and copied; right: RGB colour, with various shades selected and copied

In some areas where the ink has been washed away, there are still marks left by the quill pen. The traditional way of reading these is to take the manuscript to a window, preferably in the early morning or late afternoon, and tilt it until the marks show up white. The artificial way is to photograph them under raking light. This is effectively a form of shadow stereo.[44] Though this technique also picks up all the hills and valleys in the manuscript surface, it can be effective in recording relatively flat areas. Compare here the information given by the UV image and that given by the raking

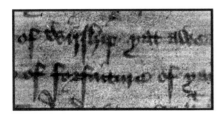 

Figure 3.10   York City Archives, A/Y Memorandum Book, fol. 254v, detail of water-damaged text. Left: UV image; Right: raking light, colour inverted

---

44 The marks also showed up in the Visual Spectral Comparator at a point on the scale between ultraviolet and the lower reaches of the visible spectrum – possibly some form of interference effect?

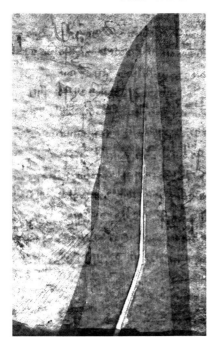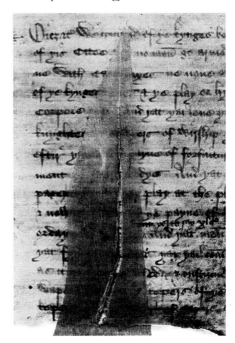

**Figure 3.11   York City Archives, A/Y Memorandum Book, fol. 54v: detail
showing writing under paper patch seen by (left) light box,
(right) UV**

light, colour inverted so that the white marks show up as black: the outlines very
clearly show the movement of the pen, which is useful when comparing hands (see
Figure 3.10).

Where the writing has been obscured by a paper patch, some information may
be recovered by photographing it on a light-box. The drawback here is that the
image records the writing from both sides of the parchment, and the contrast is
thin in comparison with an ordinary image, and thus less workable. It also picks up
irregularities in the surface texture of the parchment. Again, using the light-box and
UV may give complementary information (see Figure 3.11).

Recently I have enlisted the help of Trevor Emmett from Anglia Ruskin University's
Department of Forensic Science, who introduced their Video Spectral Comparator to
the manuscript.[45] The VSC is an imaging device for examining questioned documents
using a range of multispectral sources from 'the visible and near infrared regions

---

45 The best description is how this works is on the FBI website: <http://www.fbi.gov/
hq/lab/fsc/backissu/oct1999/mokrzyck.htm>. It is 'an imaging device that includes a color
charge coupled device (CCD) video camera, a black and white CCD video camera, excitation/
barrier filters, and various radiant energy sources (tungsten, halogen, and fluorescent lamps)'.
It displays its results on a 21-inch LCD flat screen. For a detailed spec, see the manufacturer's
website: <http://www.fosterfreeman.co.uk/products/documents/vsc5000/vsc5000-technical.
html>.

of the spectrum carried out with incident and transmitted UV, visible and infrared illumination up to 1000nm'. This is operated by a slider which shows the effects of the various wavelengths in an image of the writing on screen. It is used by archivists and librarians, but its main market is the police and the immigration service. One drawback from our point of view is that though it has an 85x optical zoom, since it is customized for forensic document examiners it will only inspect and record small areas of its target in close-up. This is partly due to the fact that some of the light sources can illuminate only a fairly small area effectively.[46] It is not possible to image a whole sheet of A4 at high magnification: you have to stitch together a patchwork of images, each of which will look slightly different in tone. In addition, its digital output is in bitmaps. Some of its operations are also redundant if you want to work on the saved images in Photoshop, as they replicate features like Contrast, Sharpen, Despeckle, Rotate, and various types of layering and measurement.[47] But it is an excellent exploratory device.

It is said to be particularly helpful in its IR range for 'revealing concealed or masked information and detecting alterations to documents by revealing the use of different inks'.[48] Our manuscript did not respond particularly well to this, but one very useful feature was that by sampling the ink at various points, the VSC produces a graph profile which reveals the chemical composition of the ink. Unsurprisingly, the main ink turned out to be conventionally iron-based, and the profiles of Hand A and Hand B (see below) suggested that they used the same ink-horn, or at least had the same supplier. There was no evidence that, as has been suggested, some heavy overwriting of individual letters was made in the late nineteenth century, when the chemical composition of the ink would have been different.

A palimpsest

So far, this illegibility was produced by accident. The second kind was intentional, and leads us to the really challenging part of the investigation. The manuscript is a partial palimpsest, for good historical reasons.

The *Ordo paginarum* was an official document with a quasi-legal function, but it recorded and controlled an evolving event. The list of pageants, and the guilds which were responsible for them, did not remain static. For financial and artistic reasons, guilds combined and recombined responsibilities for a pageant, and updated the scripts where they felt it was necessary, always with permission from the City Council. This process went on for at least 150 years. And each change is reflected in the document, as the Council's clerical staff[49] erased, overwrote and inserted information (see Figure 3.12).

---

46 Information from Bob Dartnell of Foster and Freeman.

47 The VSC also has a device for 'visualising indented writing or embossing', though the makers suggest that 'shallow indentations and those not visible at all, are more effectively examined using an electrostatic imaging technique'.

48 See Foster and Freeman website at <http://www.fosterfreeman.co.uk/products/documents/vsc5000/vsc5000-1.html>.

49 Probably the Deputy Common Clerk: see M. Twycross, 'Forget the 4.30 a.m. Start: Recovering a Palimpsest in the York *Ordo paginarum*', *Medieval English Theatre*, 25 (2005

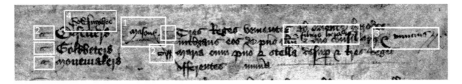

Figure 3.12   York City Archives, A/Y Memorandum Book, fol. 253r, detail: entry for the Goldsmiths' Pageant of *The Three Kings*, showing alterations

This entry shows various typical forms of alteration:

1. The Goldsmiths were originally responsible for two pageants: in 1431 the *Masons* took over one of them.
2. The *two paraphs* in the description show two separate pageants, the *three paraphs* to the left show the three guilds responsible for them.
3. Two *additional characters*, a son of Herod and a messenger, were added at a later date.
4. The original guild names were often written in their French form; later the Common Clerk occasionally added the *English* version.

Much of the work that has been done on the *Ordo* is on changes in guild attributions, many of which can be dated from external evidence.[50] There are, however, equally drastic changes in the descriptions of the pageants themselves; but fewer people have worked on these, partly because the manuscript is in such a mess, and this obscures the full nature of the problem.

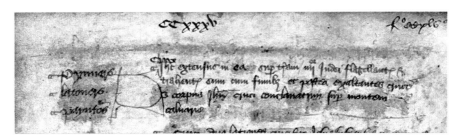

Figure 3.13   York City Archives, A/Y Memorandum Book, fol. 254r, detail: the erased entry for the Millers' pageant, and the altered entry for the *Crucifixion* Pageant of the Pinners, Latoners, and Painters

---

for 2003): 98–152.

50 See R. Beadle and P. Meredith, *The York Play: A Facsimile of British Library MS Additional 35290, together with a Facsimile of the 'Ordo Paginarum' Section of the A/Y Memorandum Book* (Leeds: University of Leeds School of English, 1983), pp. liii–liv, lvi–lix; P. Meredith, 'The *Ordo paginarum* and the Development of the York Tilemakers' Pageant', *Leeds Studies in English*, ns 11 (1980): 59–73; M. Stevens and M. Dorrell (Rogerson), 'The *Ordo Paginarium* [sic] Gathering of the York A/Y Memorandum Book', *Modern Philology* 72 (1974–5): 45–59.

For example (one of many), at the top of folio 254r there is evidence of a major alteration (see Figure 3.13). A complete pageant has been erased, the Millers' *Dicing for Christ's Garments*. This was amalgamated in 1432 with another group of pageants to produce a composite pageant of *The Condemnation of Christ*.[51] The entry for this new pageant is on the facing page, heavily erased and overwritten.

The next two pageants have been merged into one. We know from other evidence that this happened in response to a petition to the mayor and aldermen on 31 January 1421/2 by the guilds concerned.[52] The image clearly shows that two hands have been at work recording the pre- and post-amalgamation situations: the first made the original entry in 1415, and the second made the alteration, overwriting the erasure of the first. In this transcription, the second is indicated in italic, the first in roman type.

¶ *Pynners*   *Crux/* Ih<u>esus</u> extensus in *ea* sup<u>er</u> t<u>er</u>ram / iiij^{or} Iudei flagellant<u>es</u> &
¶ *Latoners*   trahent<u>es</u> eum cum funib<u>us</u> *et postea exaltantes cruc<u>em</u>*
¶ *Payntou<u>rs</u>*   *& corpus Ihesu cruci conclauatum sup<u>er</u> montem*
             Caluarie

On fol. 255r there is another, shorter list which was written slightly later than the original 1415 main list, but which was not used to record alterations (see Figure 3.14). It therefore preserves an earlier stage of the pageant sequence. Here it clearly shows the pre-1422 situation with three pageants:

¶ Milners   P<u>ar</u>ticio vestime<u>ntor</u>um christi
¶ Payntou<u>rs</u>   Expansio & clauac<u>io</u> chr<u>ist</u>i
¶ latoners   Leuac<u>io</u> chr<u>ist</u>i sup<u>er</u> monte<u>m</u>

However, the surviving script (British Library Additional MS 35290) gives the amalgamated version of the pageant, because it dates from the late 1460s or early 1470s, well after these alterations were made.

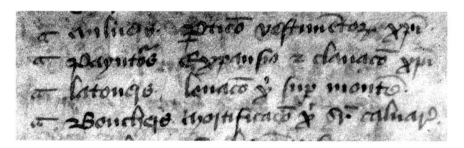

Figure 3.14   York City Archives, A/Y Memorandum Book, fol. 255r, detail: Short list entry for the Millers' *Sharing of Christ's Garments* and *Crucifixion* Pageant of the Pinners, Latoners, and Painters

---

51 See A.F. Johnston and M. Rogerson (eds), *Records of Early English Drama: York*, 2 vols (Toronto: University of Toronto Press, 1979), pp. 48–50.

52 Ibid., pp. 37–8.

It is conspicuously clear that there are two hands at work on this section of the manuscript, not one hand correcting himself (see Figure 3.15). The original, Hand A, wrote a version of Anglicana; the second hand B, a tidy version of Secretary. Besides this entry, Hand B was busy making alterations across the whole document. But whose hands were they?

 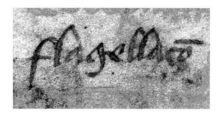

Figure 3.15 **York City Archives A/Y Memorandum Book: (a) Hand A (note Anglicana 'a' and 'g'), and compare (b) Hand B (that of Burton – note the secretary-hand 'a' and 'g')**

Hand B, the corrector, is probably that of the Common Clerk from 1415 to 1435/6, Roger Burton. Thanks to on-screen enlargement I was able to compare a range of samples of his writing. He seems to have written these alterations to the *Ordo*, the Short Pageant List, and, conveniently, a *History of the Archbishops of York*, said to be *propria manu* ('in his own hand'), signed and notarized, which almost immediately precedes the *Ordo paginarum* in the A/Y Memorandum Book (see Figure 3.16).

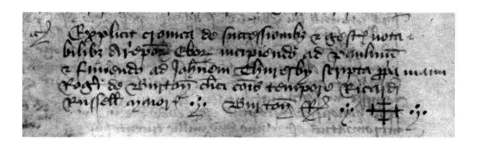

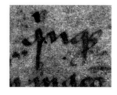 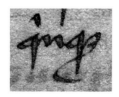 

a.   b.   c.

Figure 3.16 **York City Archives, A/Y Memorandum Book: Roger Burton's hand. Top: Explicit from *History of the Archbishops of York*, fol. 246v; Bottom: a. from Short List, fol, 255r; b. from *History of Archbishops* fol. 246r; and c. (b) overlaid on (a)**

It is clear that Burton (Hand B) was not the person who wrote out the original document (Hand A): not only do they write different scripts, their *ductus* is quite different (see Figure 3.15). Hand A is so far unidentified. What we seem to have here is the Chief Executive (modern term for Town Clerk) making alterations to a document which he had ordered someone else to copy, but over a subsequent period of some twenty years.

It is sheer good fortune that we happen to have the dated records of the intent to amalgamate both sets of plays, the eventual *Condemnation* and the eventual *Crucifixion*: but there are many more alterations which cannot be dated from external evidence. The obvious thing would be to find out who entered them in the *Ordo* list, and when they were in a position to be asked to do so. It is not, of course, necessary to put a name to the scribes, though some occasionally sign their entries; a sequence of dated entries is enough. It is possible to test one's educated guesses from a limited set of civic documents, but in order to do it thoroughly, we need to establish a database of scribal hands preferably from all the official documents emanating from York in the fifteenth and sixteenth centuries. I have made a start on this by my current campaign to digitize the early Freemen's Register (York City Archives MS D 1),[53] commissioning DIAMM to use the same equipment as we used for the A/Y Memorandum Book to produce the same high resolution in the images – overkill perhaps for viewers who merely want to read the names (and we hope it will be of interest to family historians) but essential for the necessary detailed palaeographical work. It should be the first such contribution to the understanding of the scribal culture and organization of England's second city in the later Middle Ages.

A major feature of these alterations and additions is that they seem in some cases to show an original sequence of one-episode pageants (possibly tableaux?) turning into multi-episode productions which are recognizably the plays as we know them from the late-fifteenth-century script. Sometimes this is done by the amalgamation of episodes, as with the *Crucifixion* above. Sometimes extra characters are added who demand an extra scene for themselves: the 'Centurion expounding the marvels at the death of Christ' in the Carpenters' pageant of the *Resurrection*; or the 'Woman accusing Peter' in the Bowyers' and Fletchers' pageant of the *Mocking of Christ*. Both are present in the scripts. But, as this manuscript reveals, they were not always there.

So here is an image recording an historical and, probably, a cultural process.[54] The fact that it happens to reflect the history of the mystery plays is incidental at this point, though it will become essential to that history. The important thing to note here is that, as Andrew Prescott has stressed in his chapter, a manuscript can show stages

---

53 The original transcription by F.F. Collins, *Register of the Freemen of the City of York*, 2 vols *Surtees Society Publications 96* and *102* (1897 for 1896 and 1900 for 1899), is now online for British History Online at <http://www.british-history.ac.uk/>. The transcription is an excellent resource but needs updating.

54 For a detailed discussion of the nature of his alterations, see M. Twycross, 'The *Ordo paginarum* revisited, with a digital camera', in D. Klausner and K. Sawyer Marsalek (eds), *'Bring furth the pagants': Studies in Early English Drama Presented to Alexandra F. Johnston* (Toronto: University of Toronto Press, 2007), pp. 105–31.

in a process, though in this case, the 'complex montage' is not piecing together a final definitive version, however dodgy, but reacting to changing circumstances.

So much for the additions. What of the erasures? My original project was to strip down the *Ordo* as we have it, and as it appears in all printed editions, to its original 1415 form. But to do that we need to find out what was underneath the palimpsest.

This may not eventually be totally possible. It appears from initial attempts that one has a better chance the longer the original has been left untouched, as the ink has longer to sink into the parchment, and presumably to change chemical composition. The Archimedes texts had several hundred years before they were removed to make way for the Euchologion. The entry for the Millers' pageant was removed after only twenty, and is proving recalcitrant, though I have managed to reconstruct parts of it. I have however had considerable success in recovering the writing underneath the erasure and overwriting at the top of folio 255r (see Plate 16).

This is the last paragraph of the proclamation made by the Sheriffs on the Eve of Corpus Christi. As it stands, it reads:

> **fraunchis & þaire bodyes to prisoun And þat** all maner of craftmen þat bringes furthe
> ther | pageantez in order & course by good players well arayed & openly spekyng vpon
> payne of lesyng | of Cs to be paide to the chambre without any pardon And that euery
> player that shall play be redy | in his pagiaunt at convenient tyme that is to say at the
> midhowre betwix iiij[th] & v[th] of the cloke in the | mornyng & then all oþer pageantes \go/
> fast folowyng ilkon after oþer as þer course is without tarieng | sub pena facienda camere
> vj [s] viijd

The details about 'good players well arayed & openly spekyng', which suggest quality control by the Council, and about the 4.30 a.m. start have been repeated in all the standard works on the York Cycle, including my own, and attributed to 1415. But it is clear from the image that everything after 'fraunchis & þaire bodyes to prison And' is written in over an erasure in a later hand. This was scrupulously footnoted by the 1979 *Records of Early English Drama* edition, and discussed briefly and even tentatively dated by the 1983 paper facsimile edition,[55] and nobody in the medieval theatre confraternity paid the slightest attention to the possible implications. However, by deploying a variety of techniques using both UV and RGB images (see Plate 16), I have managed to retrieve the original 1415 entry, and this is what it says:

> fraunchis & þaire bodyes to prisoun And þat ylk a player þat shall [?sall]
> play þat he be redy in his pageant at ....able tyme of payne of
> inprisonment & þe forfayture to be raysed þat is ordand þer fore

No 4.30 a.m., no instructions on theatrical expertise, costume, or vocal delivery.[56] By comparing the hand that made the alteration with other samples from the York House Books, I identified it as almost certainly belonging to William at Esshe, Deputy Common Clerk of the City between 1511 and 1519: so not only was it not 1415, it was a full century later.

---

55 Johnston and Rogerson, *Records of Early English Drama: York*, pp. 24–5; Beadle and Meredith, *The York Play: A Facsimile*, p. liv.

56 I discuss the implications of this in 'Forget the 4.30 a.m. Start'.

This retrieval depended on a combination of RGB and UV images. UV gives what at first seems to be only an image of the erasure; but by manipulating the levels on the Blue channel, the ghost of the erased writing begins to appear.[57] This is however tangled up illegibly with the overwriting. To get rid of that, I selected the colour of the ink in the RGB image, enhanced the contrast, and then inverted the result so that the writing became white. I then layered the white on top of the UV image and whitened it further until the whole of the over-writing was covered. This made the under-writing easier to see, like a garden viewed through a white-painted fence. The mechanics of pattern recognition swing into action, and the brain supplies the missing bits by interpolation. Cognitive psychologists know this as the Occlusion Heuristic.[58] Dr Craig-McFeely, recovering musical notation from palimpsests, turns the over-writing into a background-coloured parchment shade, but I found that it works best if the overlying body is actually visible and preferably in strong contrast. Interestingly, the scholars working on the Archimedes Palimpsest found the same:

> The imagers were working on the assumption that they were supposed to 'strip away' the prayer book text. However, the scholars pointed out that there was no point in stripping away the prayer book text unless one could literally read the Archimedes text underneath the individual prayer book characters. It was merely confusing to them to make the prayer book text look like parchment.[59]

This chimes with the observations of the cognitive psychologists. Clearly they and the palimpsest restorers need to talk to each other.

Copying the colour of the UV writing onto a blank canvas (preferably slightly tinted so as to allow the white to continue to stand out) removes further distracting background noise. In reading, pattern recognition is helped by context, and once the general sense becomes clear, other shapes fall into place. This is also a case where whole-word pattern recognition (zoom out) is more likely to work than piecing together individual letters, though there was a fair measure of that as well. This was helped by copying possible words, e.g. 'inprisonment', 'forfeyture', in the same hand and overlaying them to see if they matched. In this case, the only other sample in English (all the rest was in Latin) was on the preceding page, which was almost totally washed out, so it was crucial that the UV images from that page should be as sharp as possible. Some of the words were also available in outline in the raking-light images. Fortunately a legal proclamation is fairly formulaic and quite a number of the words were repeated.

Even the showthrough can be pressed into service: one particular shade of blue-green shadow on the verso turned out to be the ink from the under-writing, which when reversed gave a blurry but useful supplementary reading.

One reason why this erasure is easier to retrieve is that the corrector had more information to fit into the space, and wrote naturally in a smaller hand. The over-writing lies partly between the original lines, not on top of them. The over-writing

---

57 The Filter procedure **Find Edges** can sometimes produce some startling results, but these are more useful as a guide for extracting what is there.

58 See Coren et al., *Sensation and Perception*, pp. 258–9, 282.

59 See <http://www.archimedespalimpsest.org/>.

in the Archimedes Palimpsest luckily lies at right angles to the original, as the thirteenth-century scribes folded the sheets in half to make a smaller book, so again much of the erased writing is on a blank space. It is much more difficult to retrieve where the over-writing lies directly on top of the under-writing.

This type of manuscript archaeology, unlike real archaeology, is not destructive. As we dig down using the electromagnetic spectrum as a spade, we bring the underlying layers to the surface without destroying the original. The histories of the Archimedes Palimpsest or the palimpsests of the DIAMM Project are codicologically interesting in their own right, but the main drive of those investigations is to recover the prioritized document underneath the later layers. Here the various chronological layers are of equal importance: the 1511–19 version of the proclamation is as significant as the 1415 version it superseded. But even more interesting is the fact that the change was perceived to be necessary. We are privileged to be able to map out a multi-layered chronological narrative while leaving the original document intact.

Chapter 4

Representations of Sources and Data: Working with Exceptions to Hierarchy in Historical Documents

Donald Spaeth

In 1990, Steven DeRose et al. proposed that a text is best represented as an 'ordered hierarchy of content objects' (OHCO).[1] This definition has been influential, with one commentator describing this article as the *Principia* of markup studies.[2] The hierarchical model persists in XML, now recommended by the Text Encoding Initiative and the World Wide Web Consortium (W3C). Yet markup specialists have long known of exceptions to the OHCO thesis. Problems of multiple and overlapping hierarchies have attracted the most attention. These may occur because encoders wish to maintain multiple views of a document. But they are also inherent in the text, as in plays where the structures represented by acts, scenes and speeches and by the presentation of the text in verse lines unfold side by side.[3] Examples of multiple and overlapping hierarchies have been found in studies of poetic scansion, semantic structures, scribal variants and the notebooks of Ludwig Wittgenstein.[4] Fragmented texts, implied and ambiguous data, and cross-references present further problems which violate the hierarchical assumptions of OHCO. This chapter considers instances of such exceptions to hierarchy occurring in historical documents, and explores their implications for the encoding and analysis of data embedded within texts.

---

1 S.J. DeRose, D.G. Durand, E. Mylonas and A. Renear, 'What is Text, Really?', *Journal of Computing in Higher Education*, 1 (1990): 3–26.

2 P. Caton, 'Markup's Current Imbalance', *Markup Languages: Theory & Practice*, 3 (2001): 1–13.

3 D.T. Barnard, R. Hayter, M. Karababa et al., 'SGML-Based Markup for Literary Texts: Two Problems and Some Solutions', *Computers and the Humanities*, 22 (1988): 265–76.

4 A. Renear, E. Mylonas and D. Durand, 'Refining Our Notion of What Text Really Is: The Problem of Overlapping Hierarchies', in S. Hockey and N. Ide (eds), *Research in Humanities Computing*, vol. 4 (Oxford: Clarendon Press, 1996), pp. 263–77; C.M. Sperberg-McQueen and C. Huitfeldt, 'GODDAG: A Data Structure for Overlapping Hierarchies', in P. King and E.V. Munson (eds), *DDEP-PODDP 2000*, Lecture Notes in Computer Science 2023 (Berlin: Springer, 2004), pp. 139–60; D.T. Barnard et al., 'Hierarchical Encoding of Text: Technical Problems and SGML Solutions', *Computers and the Humanities*, 29 (1995): 211–31; Text Encoding Initiative, 'SIG: Overlap' <http://www.tei-c.org.uk/wiki/index.php/ SIG: Overlap>, accessed 21 May 2006.

Historians who use computers have most often taken a data-oriented view of their sources, rather than a text-oriented view. They have studied well-structured 'roll-call' documents, such as census enumerators' books and pollbooks, which take the physical form of tables, or sources such as parish registers which are sufficiently regular to be easily represented as matrices. Less regular sources have been shoehorned into the same table structure. Advocates of source-oriented data processing have long criticized the data-oriented approach, arguing for the need for specialist historical software, such as Kleio.[5] XML appears to hold considerable promise for historians who wish to integrate data-oriented and source-oriented views of historical documents, permitting data structures to be represented, while remaining true to the form of these documents as texts.[6] Many historical documents, such as depositions and charters, take the form of texts, but nonetheless contain clearly identifiable data elements and are reasonably regular in structure. This chapter explores one such category of documents, probate records, and particularly the probate inventory, using a small XML database of records from seventeenth-century Thame, in Oxfordshire. The database contains around 300 inventories, listing over 30,000 domestic, agricultural and trade goods.[7]

Unlike bibliographies, invoicing systems, and other domains commonly used to demonstrate how data may be represented in XML, historical documents contain data that are both mixed and semi-structured. Data are mixed when textual information and data elements are intermingled. A document is a text which has data elements embedded within it. Data values may appear anywhere in the text, at any level of the hierarchy, and not just at the 'leaves' which represent the tree's furthest reaches. Besides being inefficient to search, mixed data can also cause difficulties at the analysis stage. Semi-structured data are less predictable than the table structure with which historians using databases and statistical packages are most familiar. Although there are discernible data elements, particular elements may occur at different points of the hierarchy or be omitted entirely. The boundaries of data elements themselves may be ambiguous and uncertain. The depth of the data hierarchy is unknown, since elements may be embedded within other elements. Indeed, the data may not be fully hierarchical.[8] Historical data have all of these characteristics of semi-structured data.

---

5 M. Thaller, 'The Historical Workstation Project', *Computers and the Humanities*, 25 (1991): 149–62; *Kleio version 5.1.1* (Queen Mary and Westfield College, 1993); C. Harvey and J. Press, *Databases in Historical Research* (Houndmills: Macmillan, 1996), ch. 7.

6 D. Greenstein and L. Burnard, 'Speaking with One Voice: Encoding Standards and the Prospects for an Integrated Approach to Computing in History', *Computers and the Humanities*, 29 (1995): 137–48; D. Greenstein (ed.), *Modelling Historical Data* (St Katharinen: Scripta Mercaturae Verlag, 1991).

7 The database is described in D.A. Spaeth, 'Representing Text as Data: The Analysis of Historical Sources in XML', *Historical Methods*, 37 (2004): 73–85. I am grateful to the Thame Research Group for permitting me to use their transcripts of probate records.

8 S. Abiteboul, P. Buneman and D. Suciu, *Data on the Web: From Relations to Semistructured Data and XML* (San Francisco: Morgan Kaufmann, 2004); P. Buneman, 'Semistructured Data', *Proceedings of the Sixteenth ACM SIGACT-SIGMOD-SIGART Symposium on Principles of Database Systems* (New York: ACM, 1997), pp. 117–21.

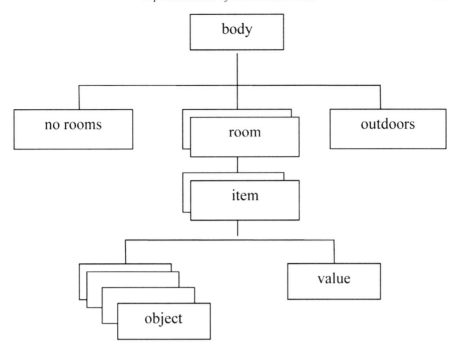

Figure 4.1   A data tree for a probate inventory

The remainder of this chapter is divided into three parts. First, we will briefly examine the probate inventory as a source, giving examples of its potential uses. Then we will give examples of exceptions to hierarchy, particularly those resulting from implied and fragmented data, and discuss alternative approaches to encoding them. Finally, we will consider the use of XQuery and XPath to interrogate data with hierarchical anomalies. XQuery proves to be a highly powerful tool for dealing with hierarchical and semi-hierarchical data, but its power and flexibility mean that extra care must be taken at the encoding and processing stages to minimize risk of incorrect results. The goal is to identify markup approaches which permit researchers to interrogate native XML databases without advanced programming skills, just as they would interrogate the structured databases with which they are more familiar.

The historical domain

Probate inventories are lists, with values, of the moveable property that individuals owned when they died.[9] Historians have made extensive use of them to study wealth, agriculture, consumption and material culture, among other topics. A number of studies have relied heavily upon quantitative analysis, in which project-oriented methods have dominated over source-oriented data processing. Most studies have

---

9 T. Arkell, N. Evans and N. Goose (eds), *When Death Do Us Part* (Oxford: Leopard's Head, 2000).

Table 4.1   Percentage of halls with hearth

	1600–24	1625–49	1650–74	1675–99
% of houses with at least one hall	95	92	90	68
% of halls with hearth	68	59	64	56
Total number of inventories listing rooms	58	62	48	38

Source: Spaeth (2004)

extracted data elements and represented them, often in a coded form, in structured databases suitable for quantitative analysis.[10] While this has led to the loss of considerable contextual information, it has meant that these researchers have not had to address directly the complex structure of the documents.

An inventory normally takes the form of a hierarchy. After an introductory paragraph, which records the date and the names of the deceased and the appraisers, a typical example lists the contents of the house, room by room, as well as belongings found in outhouses, the shop, the yard, and surrounding fields. Goods are grouped into 'items' (from the Latin for 'also'), each of which is assigned a value. The document's structure, in which inventories contain rooms, rooms contain items, and items contain objects and values, can be represented as a data tree or graph (see Figure 4.1). Tables 4.1 and 4.2 demonstrate the kinds of information which can be extracted from inventories. Details of room contents allow the organization of houses and the functions of particular rooms to be studied. A full-text database of inventories also can be used to study how appraisers represented household contents. The grouping of objects into items, and even the presence of room details, reflected choices made by appraisers.[11] An accurate picture of the reality and representation of houses depends upon the encoding system adopted and upon the degree of correspondence between the representation found in the document and the physical layout of the house.

---

10 C. Shammas, *The Pre-Industrial Consumer in England and America* (Oxford: Clarendon Press, 1990); L. Weatherill, *Consumer Behaviour and Material Culture, 1660–1760* (Routledge, 1988); A.H. Jones, *Wealth of a Nation To Be* (New York: Columbia University Press, 1980). For an exception, see M. Overton, 'Computer Analysis of an Inconsistent Data Source: The Case of Probate Inventories', *Journal of Historical Geography*, 3 (1977): 317–26; M. Overton, et al., *Production and Consumption in English Households, 1600–1750* (Routledge, 2004).

11 I am currently preparing an article on appraising its intellectual implications, with the provisional title, 'The Middling Sort Make Sense of the World of Goods: Identification and Differentiation in Seventeenth-century England'.

Table 4.2   Choices made by Thame appraisers

	Rooms? (by invent)	>1 items (by room)	Counting (by object)	Descriptors (by object)	Lumber (by item)
Thame	68%	43%	34%	21%	10%
Panel	69%	42%	38%	21%	7%
Trinder	85%	51%	43%	13%	3%
Stone	86%	57%	37%	21%	9%
Louch	100%	48%	42%	16%	8%
Jemett	73%	57%	36%	19%	7%
Parslow	38%	33%	32%	35%	9%
Peck	89%	15%	40%	22%	23%

Source: Thame XML Database

Markup

XML represents a text as an ordered hierarchy of content objects, known as elements. An element may contain data values (PCDATA) and child elements, so long as each child element is fully contained within its parent and siblings do not overlap. The end tag, which represents the completion of a child element, must occur before the end tag which marks the end of its parent. Child elements may, in turn, contain their own children, which are grandchildren of the original parent. This simple system provides an elegant means of representing data. A relational table may be represented by viewing an element as the container for a table, the element's children as records, its grandchildren as fields, and the data values within the grandchildren as the field values. This structure is at least partially self-documenting because the names of the elements in the hierarchy represent the table, record and fieldnames; exceptions require further documentation, however. Restrictions can be placed upon the number and order of values using a schema (such as a DTD or an XML Schema), although it is advisable to keep restrictions upon semi-structured data to a minimum.

There are two alternative ways to represent data in XML. A table-based approach imposes a structure upon the data by preparing a template of elements in advance, into which the data are transcribed. The order and structure of elements are fixed. This approach is often used in published examples of XML databases, which have been written for database specialists who wish to represent legacy or new data in XML.[12] It is little different than entering data into a conventional relational database. The logical view of the data is allowed to take precedence, and aspects of the physical representation of the data which do not align with this logical view are

---

12 E.g., W3C, 'XML Query Use Cases: W3C Working Draft, 15 Sep. 2005' <http://www.w3.org/TR/xquery-use-cases/>. See also the useful discussion in R. Bourlet, 'XML and Databases' (updated September 2005) <http://www.rpbourret.com/xml/XMLAndDatabases.htm>, accessed 13 December 2007.

ignored. This approach raises no hierarchical difficulties and will therefore receive no further attention here. Alternatively, a text-based approach exploits the hierarchical nature of XML to represent directly the hierarchies found in the documents. In a purely source-oriented model, the transcribed text is preserved unaltered, without modification, addition or omission. XML elements are inserted into the file to make the data structures within the text explicit. This approach creates a mixed data file, with text present at all levels, including words (such as 'Imprimis' and 'Item') which are structural signposts rather than data. In addition to the data found in the text, data such as identification numbers, normalized forms and classifications, if needed, may be introduced as attributes. The text-based approach has the advantage that, if the markup is later stripped from the file, the original text remains intact. It is nonetheless recognized that the database is only a representation of the source and that some questions, especially those that concern the physical appearance of the document, may require the researcher to view the original source. However, the text-based approach relies upon the alignment of logical and physical views of the data. Hierarchical exceptions, in which data elements do not appear in the source where expected, will cause problems for analysis.

A simplified encoded inventory is shown in Figure 4.2. This hierarchy may be represented schematically as follows, in which elements which may repeat are starred:

```
inventory*
    body
        room*
            item*
                object*
                value
```

Although most inventories follow this structure, there are exceptions. Levels of the hierarchy may be omitted entirely, or it may be unclear where a level begins and ends. In Thame, appraisers chose not to organize items by room location in one-

---

```
<inventory>
The inventory of the goods of <deceased< <name> John Small</name>.</deceased>
prepared on <date> 14 April 1640 </date>
<body> Li s d Imprimis <room name="hall"> in the hall
<item>
two <object quantity="2"> joined tables </object> and
six <object quantiy="6"> jointed stools </object>
appraised at <value>12s.</value></item><room>
<room name ="chamber">In the chamber <!--etc. --></room>
</body>
</inventory>
```

Figure 4.2   An encoded inventory

1. Cooke lacks status
<app> <name> Steven Cooke <name></app>
<app> <name> John Springall </name> <status> yeomen</status> </app>

2. Adding a group wrapper
<group type="app" status="yeoman">
<app> <name> Steven Cooke <name></app>
<app> <name> John Springall </name> <status> yeomen</status> </app>
<group>

Figure 4.3   Dealing with implied data

third of inventories. Even if they did list by room, most inventories contained some objects whose exact location in the house is unclear. These are instances of semi-structured or ambiguous data rather than serious exceptions to hierarchy, and these are easily resolved by introducing virtual rooms, such as <norooms> and <other> which take the place of <room> in the hierarchy. A more serious structural problem occurs when data values are not explicitly stated, although they are implied by the syntax of the text. Instances of implied data are common. For example, an inventory may record that goods were appraised by 'Steven Cooke and John Springall yeomen'. Similarly, a group of domestic goods may be covered by an overall description at the start, such as 'All of the pewter, at 7d per pound, two dishes, three bowls, a candlestick.' The first example leaves no doubt that both men enjoyed yeoman status (a middling farmer, below gentleman), but a markup system which relies solely on the text to provide the data will be missing a status for Cooke. Attributes provide an easy solution, but a more elegant alternative might be to code the linguistic structure explicitly, by introducing an additional level of the hierarchy, which serves as a wrapper (as in Figure 4.3).

Non-adjacent text presents a more serious exception, since it means that the hierarchy is fragmented. This may occur when one sibling is interrupted by another, before it has itself finished. The inventory of Robert Maund provides a good example.[13] (See Figure 4.4: the inventory has been simplified and line numbers have been added for readability; see Plate 17 for a facsimile of the original document).

The data model assumes that all of the goods in a room will be listed together. Yet in this inventory the contents of two rooms – the kitchen and chamber over the kitchen – are fragmented. To complicate matters further, the bedding from three chambers (lines 5–7) is listed together in a virtual room (line 8), separate from the other objects in these rooms. A strict source-based markup system fails because the logical and physical structures of the document are not aligned with one another. To put the problem differently, the representation of the house constructed by the appraisers differs both from the physical layout of the house and from the logical

13 Oxfordshire Record Office, PEC 46/2/26.

Inventory of Robert Maund, taken 16 April 1660
1. In the hall [etc.]
2. In the parlour [etc.]
3. In the **kitchen**, a knife, tubs, barrels, spinning wheels [etc.], 1Li 15s
4. In the brewhouse [etc.]
5. In the chamber [etc.]
6. In the chamber over the parlour [etc.]
7. In the chamber over the kitchen, 2 bedsteads, 2 trunks [etc.], 1Li 1s
8. Upon the bedsteads in these rooms, 2 featherbeds, 5 feather pillows [etc.], 5 Li 15s
9. More in the **kitchen**, 12 pewter platters, 1 pewter basin [etc.], 5Li 10s
10. In the chamber over the kitchen, 9 pairs of sheets, 2 pillowberes [etc.], 5 Li 2s

Figure 4.4   An inventory with fragmented hierarchy

structure of the data. Implementation of a simple markup system based upon the expected hierarchy would lead each part-room to be encoded as if it were a complete room, with the consequence that an extra kitchen and chamber would be added to the house. A count of rooms would find three more than were physically present in the house, while understating the number of objects in each room.

It must be stressed that, although not unique, this inventory is a relatively uncommon exception to the normal hierarchy. Unlike better-known examples of multiple hierarchies in literary texts, only one view of the data is valid in most of the database. Only in a few cases do the logical and physical structures represent different views of the same document, and these apply only to a section of this document. An encoder may therefore be reluctant to impose a more complex system of markup on the data, when this will be needed only in exceptional cases. Set against this must be the likelihood that the presence of exceptions will complicate analysis of the data.

There are several solutions to the problem of fragmented hierarchy, each of which has implications for the analysis of the marked up data.[14] We have already set aside encoding the rooms precisely as they occur in the source, since treating fragmented rooms as if they were complete will produce misleading results. Yet, we would be equally reluctant to adjust the text so that it conforms to the expected logical structure. This would conflict with the source-oriented ethos and obscure the representation chosen by appraisers. Another option is to mark up the *hierarchy* exactly as it appears in the text, so that rooms are literally located within other rooms, even though this violates the expectation that rooms are siblings. The chambers are then encoded as children of the kitchen. Although unorthodox, this has the advantage of recording the structure of the original text, and perhaps also the

---

14 Semantic web technologies may provide an alternative solution, by allowing the definition of multiple ontologies. These technologies, and their application to historical documents, are discussed in ch. 5, below.

physical construction of the house and its representation. Chambers were sometimes added above existing rooms, so there is a sense in which they can be regarded as contained within them. Reading the inventory, we can see that appraisers went from the kitchen to the brewhouse, then upstairs to the chambers, finishing with the chamber over the kitchen, before returning downstairs to the kitchen, where it appears that they discovered goods that they had missed the first time. It is likely that there was a door between the kitchen and the brewhouse, and that there was at least one staircase, perhaps leading from the brewhouse. It is not entirely clear why the appraisers returned to the chamber over the kitchen; perhaps a second pass through the chambers to list the bedding led them to discover more objects. Using markup to embed some rooms in others may therefore reveal historical features of the inventory, even though it fails to conform to the logical model. As tempting as this option may be, nesting elements which logically are siblings can produce unintended consequences for analysis, so that objects located within the inner rooms may be counted twice. It would not work with this inventory, in any case, because the chamber over the kitchen is also fragmented.

```
(a) Approach 1
<partroom name="kitchen" id="r1"> ... data ...</partroom>
... other rooms ...
<partroom id="r2"> ... data ...</partroom>
<join result="room" target="r1" r2"/>

(b) Approach 2
<room name="kitchen">
... items ...
<item target="i1"/.
</room>
... other rooms ...
<detachedroom id="i1"> ... data ... <detachedroom>

(c) Approach 3
<room name="kitchen" status="fragment" part="1">
   <item> ... data ... </item>
   <item view="data"> ...data ...</item> </room>
<room name="chamber"> ... data ...</room>
<room name="kitchen" status="fragment" part="2">
   <item view="source"> ... data ... </item><room>
```

Figure 4.5   Three approaches to encoding fragmented hierarchy

This leaves three different approaches for more detailed consideration; these are summarized in Figure 4.5. The first two approaches give one view of the data priority, but add tags which enable the other view to be reconstructed, if necessary. It is assumed here that the source view is given priority, but this is not essential.

The first approach follows the TEI's recommendations for encoding multiple hierarchies.[15] An ID attribute is added to each of the affected room elements, and the <join> element is then used to put the parts together, using the target attribute to locate the IDs. The room fragments are encoded as <partroom> elements so that an XPath search for <room> fragments does not mistake the fragments for complete rooms. A <join> element is then used to stitch together the part-rooms. At present, a schema is required to define the ID attribute, but work is underway to remove this requirement.[16] Approach 2 is similar but is intended to be more intuitive. A cross-reference is inserted where the data should appear logically, enabling it to be fetched from its position in the document. The detached fragment is again 'hidden', in a <detachedroom> element, so that it is not mistakenly treated as a room in its own right. Since this approach also relies upon an ID attribute, a schema is needed.

In the first two approaches, the text fragments occur only once in the encoded document. The third approach is simply to encode both views, so that the problematic text appears twice, once in its original position and again in its logical position. Attributes are then used to label the two views as either 'data' or 'source', depending upon which view is given priority. This approach is the only one to change the original text; if the markup is removed, two instances of the detached fragment will appear. It goes without saying that, whichever approach is adopted, proper documentation is essential. The chosen markup approach will clearly have implications for data analysis: simple queries based on an incomplete understanding of the data structures will produce unexpected results.

Processing

XML data can be interrogated using the XPath, XQuery and XSLT languages developed by the W3C. XPath and XSLT have been W3C recommendations since 1999; at the time of writing XQuery is still only at the candidate recommendation stage, but several implementations are available.[17] XQuery may be thought of as SQL for XML data. It offers many of the features one would expect of a relational database, although its lack of an update facility leaves XSLT as the preferred tool for transforming data. XSLT is particularly good at modifying particular parts of the data structure, even when the data are irregular, because it is event-driven and recursive rather then procedural.

---

15 C.M. Sperberg-McQueen and L. Burnard (eds), *TEI P4: Guidelines for Electronic Text Encoding and Interchange [XML Version]* (Oxford: Text Encoding Initiative Consortium, 2002) <http://www.tei-c.org/release/doc/tei-p4-doc/html/>, ch. 31, accessed 13 December 2007.

16 W3C, 'xml:id Version 1.0: W3C Recommendation 9 September 2005' <http://www.w3.org/TR/xml-id/>, accessed 15 December 2007.

17 W3C, 'XQuery 1.0: An XML Query Language: W3C Candidate Recommendation 3 November 2005'; 'XSL Transformations (XSLT) Version 1.0: W3C Recommendation 16 November 1999'; 'XML Path Language (XPath) Version 1.0: W3C Recommendation 16 November 1999'; all at <http://www.w3.org/>, accessed 15 December 2007. The queries in this article were tested using the open-source version of 'The Saxon XSLT and XQuery Processor', Saxon SB-8.7.1, developed by Michael Kay, downloaded from <http://sourceforge.net/project/showfiles.php?group_id=29872>, accessed 21 May 2006.

Templates are used to retrieve and change only those elements that match specified patterns, rather like a mechanic removing and replacing parts. Both XQuery and XSLT rely upon XPath to select particular 'nodes' from the data hierarchy and to navigate between nodes.[18]

Although there are some similarities between XQuery and SQL, those familiar with traditional databases will find that the experience of querying XML data is very different. The relational model is relatively simple. In XML, as we have seen, the same data can be represented in several ways, and this flexibility complicates analysis, even with regular data. Complex markup makes matters worse. It may be necessary to look in several places for the same data; if the data are fragmented, then they need to be reassembled before analysis can continue. This implies a two-stage process, in which the data are first assembled, probably using XSLT, producing a working file which has the expected logical structure. Alternatively, one can interrogate the data directly, using XQuery to build up complex queries, which perform multiple passes through the same data. A single query may include several XPath expressions, each of which passes through the entire data or a defined subset. As in SQL, the results of one query may immediately be used as input to another. There is, however, a price to pay for such flexibility; queries can be both difficult to construct and slow to process.

XPath handles semi-structured data, in which elements may appear in unexpected places, well, using axes. The descendant axis will retrieve specified elements anywhere they occur in the hierarchy. The ancestor axis can then be used to climb back up the tree as far as needed to retrieve contextual information. Thus, the expression

doc("example.xml")//room[@name="kitchen"]//object

will retrieve all objects found in kitchens. (The double-slash is a shortcut for the descendant axis.) However, the power of the descendant axis carries its own risks, for one can easily retrieve elements that one does not want, because they share the same name. This drawback can be addressed by using attribute values or parent element names to contextualize, and thus refine, a search. Nonetheless, care must be taken when marking up the data, to ensure that one will be able to retrieve all of the data one wants, but no more. The element name is itself data in a way in which a field name in a relational database is not.

Data are retrieved from an XML database by using either an XPath expression on its own or a FLOWR (or 'flower') expression, seeded by XPath, to iterate through the data. XPath on its own is quite limited, so FLOWR expressions are needed to reorder, join and present results. However, there are important differences between the ways in which XPath and FLOWR handle data. A crucial feature of XPath 1.0 is that it removes duplicate nodes, namely those which not only have the same name and value, but also the same identity, essentially the same position in the data file. In contrast, FLOWR expressions do not remove duplicates. It is for this reason that

---

18 M. Brundage, *XQuery: The XML Query Language* (Boston: Addison-Wesley, 2004); M. Kay, *XSLT Programmer's Reference*, 2d ed. (Birmingham: Wrox, 2001), 75–81; W3C, 'XQuery Update Facility, W3C Working Draft, 8 May 2006' <http://www.w3.org/TR/xqupdate/>.

(a) Joining room fragments

```
let $root := doc("test.xml")
for $join in $root//join
let $result := $root/id(data)($join[@result="room"]/@target))/*
let $merge :=
<room>{ attribute name {data($result/../@name)[1]}}
{$result}
</room>
return $merge|$root//room
```

(b) Counting objects in source-oriented view

```
for $a in doc("newtest.xml")//room
return count($a/item[@view="source" or not(@view)]/object
```

(c) Counting objects in data-oriented view

```
for $a in doc("newtest.xml")//room[@part="1" or not(@part)]
return count($a//object)
```

Figure 4.6   XQuery solutions

embedding one room in another, as suggested above, produces unpredictable results. The objects in the embedded room will be counted once if retrieved using XPath, but in some contexts twice if a FLOWR expression is used.

What implications do the three markup approaches that I outlined earlier have for retrieval using XPath/XQuery? In each case, it is possible to devise a single XQuery which brings together the room fragments and treats the kitchen as a single room. However, it is easier to query the third approach than the other two, as can be seen from the examples in Figure 4.6. In query (a), a fragmented room encoded with a join (Approach 1) is stuck back together again. Queries (b) and (c) count the number of objects per room, depending upon whether a source-oriented or data-oriented view is adopted.

Markup approaches 1 (Figure 4.5(a)) and 2 (Figure 4.5(b)) are more difficult to query because it is necessary to retrieve data whether or not they conform to the logical model, while ensuring that the data fragments are recovered in the correct position. The query shown in Figure 4.6(a) constructs a new room (the kitchen) using the information contained in the <join> element (Approach 1); the @target attribute values serve as pointers to the <partroom> elements assigned those ID numbers. This new room (constructed in the $merge variable) is then added to other (unfragmented) rooms in the last line of the query. Although I am sure that this query could be written more elegantly, it demonstrates the difficulties of querying complex data in XML. The queries in Figures 4.6(b) and 4.6(c) count the number of objects in each room, including a fragmented room, encoded according to Approach

3 (Figure 4.5(c)). These solutions are relatively simple, because only one pass is required through the data and no elements need to be constructed. Attributes are used to switch on one view of the data and switch off the other. A simple Boolean OR in the XPath predicate ensures that both normal data (which lack the @view attribute) and fragmented data are retrieved. The final query is particularly simple, since the detached room fragment (coded as part="2") can be ignored entirely.

It is often said that a system of markup reflects the purpose of the researcher. XML's flexibility means that even researchers who share the same objectives can represent data very differently. As we have seen, there are approaches to marking up even complex and irregular sources which permit easy and consistent analysis of native XML data, with the potential to permit historians to use XQuery without needing specialist programmers.

Concluding reflections

Although XML is relatively young, markup has a much longer history. Appraisers marked up inventories, using words, symbols and layout to organize and present information about a house and the goods within it. The inventory can be seen as a representation of a house and of the spaces within it. A statistical file, relational database and XML database may each, in turn, represent the inventory and, at one step removed, this house. Each of the representations is different. None provides a complete description of the house, any more than a transcript of an inventory, however accurate, fully captures the original handwritten document.

The debate between source-oriented and data-oriented approaches to historical data processing reflects the conflict between the complexities of historical sources and the need to simplify data for the purposes of analysis. The approaches to markup explored in this chapter have all addressed this tension, even when markup is used to delay the choice until the point of analysis. The appraisers of the goods of Robert Maund, and indeed all appraisers, faced similar challenges in reconciling the competing demands of listing and valuing goods. But they did not have to fit the information they recorded into a database.

PART II
VIRTUAL HISTORIES AND
PRE-HISTORIES
FINDING MEANINGS

Chapter 5

Finding Needles in Haystacks: Data-mining in Distributed Historical Datasets

Fabio Ciravegna, Mark Greengrass, Tim Hitchcock, Sam Chapman, Jamie McLaughlin and Ravish Bhagdev

Keyword-orientated searching is an integral component of research information strategy in the arts and humanities – as organic as looking up a word in a dictionary or browsing the index of a book. Perhaps because it is cognate to such familiar activities, we have subconsciously adapted to it, becoming skilled at wrenching relevant information from simplistic interfaces, avoiding ambiguous text-strings, and combining terms to avoid redundancy of retrieved information. Yet, although we necessarily make use of the meticulously refined ranking mechanisms of the Internet's commercial search engines, and exploit the preponderance of uncommon acronyms and compounds words that pervade the material on the web, many scholars in the arts and humanities are frustrated by the limitations of keyword-orientated searching and suspicious of the underlying ranking schema. This is because they find words rather than meaning. Meaning, however, is essentially about information structure and context. It is rare for a researcher in the arts and humanities to desire the indiscriminate retrieval of every occurrence of a particular text-string. Far more common is the need to discover a particular type of record, produced in a peculiar set of circumstances, within a given context. Yet such information is generally not available in keyword-orientated search environments. Arts and humanities scholars make do, grateful for the results which they achieve over the Internet through keyword-orientated searching. This is despite the difficulties in finding the right search term for string-matching (which become so much greater with pre-modern non-standard orthographies, different lexicons and lexemes, and a greater propensity to mixed linguistic environments), and the inherent frustrations of synonymity, homonymity and data redundancy. We live with these limitations, but the reality is that keyword searching discards information which, for arts and humanities scholars, determines the relevance of the data they are seeking.

The situation is further complicated when keyword-orientated searching is applied to bespoke databases, accessed through application-specific interfaces. This is typically how humanities computing resources have developed, accessed through application-specific interfaces. They have generally been developed as responses to very specific academic questions, and therefore often provide distinctive methods of interrogating their data. When projects are completed, and when their specific questions have been answered, the data is most commonly consigned to online repositories which do not preserve the functionality of the original interface. In addition, their disparate nature means that they are peculiarly difficult to search effectively using keyword-orientated search services of the kind relied upon for general Internet information retrieval. Even if the information is in the form of text (and, as is clear from other contributions to this volume, this would often not be the case) and available in a distributed fashion, it often has not been indexed. When it has, the context of the information has been disregarded, even though well-designed databases contain a wealth of such information, either implied in their structure or declared explicitly in markup. This persistent information loss creates a situation where humanities computing resources do not constitute a coherent or accessible body of online knowledge.

To what extent can Semantic Web technologies provide a solution to this problem? The 'Semantic Web Vision' is, briefly, an attempt to extend the existing World Wide Web to allow much more of the information in web pages to be intelligible to machines.[1] The objective is that software programs, or 'agents', should be able to navigate, digest, categorize and exchange information from different websites in a more sophisticated way. The process is commonly described as the 'mining of knowledge' as distinct from the 'retrieval of data' of the kind achieved by keyword-orientated searching. Such agents already exist; and the principles of the Semantic Web have already begun to be applied in other academic disciplines. The Advanced Knowledge Technologies Project is one such interdisciplinary research collaboration, focused upon the advanced management and mining of knowledge, funded by the EPSRC (Engineering and Physical Sciences Research Council).[2] The Natural Language Processing Group at the University of Sheffield is a constituent part of that project.[3] Among its outputs has been Armadillo, an agent designed to provide machine-readable content for the Semantic Web. It produces automated domain-specific annotation of large repositories in a largely unsupervised way, extracting information from different sources and integrating the retrieved knowledge into a repository which can be used both to access the extracted information and to annotate the pages whence the information was identified. By linking back to the original data, the user can verify the correctness and provenance of the information concerned.[4] The methodology has been applied, for example, to technical documentation accompanying jet engines to enable engineers world-wide to find their way swiftly to the data relevant to their particular needs. It has also been developed to help investigate emerging issues, and to enable the life cycle (in information terms) of an engine to be stored and interrogated, linking interrelated data and documents

---

1 Among the many surveys, see G. Antoniou, and F. v. Harmelen, *A Semantic Web Primer* (Cambridge, MA: MIT Press, 2004).

2 N. Shadbolt and K. O'Hara, *Advanced Knowledge Technologies: Selected Papers* (Southampton: University of Southampton Department of Electronics and Computer Science, 2004).

3 <http://nlp.shef.ac.uk> (all urls accessed on 7 September 2007).

4 F. Ciravegna, S. Chapman, A. Dingli, Y. Wilks, 'Learning to Harvest Information for the Semantic Web', in *Proceedings of the 1st European Semantic Web Symposium* (Heraklion, 2004).

in a variety of different media and in a very interrelated fashion. It is not difficult to envisage circumstances in which data mining, using Semantic Web agents, would be relevant, timely and crucial. If one could locate all the chicken farms in a particular region and map them, using such data-mining technologies, the response to an incident of avian flu (to take a hypothetical example) would be considerably enhanced. Emergency response is another of Armadillo's existing applications[5]. The potential for the application of such technologies is considerable.

To what extent can they *also* be used to move beyond keyword-orientated searching when consulting distributed scholarly research materials? In principle, the Semantic Web's key objective – automated information exchange – faces the same problem of the 'de-contextualization' of information. This is why its technologies include techniques and standards for retaining the context of data between different websites, media and domains. Can we not apply them to provide a framework for historical and pre-historical research, allowing us to ask questions and evaluate data in ways which were previously very difficult? That was the objective of the collaborative research project, funded by the AHRC ICT programme, completed in September 2007, of which this paper is the outcome.[6]

It is easy to be mesmerized into thinking that Semantic Web technologies, in themselves, provide revolutionary techniques for properly interpreting the context of data. They do not. One of the main languages of the Semantic Web is the Resource Description Framework (RDF), a standard defined by the W3C, and based upon Uniform Resource Identifier (URI) and Extensible Markup Language (XML) standards.[7] So one of the primary functions of a Semantic Web agent such as Armadillo is to perform information extraction on large bodies of data in order to generate facts (or statements) expressed in RDF. Such data-extraction techniques do not, of themselves, however, constitute the Semantic Web. They are simply one of many methods that can be employed to create content for it. In practice, Armadillo's generic data-extraction facilities were seldom used in this particular project. Humanities computer resources do not benefit from such techniques because they are usually highly structured to begin with. The datasets that we accumulated to create our 'haystack' were, in this respect, very typical of what we might expect to find among the various distributed resources available in electronic media in a particular historical or archaeological domain.

It comes as no surprise to humanities research practitioners that there is generally no one electronic archive or dataset that will meet all their research needs in answering a particular question. That would be like discovering that all their answers were discoverable within one archive, or one archaeological site. We expect to use a variety of sources, not all of them particularly well suited to answering the question we are asking. We are not working towards a 'set of sets' or electronic pansophy, the equivalent of all the historical materials available from all periods, places, individuals,

5 S. Potter, Y. Kalfoglou, H. Alani et al., *The Application of Advanced Knowledge Technologies for Emergency Response*, in 4th International Information Systems for Crisis Response and Management (ISCRAM 07) (Delft, 2007).

6 <http://www.hrionline.ac.uk/armadillo/>.

7 <http://www.w3.org/RDF/>.

institutions, in the past. To imagine such a utopia is to understand why it will never happen. Our representation of the past is an *imagined* plenum, fundamental to our conceptualization when we refer to an entity such as 'eighteenth-century London' or 'Augustan Rome'. The 'haystacks' of data with which we interrogate that imagined plenum are congeries, put together in contingent fashion to help us in that imaginary process. They have no more ontological value than the fact that this or that bundle of papers happened to find its way into this or that archive. Archaeological site materials, by contrast, do have ontological value by virtue of where objects are located in the ground, a value which can be recorded and interrogated. But once that recording and interrogation has taken place, the information joins the historical 'haystack' of materials, as contingent and as contextual as the rest of it. Our particular test-bed of sources was constructed around those available that related to eighteenth-century London. We initially selected 12 datasets, the basis for our test-bed choice being the Proceedings of the Old Bailey Online, a substantial database of the published reports of over 100,000 trials before the principal court of London, spanning the period from 1674 to 1834.[8] It is 'the largest body of texts detailing the lives of non-elite people ever published' for the pre-modern period, according to its editors, one of whom (Tim Hitchcock) was involved in the Armadillo for historians project from its inception. Four other datasets were located among deposits with the Arts and Humanities Data Service (AHDS), of which only one was functionally consultable in public media.[9] Other datasets were provisionally identified from other providers, mostly from the academic/public sectors, but with two resources potentially being offered from the private/commercial sector. In the event, however, none of them was incorporated into this initial demonstrator.

The majority of these materials were, in reality, comma-separated variable files. The Prerogative Court of Canterbury wills, for example, was a painstakingly-constructed index to all the 1,015,603 wills (for individuals who were not uniquely from London, but from across the British Isles) held in that source at the National Archives. The brief details include the testator's name, occupation and address along with the unique identifier which enables the user to access the original images of the document online. The Index to the Eighteenth-Century Fire Insurance Policy registers, by contrast, was a more limited inventory of that proportion of the estimated 1.25 million fire insurance documents issued by the Sun and Royal Exchange

---

8   <http://www.oldbaileyonline.org/>.

9   These were (with the AHDS accession reference): The Marine Society Registers (Long-term Changes in Nutrition, Welfare and Productivity in Britain – Heights and Ages of Landmen Volunteers Recruited to the Marine Society, 1756-1814 (hist-2132-1)); the Prerogative Court of Canterbury Wills for the Eighteenth Century (Prerogative Court of Canterbury Wills, 1384-1858 (hist-4816-1)); Eighteenth-century Fire Insurance Policies (Index to Eighteenth Century Fire Insurance Policy Registers (hist-1838-1)); and the Westminster Historical Database (Westminster Historical Database, 1749-1820 – Voters Social Structure and Electoral Behaviour (hist-3908-1)). The latter was also available on a CD-ROM from Bristol Academic Press (2000) to accompany C. Harvey, E.M. Green and P.J. Corfield, *The Westminster Historical Database: Voters, Social Structure and Electoral Behaviour* (Bristol: Bristol Academic Press, 1998). We are grateful to all the editors of these datasets for the opportunity they have provided for our research enquiry.

insurance houses covered by the period from 1777 to 1786. The database provides very summary information of the name(s) of the policy-holder(s), their address(es) and occupation(s), a unique identification number and the total sum insured. The data is, once again, not limited to London, though it tends to concentrate in the southern counties of England. The Westminster Historical Database is more complex, and consists of tabulated voter data from surviving poll books from elections in the Parliamentary constituency of Westminster, correlated with evidence from the city's rate-books. The right to vote in the Westminster constituency lay, somewhat unusually in the unreformed English electoral system, with adult male rate-paying householders. Thousands of them participated in each of the 12 elections between 1749 and 1820. The database contains individual-level data on pre-reform electoral behaviour for the constituency between 1749 and 1820, and consists of 23 tables in standard relational format. Of these, 12 are electronic editions of the surviving Westminster Poll Books for the years between 1749 and 1820, enhanced through the addition of supplementary name and occupational codes. A further nine tables summarize the selected Westminster Parish Rate Books which complement the Poll Book tables and which, through record linkage, enable a much fuller representation to be made of Westminster's voters, their social standing and political preferences. A further two tables contain coding schema for names and occupations respectively. The Old Bailey Proceedings Online, by contrast, is a highly-structured XML-coded text repository, which uses over 40 different tags and attributes to describe criminal proceedings and their outcomes. There is, quite simply, no way that any generic software solution could properly integrate these highly complex and specialized databases without human intervention. In what ways would Semantic Web technologies help to solve the problem of integration?

The first step was to construct small, bespoke scripts to generate RDF from each of the datasets so as to represent their fields. This was done using Extensible Stylesheet Language Transformations (XLST), quite a simple process which retained the underlying data structures more faithfully than even the most sophisticated generic approach.[10] The more complicated issue is how to create a data model which can sensibly contain the information from the various different fields and relate them one to another. In effect, the essence of the Semantic Web is about drawing data from a variety of differently structured sources and rendering it intelligible within a single, unified matrix which defines the relations of the parts to one another, and to the whole. This matrix is most commonly described as an 'ontology'. The term 'ontology' has a specialized meaning here within computer science. It has been variously defined, but most concisely as 'an explicit specification of a shared conceptualization'.[11] Ontologies are expressed using another W3C recommendation, Web Ontology Language (OWL). OWL is, in reality, a 'dialect' of RDF, a 'machine-', rather than 'human-' readable language. Fortunately, however, there are a number of

---

10 <http://www.w3.org/TR/xslt>.

11 R. Studer, V.R. Benjamins and D. Fensel, 'Knowledge Engineering: Principles and Methods', in *IEEE Transactions on Data and Knowledge Engineering* 25, 1/2 (1998): 161–97; building on T.R.A. Gruber, 'A Translation Approach to Portable Ontology Specification', *Knowledge Acquisition*, 5/2 (1993): 199–220.

tools readily available for constructing and viewing ontologies written in OWL of which the most commonly used are Protégé, developed at Stanford University, USA, and KAON, developed at Karlsruhe in Germany.[12] Ontology design is a developing and highly involved field in its own right. There is a substantial literature specifically devoted to it, and a debate about 'best practice' in creating ontologies which reflects (at least in part) the differing approaches of philosophers, linguists and computer scientists to the fundamental question of human knowledge representation.[13] Creating ontologies, however, lies at the heart of the Semantic Web. It makes feasible the task of asking intelligent questions of multiple sources simultaneously. To provide a specific example from our distributed datasets, the Old Bailey Proceedings Online offers a limited facility to search for names mentioned in a collection of accompanying sources, in particular the 'Ordinary's Accounts'. The Ordinary of Newgate was the prison chaplain, whose duty it was to provide spiritual care to prisoners condemned to death. One of the perquisites of the chaplain's post was the right to publish the prisoner's final confession together with an account of his life. This proved to be a profitable, if gruesome, sideline and around 2,500 such accounts were published in the century following the inception of the Old Bailey Proceedings. But such record linkage is only possible because it has been specifically integrated into the Old Bailey site. It is not extensible, and only the engineers of the Old Bailey site have the ability to add further resources to it. However, there are other datasets (such as the wills registered at the Prerogative Court of Canterbury) where those condemned to death and ultimately hanged at Newgate will also appear. Historians might reasonably want to consult these at the same time, but they have no way of doing so. This is despite the fact that a more or less equivalent conception of 'person name' existed in both. So, by defining our own idea of 'person name' in an ontology existing outside and independently from all these records we can solve this problem. Once populated with instances from both collections, searching our new aggregated list would effectively consult both sources at once.

The real power of ontologies only becomes apparent, however, when we begin to add additional concepts, and (most importantly) to define the relationships between them. So, for example, we might add OWL classes for 'age', 'occupation' and 'gender' which appear in various ways in more than one of our selected datasets. Instances (for example, the named individuals) of classes in an OWL ontology are expressed in RDF. The nature of RDF allows us to associate this information explicitly with the relevant 'person name' when a particular resource provides such details. So whereas a conventional keyword search indexer would record the individual text-strings involved, but lose the association between them, an ontology retains the information and the relationships across multiple repositories to match up to the concepts we have defined in it, and so we begin to create a search tool

---

12 <http://protege.stanford.edu> and <http://kaon.semanticweb.org>.

13 We cannot reflect the intensity of these debates in this article. A convenient introduction to ontology design for arts and humanities practitioners who are non-specialists is provided, however, by D.L. McGuinness and N.F. Noy, 'Ontology Development 101: A Guide to Creating your First Ontology', in *Stanford Knowledge Systems Laboratory Technical Report KSL-01-05* (Stanford, 2001), available online from <http://www-ksl.stanford.edu/publications/>.

capable of assisting a scholar in tracing an individual across the distributed historical records. The aspiration of Semantic Web engineers is that ultimately such ontologies will proliferate and be capable of mapping one onto another in the equivalent of an ontological forest of knowledge mappings. In the arts and humanities, however, we are nowhere near such elaboration, and there are good reasons to think that, because of the essential ambiguity and complexity of the material with which we deal, and the open-ended nature of its domains, such intricacy will never happen.

In reality, there are very few bespoke ontologies for any arts and humanities domains yet available. VICODI is the exception, specifically developed for ontology mapping of European history from its origins to the present. It took 24 person-months to build and was principally designed in the UK by Richard Deswarte (UEA) and Jan Oosthoek (Newcastle).[14] It is a thoroughly professional ontology. Its concepts are clearly formulated, its classes, constraints, elements of cardinality and dependency are properly defined. Careful consideration has been given to a very wide range of mutualities. The first difficulty encountered by the VICODI team was that there was no commonly accepted 'canon' or corpus of writings on European history from which to develop the conceptual framework, such as a botanist might be able to elaborate an ontology from a taxonomy of plants. The second, related problem was whether the ontology was designed to represent knowledge in the form of primary sources (the 'raw materials' to which historical understanding relates) or to the historical literature (the 'history') which has been written about it. This is not to say that Europe's historians do not have something of a specialist vocabulary ('classical', 'medieval', 'contemporary' are all part of commonly utilized terms of art to delineate period, for example) but it is a vocabulary which is shared with the general public (for whom the terms sometimes designate something rather different) and it delineates a meta-understanding which is context-dependent and essentially contested. It is salutary to remind oneself at this point of the extent to which scientific ontologies are dependent on the support of powerful institutions to authenticate their use. Even the Linnean classification of plants acquired its preeminence because of the authority accorded it by the European learned societies of the later eighteenth century. Greenwich Mean Time as a classification for global time and space required the heavy hand of a maritime empire to become a recognized standard. There are no historical or archaeological bodies, let alone humanities institutions with that kind of weight and authority, precisely because the relationship between knowledge and power is different. One of the initial experiences of the VICODI team was one which we also discovered in our ontology development for the Armadillo agent. Ontological concepts and relations rapidly mushroom to become quite unmanageable. So the notion of an ontology has to be restricted to a small number of generic concepts. In the case of the VICODI ontology, it was limited to a well-structured number of generic concepts around a temporal matrix – categories of historical instance which might be temporally disposed in some way or another. The categories of instance are themselves kept very simple and broad, and not sub-divided (see Figure 5.1).

---

14 <http://www.vicodi.org>. The prototype version of the ontology applied to a small selection of secondary materials is available from <http://www.eurohistory.net/>.

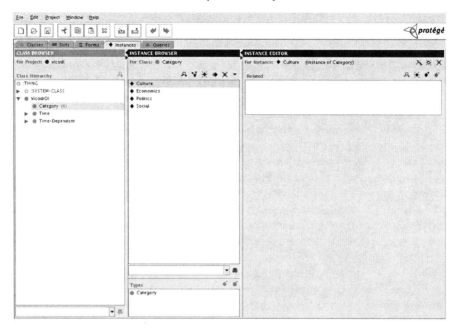

Figure 5.1   VICODI ontology of 'categories'

Military historians might well say, for example, that this ontology does not represent their knowledge. And since there is potentially a 'history' of every science, of every aspect of our lives, of every element in our universe, such objections are inherent in any subject domain which is open-ended, a problem which was recognized by natural philosophers at least as early as the seventeenth century when they attempted to formulate taxonomies of human knowledge on an encyclopedic basis. The VICODI engineers found that they could not model the essential ambiguity and complexity of the historical world through a conceptual ontology. It had to be undertaken through the property relationships of instances.

As an example of that complexity and ambiguity, let us examine how the VICODI ontology handles historians' use of time. We all use time in a remarkably flexible way, content to function in a world in which we can refer to events both very vaguely and very precisely. Historians are no different, evoking precise calendar time at one moment ('31 October 1517'), allusive time in the next ('a century later in 1617'), implicit time ('Philip Melanchthon's funeral oration for Luther'), mythic time ('rather doubt that the event actually happened') and iterative time ('the period of the reformation'), all in ways that are thoroughly comprehensible to a human reader but completely incomprehensible to a machine. VICODI tries to handle this problem with three interrelated senses of time. It has a precise notion of 'calendar time', and then establishes a huge range (14,492) of 'time-interval' instances (a 'time-interval' being anything from a year to a period of years) to create periods of calendar time, allowing for a third possibility of a 'fuzzy temporal interval' at some future stage, with the application of fuzzy set-theory mathematics to the representation of temporal imprecision (see Figure 5.2).

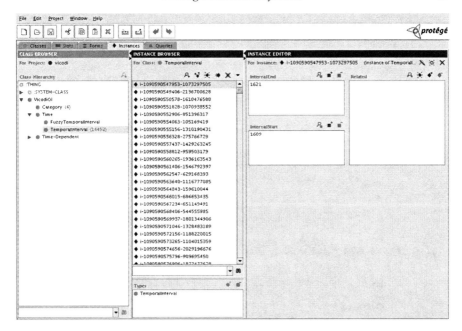

Figure 5.2 **The VICODI representation of the time-interval for the 'Nine Years' Truce in the Netherlands (1609–1621)'**

The problem that the VICODI ontology designers were grappling with is a particular instance of the fact that historians and historical writing do not have a 'correspondence' relationship with their evidence. We might assert that the protestant reformation began with the nailing of Luther's 95 Theses to the door of Wittenberg cathedral on 31 October 1517, but that would not correspond to any perception that any contemporary might have had of the significance of this iconic event, which might not, in any case, have actually taken place. They would not have used the word 'protestant', which was a later neologism. They would not have recognized this as the 'reformation', even though that was something which had been often discussed and ardently debated for over a century before. Idealist philosophers have taught historians to think about their relationship with their evidence as one of 'coherence' – i.e. that their picture of the past is one that achieves its ontological status through being internally coherent, congruent with the evidence as presented, but not making claims to be the only picture capable of being painted, the only story told of these events.[15] So we should judge the utility of a Semantic Web ontology not in terms of the extent to which it is able to map some putatively objective virtual taxonomy of the past, but by the degree to which it performs a practical and pragmatic utilitarian function of helping to find needles

---

15 H. Putnam, *Reason, Truth and History* (Cambridge: Cambridge University Press, 1981); D. Davidson, 'A Coherence Theory of Truth and Knowledge', in E. LePore (ed.), *Truth and Interpretation: Perspectives on the Philosophy of Donald Davidson* (Oxford: Blackwell, 1986), pp. 307–19; J. Tosh, *The Pursuit of History*. 3rd edn (Longman, 2002).

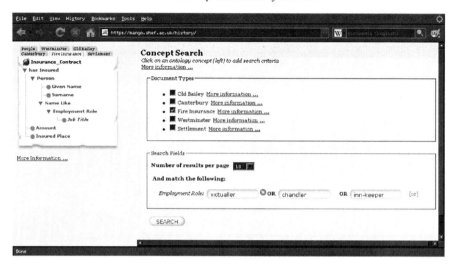

Figure 5.3   The Armadillo ontology (fire insurance contract data)

of relevant information in 'haystacks' of primary material with information of varying, but considerable, amounts of contextuality within it.

The Armadillo ontology set out, therefore, with the more pragmatic aim of simply mapping the 'oracles' (the various fields into which the data had been divided) for each of the datasets for the test-bed study. In the case of the fire insurance documentation, this meant a relatively simple ontology indicating the fields into which it had been divided (see Figure 5.3). With the Old Bailey Proceedings, the ontology was necessarily much more complicated, and this had knock-on effects for the speed and performance of the tool (see Figure 5.4). The ontology presented to the user (on the left of the figure) reflects the extent of the cross-field searching available between one set and another. The resulting demonstrator is available from the project web page. There are various potential fields in the documentation which, in the limited amount of time available to us, we did not succeed in mapping into the ontology, most notably that of time and time-intervals. We had learnt valuable lessons, however, from VICODI in how to approach that particularly difficult issue.

From the demonstrator that we have created, it is difficult to evaluate the potential impact of such an agent for research purposes. We had concentrated on providing distributive searching for name-matches. In this one respect, it works quite well. If we take the example of William Bird, a watch-house keeper in the parish of St Martin in the Fields, we find the details of his family in the Settlement examinations and the Old Bailey Proceedings reveal that he was twice tried for murder before the Old Bailey court. From there, we can go on to discover who the witnesses were in his two trials, and follow their details through the records. The tool cannot guarantee, of course, that the William Bird mentioned in the Settlement examinations is one and the same as the William Bird who is mentioned in Old Bailey records. The best it can do is to offer a graphic interface, developed by Sam Chapman, which uses difference metrics to assess the proximity of semantic matches around the text-

Figure 5.4   The Armadillo ontology (Old Bailey Proceedings Documentation)

string in question, which can be helpful, especially when there are orthographic variations (something that is quite common in the spelling of eighteenth-century names). It is the user historian that must make that probabilistic decision, using their interpretative skills.

One way of imagining how such a tool might be used is to conduct a thought experiment. Let us imagine that we are interested in investigating the role of taverns and inns in eighteenth-century London. Where might we start? The fire insurance records contain the contracts for insurance on numerous taverns and inns (and we would have to search for both terms in that part of the ontology), saving the results as we went. We have immediately registered the fact that iterative searching is a key component of this kind of agent in a research environment. The need for an efficient way of saving the results is one of the clear implications of this demonstrator. The records also give details of insured individuals who were liquor-sellers. We encounter 'tavern-keeper', 'chandler', 'victualler', 'inn-keeper', etc. as possible search terms, and it is for the user, as they familiarize themselves with the resources, to discover these terms, rather than for the ontology to dictate them. The result would be a list of names (and some addresses) of inn-keepers, which may then be used to discover more about these individuals across a wider set of records. We would have to decide (for example) whether the Daniel Lawrence, contracting for two fire insurance licences, once as a victualler in Bishop Stortford (in 1775), and then again as the inhabitant of the 'Three Tuns' at Whitechapel in 1780, was one and the same as the Daniel Lawrence, victualler of the parish of St Mary, Whitechapel whose will, dated 2 November 1791 was registered before the Prerogative Court (see Figure 5.5). We would be more confident that the match was a valid one than in the case of Robert Humphrey, victualler, who signed a contract for fire insurance in 1775 and

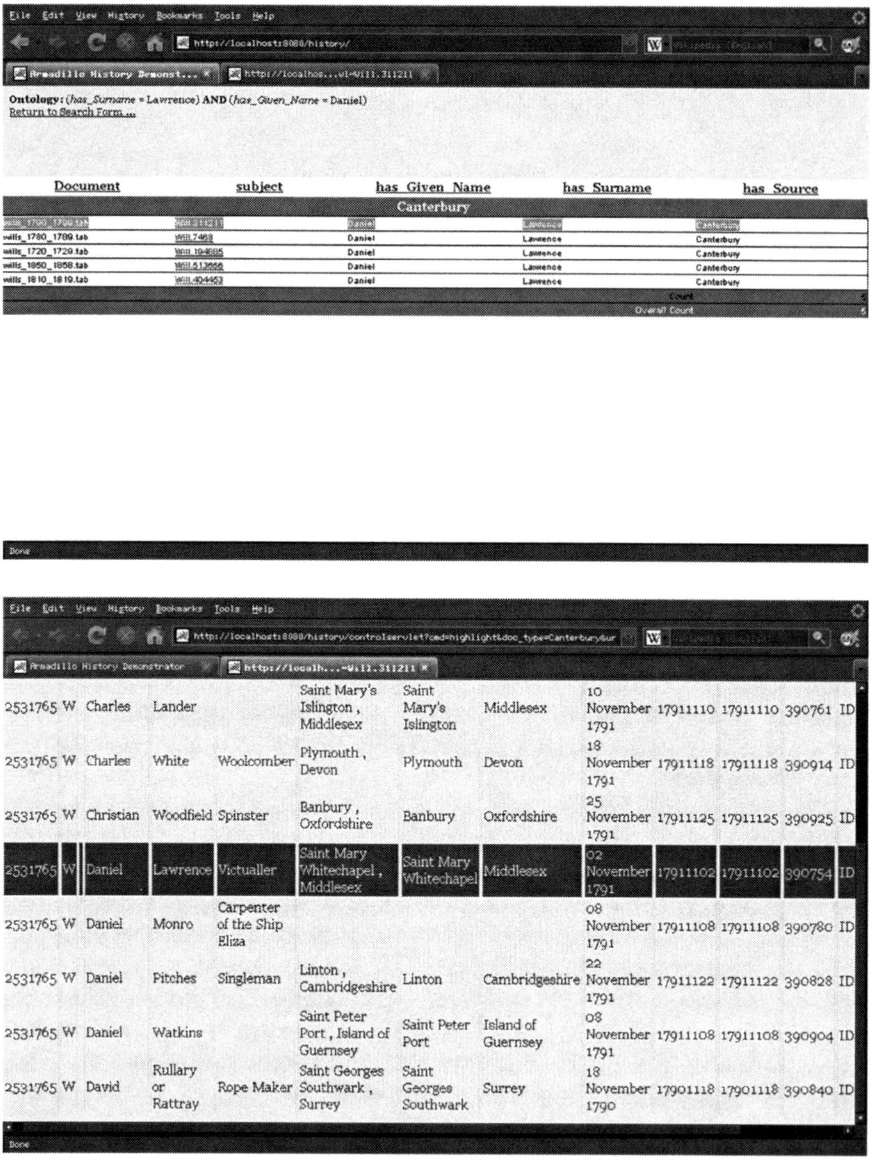

Figure 5.5   Armadillo Ontology (Canterbury wills documentation)

the Robert Humphrys who appeared before the St Martin-in-the-Fields examiners in 1750. The latter may, however (we might conclude) be very probably one and the same as the Robert Humphrys who appeared before the Old Bailey court in 1751 and who was sentenced to be transported for stealing a pair of breeches and two aprons, one of that substantial underclass of eighteenth-century Londoners whose circumstances drove them to make a life from crime, and whose lives we can only reconstruct with patient detective work and the aid of tools like this.

We have now completed an independent evaluation of the Armadillo demonstrator, devised and conducted under the direction of Professor Tim Hitchcock by Ian O'Neill. The evaluation was undertaken with graduate students in history and data developers, all of whom had some familiarity with researching using digital tools. The testers kept logs of their specific searches, enabling us to evaluate their evolving search strategies, and their achievements and frustrations in using the tools. Four user-testing sessions were then organized, each of which was in four stages. The first was a 'walk-through' in which the test-group followed a step-by-step example of a historical problem elucidated by means of the Armadillo tool. This involved a search for Middlesex pawnbroker Frank Rochfort and his family. The second stage involved a problem-only cognitive walkthrough, in which testers were given a historical problem, known to be solvable by Armadillo, and invited to use their own strategies to solve it, and in doing so to document their experiences of that process. The problem required testers to search for Joseph Vandecomb, a Middlesex chimney sweep in the 1770s, in a variety of the sources contained in the demonstrator. During the third stage, the user group was invited to construct a problem which they thought that the agent *ought* to help them to solve, based upon their knowledge of the sources and what they understood to be how the search environment worked. In a final stage, the group was given a guided comparison of the Armadillo agent with a selection of other website interfaces, encouraging a discussion of what each could learn from the other.

The conclusions from this evaluation were used to build help screens and supporting documentation for the demonstrator. They revealed both the potential of the Semantic Web approach and the severe limitations of what had currently been constructed. The speed of performance of the tool was a persistent and intractable problem. The fact is that generic and flexible conceptions of data cannot be as efficiently stored as narrow, heavily optimized and structured ones. To make an ontology work, the underlying RDF data is reduced to what are known as 'triples'. A triple is a simple statement of a single fact (for example, PersonName 32 has the surname 'Smith'). Each triple can be split into three parts (subject: predicate: object). In the case of our example, the subject 'PersonName 32' has the predicate 'Has Surname' and the object is the text-string 'Smith'. In order to consult the data contained in an RDF repository, these three pieces of information are stored together by a piece of software known as a 'triple store'. RDF documents of a modest size typically reduce to hundreds or thousands of triples. A whole data repository, encoded in a reasonably ambitious ontology of the kind that had been generated by the oracles in our documents, runs to millions. Storing and consulting these triples at high speed represents a technical challenge, and the size of the triple store grows exponentially with the flexibility and complexity of an ontology. Complex ontologies create vast numbers of triples, which (in turn) highlight the Semantic Web performance problems most harshly. Whether this problem can be resolved through the development of more efficient triple-store software remains an open question.[16]

The second problem revealed by the demonstrator was the inadequacy of the ontology implementation in the current demonstrator. The user groups fully

---

16 The Armadillo agent used the open source-code triple-store agent 'Sesame', which is still under active development – <http://www.openrdf.org>.

document their frustrations that what was provided by the agent fails to represent adequately and make fully searchable the contents of the underlying datasets; it exploited neither the horizontal relationships between different document types by (for example) date, nor all the comparable fields of data. These are limitations of the demonstrator, however, rather than the overall approach. The potential of applying Semantic Web techniques rests upon the fact that (in due course) users need not be dependent on any given interface to interrogate a range of resources. Since the contextual data is stored in a standardized format, it can be examined using a standardized query language. The emerging standard for querying RDF is SPARQL (or SPARQL Protocol and RDF Query Language).[17] It does not yet carry a W3C recommendation, but it is a 'candidate recommendation' and it, or something very like it, is sure to become the equivalent of the Structured Query Language (SQL) with which one can interrogate a relational database. The difference, however, is that an RDF resource offers much more information about its contents and structure than a set of tab-delimited data files. The basic principle remains, however, that by separating interface and resources, it would be possible to envisage a variety of interfaces interrogating different mixes of datasets for their contextual information in ways that would more adequately satisfy user needs than the current, very limited Armadillo agent is able to do, and to spread the development costs to cover a wider range of resources and combinations of user needs.

The third set of problems related to the 'black-box' nature of data mining, and user frustration with the agent returning large numbers of results with little apparent connection to the input criteria. This was, in part, the result of combining fuzzy-match searching algorithms within the agent, but also a reflection of the inherent difficulty of how one presents a hierarchy of results when they are coming from different datasets, combined with some anomalies in the way the demonstrator worked. We suppose the latter can, given time, be removed – and fuzzy search-matching was not essential to the success or failure of the agent. But the problem of how one presents the results – and the related issue of how one saves them – remains an important component for future investigation. It is linked to the question of how, once one has separated datasets and interfaces, they should communicate with one another. At present Internet applications often draw information from a variety of servers and domains, but there is no standardized method for doing so. More recently, the W3C has formally defined the concept of a 'Web Service' as 'a software system designed to support interoperable machine-to-machine interaction over a network'.[18] This is very close to the vision of software 'agents' associated with the Semantic Web, although Web Service technology is by no means limited to the Semantic Web field. Web Services use a standard called Web Service Description Language (WSDL) to explain the functions a website offers in a machine-readable format, i.e. capable of being understood by another machine. Other websites and services can then communicate with the site using what are known as SOAP messages (Simple Object Access Protocol), exchanging digital information in accordance with the respective WSDL descriptions. In this way, interfaces and datasets can be coupled with one

17 <http://www.w3.org/TR/ref-sparql-query>.
18 <http://www.w3.org/TR/ws-gloss>.

another. Taken to its logical conclusion, the interface for a given resource becomes extensible by any user. So, for example, a scholar might have a list of names they want to research using the Prerogative Court of Canterbury wills. A default interface might only offer the ability to look for one name at a time, presenting the scholar with the laborious task of entering each name separately. Using WSDL and SOAP, it would be possible to host an alternative interface which allowed lists of names to be submitted and compared to the Canterbury database through its Web Service, the results being presented back to the user in ways that the individual might specify.

In practice, we are a long way from realizing this vision of independent interfaces communicating with repositories storing the contextual information that renders the material they contain potentially so much more usable. The widespread adoption of Semantic Web technology is inhibited in a number of ways, not least by the conventions of the Web as it stands today. Aside from the challenge of creating suitable data conceptions, reflected in the discussion about ontologies above, the most obvious difficulty is still that of interface design. Users want intuitively to formulate complex queries and intuitively to understand the results they receive. This requires substantial thought, and an innovative approach. Every search environment implies a virtual representation of the query expected, and the result returned. How to reflect that representation in such a way that the end user understands precisely how it works, and why individual search results have been returned, remains a substantial challenge. The flexibility of Semantic Web searching cannot be exploited by the most obvious, and most widespread, way of achieving that representation (the single free-text search field). Its potential lies in the fact that RDF allows users to specify not just the things they are interested in, but also the relationship between those things. So any Semantic Web interface must give users some way to indicate the desired connections between different search fields. In addition, depending on the complexity of the ontology, it may not be practical to display all the possible fields at one and the same time. So there has to be a mechanism for users to select which fields interest them. The interface utilized by the Armadillo agent used a combination of these approaches, presenting a full hierarchical display of the project's ontology (see Figure 5.3, left-hand side) which is then used to add text fields dynamically to the more conventional search form (Figure 5.3, centre and left). Our user-group evaluations suggested that this was not intuitively understood. Our work has underlined the fact that the virtual representation of the contextual knowledge about the past contained in its primary materials still relies upon a simple, intuitive way of conveying that representation.[19]

---

19 Cf. R. Deswarte and J. Oostoek, 'Clio's Ontology Criteria: The Theory and Experience of Building a History Ontology', paper given at the XVIth International Conference of the Association for History and Computing, Amsterdam, 14–17 September 2005.

Chapter 6

Digital Searching and the Re-formulation of Historical Knowledge

Tim Hitchcock

In a recent error of judgement AOL released the search logs of 650,000 of its users, exposing 21 million search terms (and their results) to a keen audience. The employee responsible was quickly fired, and AOL is currently facing a volley of legal action. But what the queries revealed – more than the shopping habits of the internet generation – is the sheer randomness of knowledge online. If you explore the use of academic sites by the AOL users, they appear fully mixed with directions for hobby projects, enquiries for everyday services, and an almost ubiquitous hunt for pornography. The Old Bailey Online (<http://www.oldbaileyonline.org>), for instance, comes up in one user's history in close proximity to enquiries for recipes for chicken pot pie, chainsaw maintenance and spare parts, and the whereabouts of old US navy buddies.[1] This chapter is an attempt to explore how this liberation and resulting deracination of academic knowledge has, and will, impact on the research methodologies of academic historians. It is an attempt to chart what we are doing to history as a discipline, as a research methodology, and as a literary genre with the creation of new ways of organizing and accessing historical information. It is an exploration of the interactions between professional practice, technological change and intellectual perspectives.

*****

As a social practice, 'history' in the post-Enlightenment West represents a powerful claim to authority. As a profession, historians have created a subtle language of authentication that inextricably ties together the hierarchies of the academy, with a particular research methodology, and the outward signs of a trusted textual representation. Academic publications are designed to ensure that a broader society recognizes the authority of the historian's work. A monograph on seventeenth-century poor relief, for instance, based on a detailed reading of manuscript sources, published by Cambridge University Press, and written by a member of academic staff at a trusted institution, claims social authority on a variety of different levels; in the process, the publication medium privileges the information and knowledge disseminated. The methodologies of comparison and validation which underpin

---

1 See, for example, AOL user 10649659 <http://data.aolsearchlogs.com/search/index. cgi>, accessed 13 September 2006.

works of this sort clearly promise something akin to truth, but these are sustained and reinforced by indications of quality that are much less precisely articulated. The footnotes that climb each page certainly convey precise information for anyone industrious enough to follow them, but they also gently reassure the reader who simply skims the text.

Since at least the early nineteenth century, the methodologies of empirical history have been represented as a series of ever more precisely formulated physical objects (books and journals), with rules and expectations embedded in every sentence, every paragraph, and most obviously in every footnote, and which in turn speak loudly of the labours of the 'author' in the archives and libraries of a mature network of intellectual institutions. This evolution of a set of trusted products – books and peer-reviewed articles – has, in turn, been intertwined with the growth of institutions more broadly. Universities, libraries and archives have sprung up on every side, laying claim to social authority with every breath. When the pioneer of the county archive movement, F.G. Emmison, rode his bicycle from parish to parish across Essex and the East Midlands, recording and calendaring the contents of each parish chest along the way, he was essentially contributing to the creation of a new set of institutions which in turn helped to frame and discipline historical practice.[2]

In just the last forty years this body of professional practice, embedded as it is in a notion of empirical truth, has been confronted by the corrosive force of postmodernism, which has had an impact on both the role of the 'public intellectual' and how we read and write history. Postmodernism has forced us to question the validity of history as a 'truth claim', and to query the methodologies that underpin it.[3] Primary texts and manuscripts have been revealed as elaborate constructs, with only the most ambiguous relationship to a knowable truth, and secondary works have emerged as literary confections, in which 'truth claims' are embedded in both the use of language, and the layout of passive prose on a clear page. Nevertheless, the majority of historians remain wedded to, and practise, an older style of history writing that would be as familiar to Karl Marx as it is to us.

The commitment to at least the appearance of empiricism, and to the research practices that must be demonstrated to have been followed in order to practise it, impacts dramatically on the content of historical writing. Both the methodologies of the social sciences and the evolution of the profession have effectively given prominence to specific types of information and relationships that privilege organic archives and recondite primary sources, interpreted by professionally trained individuals, as the source of legitimate truth. In the process, our understanding of the past has been shaped in subtle ways, one facet of which is a simple outcome of the very process of delving into archival sources in order to demonstrate historical

---

2 See K. Neale, 'Frederick G. Emmison: Archivist and Scholar', in K. Neale (ed.), *An Essex Tribute: Essays Presented to Frederick G. Emmison as a Tribute to his Life and Work for Essex History and Archives* (Leopard's Head Press, 1987), pp. 1–10; and *The New DNB*, 'Frederick G. Emmison'.

3 This claim is most obviously revealed in postmodern critiques of the discipline. For a useful collection of such critiques see K. Jenkins (ed.), *The Postmodern History Reader* (Routledge, 1997).

bona fides. By grounding legitimacy on archival research, we are unconsciously led to give an unwarranted prominence to the institutions of past societies, in preference to groups and individuals defined in more inchoate ways, those who did not leave well-structured archives. Because archives are themselves almost universally the products of specific institutions, our contact with them ensures that the institutional voice is heard in all its stentorian splendour – effectively drowning out the quieter tones uttered by the individual.

The role of archives in creating the cultural authority deployed by historians is in many ways visceral and emotional in character.[4] That first moment when you are confronted by the paper and parchment remains of long-dead generations is an immensely powerful one that historians frequently romanticize. Nevertheless, there is something about walking out of an archive at the end of the day, your clothes and hands dark with rotting paper and the dust of decades, that provides an emotional link to the past. When you unwrap the parchment document enclosing the 200-year-old evidence given at a coroner's inquest, and the sand used to blot the ink spills into your lap, it is difficult to maintain an appropriate distance – regardless of whether that distance is postmodern or empirical in character. Even when dealing with the carefully conserved documents of record given pride of place in national repositories, there is something special about old texts, and manuscripts in particular. It is emotional, it is attractive, but it is also very real. As Herbert Butterfield wrote, 'the romance of historical research' lies in 'the historian's passion for manuscripts and sources [and] the desire to bring himself [sic] into genuine relationship with the actual ...'.[5] Although this claim was made some seventy years ago, it nevertheless underpins entirely current notions of historical explanation and value. Unpicking the quality descriptors used by the history panel for the 2008 Research Assessment Exercise (RAE), for example, reveals the continuing centrality of this relationship to sources, and to manuscripts in particular. A 'four-star' submission – the benchmark for truly outstanding historical scholarship – is defined firstly as being characterized *either* by originality of approach, *or* by 'opening up new sources, new data or material'; but the definition goes on to suggest that any item of work graded at this level should contain both 'new' sources and new approaches.[6]

The most impressive footnotes in any monograph are those referencing archives and the most obscure of primary sources. We judge good scholarship by its engagement with the recondite and the difficult, and like the RAE, distrust histories made more intellectually free-floating by the absence of such sources. When we endeavour to convey the essence of our profession to our undergraduate students,

---

4 For a discussion of the emotional response to archives see T. Laqueur, 'Bodies, Details, and the Humanitarian Narrative', in L. Hunt (ed.), *The New Cultural History* (Berkeley, Los Angeles and London: University of California Press, 1989), pp. 176–204.

5 H. Butterfield, *The Whig Interpretation of History* (George Bell and Sons, 1950), p. 73. See also M. Eamon, 'A "Genuine Relationship with the Actual": New Perspectives on Primary Sources, History and the Internet in the Classroom', *The History Teacher* 39/3 (2006): 32. Available online at <http://www.historycooperative.org/journals/ht/39.3/eamon.html>, last accessed 16 December 2007.

6 Higher Education Funding Council for England, *RAE 2008: Panel Criteria and Working Methods. Panel N* (January 2006), p. 60, para 71a.

we most frequently fall back on an introduction to structured sources. The image of 'history' currently being taught throughout Britain is sharply polarized between a self-conscious body of 'professional' opinion (historiography) and an ever-growing emphasis on 'original' sources.[7]

The difficulty is that the habits of mind and more explicit methodological content of this tradition are increasingly at odds with the course of technological change. We are in the middle of the process of transforming the very nature of the manuscript and primary sources upon which we rely. Digitization, new search facilities, new ways of representing and connecting information, fundamentally changes the nature of the archive – what it means and how it is used, and how we as historians experience it. If our claims to cultural authority are built on our relationship with that archive and the sources they contain, then we need to rethink how the social authority of history can be reconstituted to reflect the changing nature of those holdings.

*****

In the last ten years billions of words of printed historical text have been digitized and delivered to an eager audience in a keyword searchable form. It is now commonplace to use keyword searching in order to locate information on topics that do not normally appear in a nineteenth- or twentieth-century index, or a good card catalogue, or even a well-developed concordance. Early English Books Online (EEBO) and Eighteenth Century Collections Online (ECCO), The Times Digital Archive, Project Gutenberg and the Million Book Project and the Old Bailey Online, among a host of other similar resources, make printed text easily available and have in ten years essentially made redundant 300 years of carefully structured and controlled systems for the categorization and retrieval of information.[8] In the process these developments have also had a profound impact on the way literary and historical scholars go about doing research. A growing number of historians are now using literary sources to round out their more apparently factual accounts. And the number of literary scholars who are discovering the joys of contextualizing literature within history is similarly expanding.[9] This trend is entirely dependent on the fact that it is now possible to perform keyword searches on billions of words of printed text – both literary and historical. History conferences are becoming more literary, and literature

---

7 For a review of methodological courses taught in English universities see T. Hitchcock, R. Shoemaker and J. Tosh, 'Skills and the Structure of the History Curriculum', in A Booth and P. Hyland (eds), *The Practice of University History Teaching* (Manchester: Manchester University Press, 2000), pp. 47–59.

8 See <http://eebo.chadwyck.com/home>; <http://www.galeuk.com/trials/ecco/>; <http://www.gale.com/EighteenthCentury/>; <http://www.gale.com/Times/>; <http://www.gutenberg.org/wiki/Main_Page>; <http://www.archive.org/details/millionbooks>; and <http://www.oldbaileyonline.org/>, all accessed 17 December 2007.

9 For an excellent example of a social historian writing in a strongly empirical tradition who has recently begun to use literature more fully see M. Finn, *The Character of Credit: Personal Debt in English Culture, 1740–1914* (Cambridge: Cambridge University Press, 2003); for a literary scholar moving in the opposite direction see P. Fumerton, *Unsettled: The Culture of Mobility and the Working Poor in Early Modern England* (Chicago: Chicago University Press, 2006).

conferences are becoming significantly more historical.[10] This is particularly true for scholars working on printed English sources for the period before 1800, the vast majority of which are now available online.

The same kind of transformation in scholarly practice is also happening in relation to images. Art history used to be a highly specialized, largely museum-based discipline. But, as collection after collection goes online, historians who traditionally avoided engaging with visual sources have now discovered the ability to use graphic representations to support their texts.[11] This same transformation is just beginning in relation to the integration of material and museum objects into historical analyses and again reflects the direct intellectual impact of new search facilities. In other words, keyword searching of printed text, and, by proxy, of picture collections, has dramatically impacted on how we do research, and has demonstrably impacted on what we research about. In the process, it has resulted in the substantial deracination of knowledge, the uprooting, or 'Google-ization' of the components of what was once a coherent collection of beliefs. Embedded within the Dewey Decimal and Library of Congress systems of classification (and in all their less successful imitators) are clear disciplinary boundaries which constrain how a reader imagines their topic and the intellectual landscape through which they navigate. But, in an intellectual world dominated by new types of search facilities, historians are increasingly expected to search across a large number of different electronic sources, and to deploy fragments of knowledge in the creation of a new analysis. We choose a search term, or a collection of them, and search indiscriminately through literature, and the records of crime, through electronic catalogues, and newspapers. In the process the requirement (or even the opportunity) to understand the context out of which any individual element of information comes frequently disappears. Images suffer this fate even more completely. The heady hierarchy of knowledge created by the heroic cataloguers of the nineteenth century has become an historical artefact in its own right.

In many respects this development has been less fundamentally transformative than might be at first imagined. It has ensured that thematic history has become ever more commonplace. But this is a trend discernible from at least the 1980s, and in itself a response to the breakdown of broader historical meta-narratives. Histories of night time, cod, of gesture and salt, were conceived before the internet made them easier to write.[12] And, despite these developments, we continue to place our faith in the signs and forms of professional history, presented in an authoritative manner.

---

10 To take just a single instance, the traditionally more literary British Society for Eighteenth-Century Studies' annual conference has been actively and consistently soliciting for more historical contributions since 2003.

11 For examples of image resources that have been particularly important for the evolution of British history see <http://lwlimages.library.yale.edu/walpoleweb/default.htm>; <http://collage.cityoflondon.gov.uk/collage/app>;   <http://www.artandarchitecture.org.uk>; and <http://www.tate.org.uk>, all accessed 17 December 2007.

12 A.R. Ekirch, *At Day's Close: Night in Times Past* (New York: W.W. Norton & Co., 2005); M. Kurlansky, *Cod: A Biography of the Fish That Changed the World* (Vintage, 1999); J. Bremmer and H. Roodenburg (eds), *A Cultural History of Gesture* (Ithaca and London: Cornell University Press, 1991); and M. Kurlansky, *Salt: A World History* (Vintage, 2003).

Although most historians now use the internet as a finding tool, their footnotes remain replete with forms of reference that imply the direct and physical consultation of a printed edition. A high proportion of journal articles are now accessed online, but the references are still made to the hard copies on library shelves. By ignoring the proximate nature of electronic representations, the impact of new technology has been largely skated over and subtly downplayed.

We are now, however, faced with a new set of possibilities. Until recently almost no substantive manuscript archives have actually been posted in a full and searchable form. And even where attempts have been made to do so, little effort has been put into breaking down the archival structures involved, or to confronting the changed nature of an electronic edition. Bethlem Royal Hospital Archives and Museum, for instance, a site containing one of the largest collections of manuscripts currently available on the internet relating to eighteenth-century Britain, simply reproduces page images that must be viewed one after the other.[13] The British Library's solution to the presentation of manuscript materials again reflects a certain discomfort with the possibilities for search and presentation made available by a rapidly changing technology. Their framework for presenting digitized manuscripts presents each page in such a way that the user is forced to go through the motions of manually turning one page after another. In the process the system reassures the reader of their connection to a 'real' object, but simultaneously disguises the proximate and mediated nature of the new edition.[14]

The next generation of digitized manuscripts is unlikely to take either of these approaches. As the impediments to posting large volumes of manuscript in a searchable form disappear, and as the managerial and technical challenges of doing so are gradually solved, the uncertainty about how to search and present such sources diminishes. In a recently funded project managed by Robert Shoemaker and Tim Hitchcock, Plebeian Lives and the Making of Modern London, some 70 million words of manuscript material, encompassing eight freestanding organic archives, tied in to some 120 million words of printed text available through the Old Bailey Online, will help to create an early example of a type of resource that must become ever more commonplace. Plebeian Lives will take three London parish archives, the records of the Carpenters Company, of Bedlam and Bridewell, of St Thomas' Hospital, and the Sessions papers of the County of Middlesex and the City of London, and transcribe them from scanned images, captured from 530 reels of microfilm. This material will then be posted in a searchable form in combination with the distributed resources of the voting and tax records of Westminster, of the parish records of St Martin-in-the-Fields, and the ever growing body of material available through History On-line at the Institute of Historical Research, including the records of property holding in the City of London, of the window tax and the hearth tax.[15]

---

13 See <http://www.bethlemheritage.org.uk/web/brha.htm>, accessed 17 December 2007.

14 For an online demonstration of this technology see <http://www.bl.uk/onlinegallery/ttp/ttpbooks.html>, accessed 17 December 2007.

15 For a more detailed description of this project see <http://www.shef.ac.uk/hri/projects/projectpages/plebeianlives.html>.

In terms of the sheer amount of text being processed, this is a relatively small project in comparison to EEBO or ECCO, but it reflects an important shift from the large-scale digitization of printed material to manuscript. In combination with the evolution of new kinds of search engine which allow for distributed resources to be subject to online investigation in a more coherent manner, and with the application of simple keyword searching, the nature of the archives upon which our claims to professional expertise in part rely, are being transformed.[16] The distance between the archive as a physical entity and the ways in which we use it is increasing.

The importance of this transition is certainly as profound as that we have already witnessed in relation to printed texts. But, in some respects it is more significant. If keyword searching of printed texts makes redundant the Dewey Decimal and the Library of Congress classification systems (structures of knowledge imposed after the fact on essentially freestanding objects – books), keyword and electronic searching and analysis of large numbers of manuscript sources cut away some of the very roots and structure of organic archives. Despite their claim to a unique expertise in the use of archives, few historians actually discuss the impact of archival structures on their own thinking. Yet the hierarchical and institutional nature of most archives contains an ideological component which is sucked in with every dust-filled breath, and which informs modern historical scholarship at its most basic level. To see how digitization of manuscript materials in combination with new types of search engines could impact on the nature of history, it is necessary to explore the nature of the organic archives with which we work.

In its most commonplace formulation the archive lasted from the Renaissance to almost the present day. It gradually changed, but even into the 1960s and 1970s, an archive took much the same form as it had in the sixteenth century. Most are comprised of day books, and monthly accounts, books recording the minutes of a hierarchy of meetings, and perhaps letter books and strings of miscellaneous receipts. If you are dealing with a hospital or workhouse or prison, you might find admissions registers, and medical notebooks. But the significant aspect of these accretions of administrative practice is that the vast majority of archives were created to cater for the day-to-day needs of specific institutions, and took a recognizable and hierarchical form. In their original location, they were spread through pigeonholes and cubby holes. The nineteenth-century roll-top desk, with its many slots and drawers organized above a writing pad, forms perhaps the classic physical statement of archival organization – combining both the security of a firmly closed top with the organizational specificity of its many compartments. Even when transferred to a modern professional archive, once the 'living beast' of archival construction is slain and dissected, ready for our examination, it retains a power to determine how it is dissected and, ultimately, read. The reading that it demands necessarily privileges the institutions from which it was derived. Whether an archive is of a government, a business, an estate or a charity, the object of study which naturally presents itself is the institution from which it is derived. It is that which appears with preternatural clarity before the eyes of the scholar. Some archives were created by a single clerk, while others were the output of a number of hands, but in either case the archive

---

16 See ch. 5, above.

expresses by its nature the perspective of the institution. The person whose voice is most frequently heard whispering among the folios is that of the clerk, speaking with the interest and perspective of the institution itself always to the fore. Scholars give greater weight to the role of governments and armies, parishes and hospitals, precisely because they most frequently constitute coherent archives. At the same time, we denigrate loose communities and informal connections, because they do not speak with a single voice.

There have, of course, been attempts to circumvent this inevitable bias towards a vision of the past determined by archival coherence. History from below, the new historicism and new cultural history of the 1970s and 1980s, and the anthropological history of the sort pioneered by Keith Thomas, was intended to do just this – to reconfigure our perspective and escape the clutches of the creator of the archive.[17] These attempts have not, however, been entirely successful, and have certainly not driven an institutional perspective from the intellectual high ground. In particular, the major explanatory narratives, the meta-narratives that inform Western history, are fully reflective of the continuing importance of archival structures in the creation of historical explanations. Most Western history has been the story of the evolution of the state in its many forms. Whether we take the classic works of Edward Gibbon or Lewis Namier, the management and development of the state forms the core subject. Arguably this is a natural outcome of the state's tendency to control its own archives. The existence of a National Archive ensures that most historians will have access to and hence privilege, the state's perspective. But even if we look at social or economic or cultural or intellectual history in its apparently least 'statist' form, the impact of archival structures remains. The figures in Edward Thomson's *Making of the English Working Class* whose actions and personalities most distinctly emerge from the text are those who made it into the official files through informers' reports. They therefore become described (not unsympathetically or necessarily inaccurately) from the perspective of the clerk.[18] The questions asked, and the answers given, were the product of an intellectual agenda long dead. And however compelling Thomson's storytelling skills were, or indeed his commitment to the creation of a humane Marxist narrative, he nevertheless told a story of change that the clerk himself would have recognized. Even in history more thoroughly inflected with a cultural twist, such as Jürgen Habermas's formulation of the evolution of the public sphere, it is only by personifying change in the form of an institution (the coffee house) that the transformation of social attitudes can be described.[19] In intellectual history, we study societies and libraries; in medical history, hospitals and infirmaries.

The impact of archival structures goes beyond the simple choice of topic. Most explanations are essentially dialectical in formulation. They pitch one force against another and it is the institutions of past societies that form the shorthand in this confrontation. The conflict between capital and labour in a Marxist perspective

---

17 For an accessible and up-to-date account of many of these intellectual movements see John Tosh, *The Pursuit of History*, 3rd edn (Longman, 2000).

18 E.P. Thompson, *The Making of the English Working Class* (Gollancz, 1963).

19 J. Habermas, *The Structural Transformation of the Public Sphere*, trans. T. Burger (Cambridge, MA: MIT Press, 1991).

becomes a conflict between businesses and unions (however inchoate). When rebellion occurs, the rebels are quickly reconceptualized as an organized force (and then forced to become organized under the pressure of a state demanding someone to negotiate with). In other words, it is the archives themselves which lead ineluctably to the deep structures of analysis we apply to the past. At a fundamental level we are confronted with the limitations of speaking on behalf of the archives.

In many respects, this is no bad thing. As historians it allows us to achieve at least one of the many purposes of history writing – it allows us to speak for and memorialize the experience of at least some of the dead. But, at the same time, it exists in stark tension with another purpose of history – the explanation of the process of change. If we allow institutions to stand in for the forces at work at any given moment, we inevitably downplay the roles and definitions of individuals and groups. And even if it is society's institutions that, in reality, define and describe it, or pull together individual agency into an effective force, traditional, professional research methods lead us to locate change and agency in the interstices between the letter book and the day book, in the institution, rather than in the minds of clients and participants.

The impact of the digitization of organic archives in combination with the fundamental deracination of knowledge implied by the use of keyword searching on the corpus of digitized printed text, frees us from the habit of mind implied by the structures of the archives. If keyword searching of digitized print has broken down the boundaries between genre and categories, the equivalent digitization of manuscript archives tends to eliminate the assumptions about how societies work at a more fundamental level. By way of a historical metaphor, we are confronted with the difference between a medieval strip-map on which a single route is charted through an otherwise unknowable territory (a single journey from Norwich to London, for example, being represented in linear fashion from landmark to landmark) and a perspective map on which we are expected to chart our own journey on the basis of a wider knowledge of the landscape. At least metaphorically, we have ceased to be pilgrims on an established route and become cartographers, making our own maps as we progress. Whilst a strip-map asks us to imagine a journey, a perspective map asks us to imagine a whole countryside. And in terms of explanations of social change that is exactly what this next programme of digitization demands.

Keyword searching of printed text, in combination with the melting away of archival structures (at least in relation to how we experience the information they contain), radically transforms the nature of what historians do, and it does so in two ways. First, it fundamentally undermines several versions of our claim to social authority and authenticity as interpreters of the past. When we cease to claim a special expertise in a particular archive an important component of the justification for our existence ceases to exist. If historians speak for the archives, their role is largely finished, as the material they contain is newly liberated and endlessly replicated. Like librarians, historians are confronted with the need to redefine their social purpose. Second, the development of searchable electronic archives challenges historians to re-examine the broad meta-narratives which have developed to explain social change. If historians no longer 'ventriloquize' on behalf of the archival clerk, then they are free to rethink the nature of social change. It may well be that an institutional approach which privileges the collective agency of groups defined by rules and forms of incorporation is precisely right, but for the first time we can sensibly interrogate other possibilities.

In relation to the Plebeian Lives project discussed earlier, the opportunity of digitizing a substantial proportion of the manuscript archive of eighteenth-century London will be used to ask these simple questions: What does the world look like if social change is modelled historically as the outcome of individual interactions with institutions? What happens when institutions and archives are 'decentred' in favour of the individual? What changes when we examine the world through the collected fragments of knowledge that we can recover about a single person, reorganized as a biographical narrative, rather than as a part of an archival system?

Chapter 7

Using Computer-assisted Qualitative Data Analysis Software in Collaborative Historical Research

Caroline Bowden

Computer-assisted Qualitative Data Analysis Software (CAQDAS) is no longer in its infancy. In the early 1980s, American sociologists began to appreciate the possibilities for using computers to handle the more mechanical tasks of processing qualitative data even though, by 1984 (the year when the American journal *Qualitative Sociology* devoted a special issue to computer applications in this area), very few social scientists had access to any programs designed to undertake the tasks envisaged.[1] Ten years later, there was both a well-developed range of competing software and also a professional literature devoted to the subject, including student manuals, source books and software evaluations.[2] Such developments have, however, been much slower to be absorbed within the human sciences. Why that should be so, however, is hard to discern. For qualitative evidence permeates the historian's domain, and must influence the archaeological landscape too. Although, as this book makes clear at every turn, historians and archaeologists are concerned with quantifiable entities – time, volume, distance, weight, measure, expenditure – these are human constructs, and measurement is a matter of acculturation. If the distinguished world historian Alfred Crosby has understood it correctly, that process occurred some time in European history between 1250 and 1600.[3] That this should be so, comes as no surprise to a historian of European medicine, since the dominant philosophical and methodological framework underlying Galenic medicine was Aristotelian. And only at the very end of Crosby's period – indeed, somewhat after it for much of Europe's medicine – was the Galenic–Aristotelian consensus seriously challenged.[4] For Aristotle, *qualities* lay at the heart of things, human, natural and

---

1 See, esp. P. Conrad and S. Reinarz, 'Qualitative Computing: Approaches and Issues', *Qualitative Sociology*, 7 (1984): 34–60.

2 See, among others, I. Dey, *Qualitative Data Analysis. A User-friendly Guide for Social Scientists* (Routledge, 1993); M.B. Miles and M. Huberman, *Qualitative Data Analysis. An Expanded Sourcebook* (Sage, 1994); U. Kelle, G. Prein and K. Bird, *Computer-aided Qualitative Data Analysis: Theory, Methods and Practice* (Sage, 1995).

3 Alfred Crosby, *The Measurement of Reality: Quantification and Western Society, 1250–1600* (Cambridge: Cambridge University Press, 1997).

4 R. Porter, *The Greatest Benefit to Mankind: A Medical History of Humanity* (HarperCollins, 1997), chs 6 and 7.

supernatural. His *Organon* began with the definition of such qualities, carefully distinguishing between the 'habits' and 'dispositions' of things. Habits were the more deep-rooted qualities which, in human beings, became our virtues – our capacities for courage, justice, prudence, self-sacrifice. Dispositions were the more transitory elements which might change quite rapidly, depending on circumstance and context – in human beings, for example, the health of our bodies or the reverse. For, in Aristotle's analysis, such qualities permitted of infinite variation and were mostly bound to be considered in relative terms, as constructions of opposites. So, for most of European history, intellectual elites were readily attuned to evaluating their world in 'qualitative' ways (logically formal terms). That is even before we take into account that, with most premodern sources, what might be superficially quantified data has to be treated in a qualitative way because it generally requires sophisticated interpretation before it can yield any reliable results. That interpretation is not the preserve of one individual, but one which gains validity from a scholarly consensus. Qualitative Data Analysis (QDA) software has the potential to provide both historians and archaeologists with the tools to interpret evidence qualitatively in a cooperative environment. This chapter examines one project in the historical domain which attempts to evaluate that potential.

*****

The Health of the Cecils Project, based at Royal Holloway, University of London, was funded by the Wellcome Trust for three years to study the attitudes to, and the experience of, health care in one of the great aristocratic households of early modern England.[5] It was a good opportunity to apply the ICT applications which have become a significant part of a modern health service environment to the health-care arrangements of one of the major families in English society and politics when at the heart of their prestige and influence (c.1550–1660). The project was conceived from the start as a collaborative one, in which the research data and results would be evaluated and shared among a team. Historians are gradually becoming more accustomed to sharing their sources, and experimenting with different ways of evaluating their results, leading to joint publications in a variety of formats. But they need ICT tools to enable them to adapt their working practices and research methodologies to these changes. Those tools must be readily available, robust, capable of handling large amounts of data in a flexible fashion, easily mastered, and capable of carrying out basic quantitative, as well as more sophisticated qualitative analysis.

Any archivist is aware how difficult it is to achieve complete consistency in this kind of area. In the case of the Salisbury Papers (see Figure 7.1), they are catalogued

5 I am indebted to Ann Lewins (University of Surrey) and Dr Carmen Mangion (Birkbeck College, University of London) for their comments on an earlier draft of this paper, and to Chris Horton (Royal Holloway, University of London) for the design of the images. The research was greatly facilitated by the access granted by the Marquess of Salisbury to the Cecil Papers at Hatfield House and by the advice of Robin Harcourt Williams, librarian and archivist there. Both are acknowledged with gratitude. <http://www.rhul.ac.uk/history/research/cecils/>, accessed 20 June 2006.

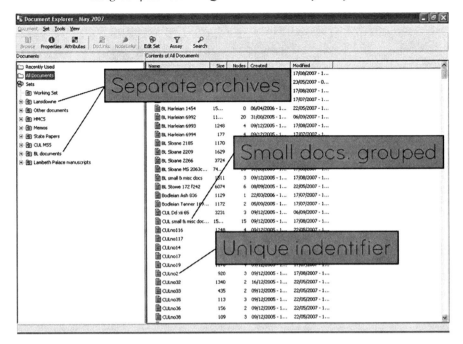

Figure 7.1   Preserving archival integrity in a QDA environment

in different ways: there is a published Calendar of most of the papers, which furnishes a point of reference. Second, each manuscript has its own enumeration, the means by which it is stored and found at Hatfield House. Third, there is a microfilm of the collection, which has its own separate enumeration. Finally, there are some manuscripts at Hatfield House which do not appear in either the microfilms or the Calendars, and do not have numbers within their bundles. So we devised a file structure which would allow for cross-referencing across the Calendars and manuscripts by means of the date of the document in question, viz: 'HMCS15990625' (where '1599' = year; '06' = month; and '25' = day). Documents from other archives were given similar headings, although it did not prove possible to include the useful date material in each of the filenames. No archive would ever be complete without its category of 'Miscellaneous' documents, those which cannot readily be assigned a place within the structure that has been defined. In our case, we found ourselves creating a 'Small & Miscellaneous' file for each collection, into which we could place brief extracts, enabling us to find small items which did not readily fit elsewhere. Although it is always possible to migrate documents from one set to another, the basic message is one that is all too easily forgotten in computer-assisted data analysis: file structures are powerful tools in the organization and retrieval of data.

The heart of QDA lies, however, in the knowledge environment (or 'coding') to be adopted for the qualitative interpretation of documentation. That requires a coding structure, and therein lies a debate among current practitioners, pertinent to any proposed application to historical documentation, about whether coding should 'emerge' from the text or be 'imposed' upon it by a predetermined research agenda.

Document Attribute Explorer - May 2007

File Edit Attribute Document

Document: [vol77nd92] + Add − Remove

Attribute: [Date [month]] + Add − Remove ↕ Invert Table

	Date [month]	Date [year]	Document Type	From	Gender of the Sender	Medical Practitioner?	To
BL Harleian 6992	April	1575	Letter	Smith, Sir Thomas	Male	-	WC Ld Burghley
BL Harleian 6993	.	.	.	.	.	.	.
BL Harleian 6994	June	1588	Letter	Huntingdon, earl of	Male	-	MC. Lady Burghley
BL Sloane 2185	.	?	Receipts	.	.	.	.
BL Sloane 2209	.	?	Receipts	.	.	.	.
BL Sloane 2266	.	?	Receipts	.	.	.	.
BL Sloane MS 2063copy	July	1611	Report	Mayerne, Dr T	Male	Physician	.
BL small & misc docs	.	.	.	.	.	.	.
BL Stowe 172 f242	April	1612	Letter plus advice	Mayerne, Dr T	Male	Physician	RC Earl of Salisbury
Bodleian Ash 836	.	?	Funeral costs	.	.	.	.
Bodleian Tanner 168 f78	June	1609	Receipt	Powle, Stephen	Male	-	NA
CUL Dd xii 65	.	?	Funeral costs	.	.	.	.
CUL small & misc documents	.	.	.	.	.	.	.
CULno116	July	1597	Letter	WC Ld Burghley	Male	-	RC Earl of Salisbury
CULno117	July	1597	Letter	WC Ld Burghley	Male	-	RC Earl of Salisbury
CULno14	September	1593	Letter	WC Ld Burghley	Male	-	RC Earl of Salisbury
CULno17	February	1594	Letter	WC Ld Burghley	Male	-	RC Earl of Salisbury
CULno19	April	1594	Letter	WC Ld Burghley	Male	-	RC Earl of Salisbury
CULno2	May	1593	Letter	WC Ld Burghley	Male	-	RC Earl of Salisbury

No Row Selected   No Column Selected

Figure 7.2   'Attributes' assigned to documents from the Lansdowne Collection in the Health of the Cecils Project

Should it be data-driven or concept-driven? Historians commonly work with an implied model of 'open' questions, beginning with a predetermined research agenda, but letting the sources direct them both as to how this should be pursued, and as to the relevant questions to ask of the historical material being consulted. Given that it is very difficult to decide in advance whether a particular source, or set of sources, is going to provide reliable answers to a preconceived question, this is the only way to proceed, and historians commonly find their most productive work comes from asking questions they would have been highly unlikely to generate in advance of looking at the material.

So, in our case, we could readily determine our research agenda as involving such questions as: Where did members of the Cecil family get their knowledge of health matters? What authorities are being quoted in the sources and thus influencing their attitudes? Who was giving the family its medical advice? What illnesses and conditions did they believe they were suffering from, or were diagnosed to be? How did they understand such notions as 'health' and 'sickness'? How did the advice given by their medical professionals compare with that given by friends and other laypeople? Is there any discernible pattern in the circumstances that led them to consult medical professionals?

Some of these questions, those of the 'what' and 'who' variety, could straightforwardly be transferred into categories that could be coded (see Figure 7.2). Others, however, are conceptually more complex, and they necessarily required a process of iteration with the documentation and refined definition before any

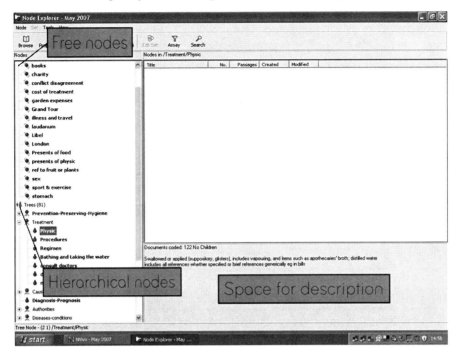

Figure 7.3 **A QDA coding structure opened to reveal the contents of a hierarchical 'node'**

coding could be applied. Often the language used to describe a condition, illness, or particular treatment was unclear, and perhaps unclear to contemporaries too. This lack of clarity needed to be reflected in the coding structures (see Figure 7.3). Some of the correspondence in our corpus indicated that the sufferer did not fully understand what was happening to them. So 'cause of illness' is a category that is particularly delicate to define, and the coding had to reflect the vague language of the text and the flawed understanding of the writers. This was where we had to work collaboratively, taking groups of documents and producing a usable coding structure on the basis of what we discovered.

An essential component of the CAQDAS medium is, therefore, that it is tolerant of considerable reiterations of the coding structure. Even so, the engagement in this project between the two researchers with social science research backgrounds, and the one early-modern historian revealed sharp divisions of approach between the desires of the former to formulate precise research questions, and the inclinations of the latter not to impose arbitrary interpretations on the meaning of the text. The point of commonality, however, was the acceptance that the language of the sources was often imprecise or unclear. Some of the correspondents in the Cecil Papers, for instance, gave only brief references to their experience of pain or an accident; or they provided an explanation of their illness which referred to the influence of astrology or humoral imbalance upon their condition. These allusions had to be

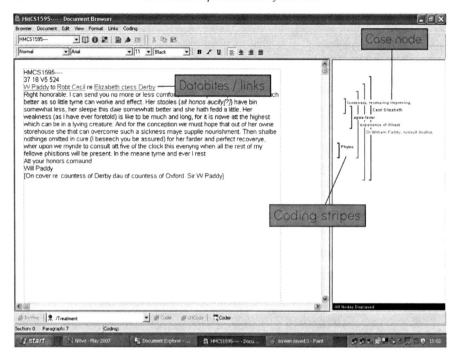

Figure 7.4   Coding indicators and data linkage in QDA software

reflected in the coding of data relating to understandings of pain. In other sources, however, the information was much more clear and detailed – where, for example, the writer of a particular source had a diagnosis of suffering from gout, and could describe to themselves and others what their experience of the condition was. Once an initial draft coding structure had been agreed through these various iterations, it was eventually approved by the whole project team. Processes of iteration can be never-ending, and it was important to keep in mind that we were not designing a universal ontology but, rather, an advanced means of patterning qualitative data in a particular environment.

NVivo permits the use of three different types of coding, called 'nodes'. There are 'free' nodes, 'tree' nodes and 'case' nodes (see Figure 7.3). Free nodes serve several purposes. They often emerge experimentally and remain as part of the coding structure if they serve a purpose, even though they may have no obvious place in the formal hierarchical representation of knowledge. 'Tree' nodes provide an environment for more structured knowledge, with some of the attributes of a semantic web ontology. They enable the grouping of nodes together in a way that allows for their structured access and analysis. So our hierarchical 'node' on 'Illnesses/conditions' was developed to group together the medical disorders using the names for them derived from the texts themselves. Similarly, the hierarchical node on 'Treatment' conjoined the various ways of dealing with ill health and the way in which contemporaries discussed the distinction between disease 'prevention' and 'treatment', notably in respect of 'regimen'. So hierarchical nodes served to link

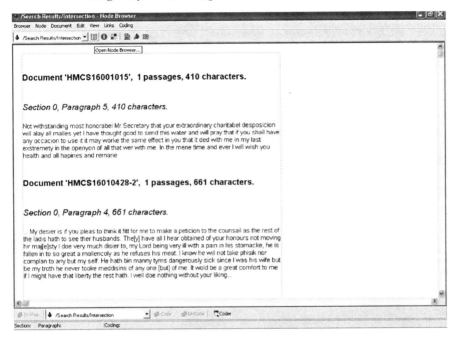

Figure 7.5   A search result in QDA software

modern ways of understanding health with premodern conceptions, rendering both accessible without their being unintentionally commingled. They aided conceptual clarity and prevented unintentional category duplication. Above all, they provided a stimulus to further discussion and research: the software became, in short, part and parcel of the way the project thought about its material. The final 'case' nodes were reserved for the 'individuals' of particular importance to the project: they might be referred to in different ways either by title, or not specifically by name at all. Through the 'case' nodes, their names can be searched for within the coding structure.

QDA software has some sophisticated tools embedded in it that allow for additional annotation and links to external resources. NVivo uses 'databites' (the equivalent of 'footnotes', or 'data-links') which allow the researcher to attach additional data or researches, annotating material internally or linking to external resources of one kind or another. In the Health of the Cecils Project we created extensive links to the *Oxford Dictionary of National Biography* (ODNB), a particularly authoritative resource for biographical information, and also to the Database of Physicians and Irregular Practitioners created by Margaret Pelling (in Figure 7.4, this is the link attached to Dr William Paddy).[6] References to Elizabeth Cecil (later countess of Derby) are linked to the genealogy created as part of the project in the specialist software WINGENEA. These links have facilitated the development of a nominal

6 Physicians and Irregular Medical Practitioners in London 1550–1640, a database publicly available from the British History website at the Institute of Historical Research <http://www.british-history.ac.uk/source.asp?pubid=107>, accessed 10 May 2006.

index in the project. Similarly, such linkage led to the creation of a glossary for the extensive specialist vocabulary in English and Latin related to 'materia medica' in the receipts and apothecaries' bills.[7]

This search (see Figure 7.5) was carried out in the context of writing a draft chapter on the contribution of lay knowledge to the health care of the Cecil family. The software enabled us to demonstrate that lay knowledge played a far more significant role in the health care of the Cecil family than we had imagined when we began our research. This was a significant conclusion in the context of our current understanding of the relationship between lay and professional medical wisdom in early modern England. We had discovered that the Cecil family, despite their great wealth and access to professional medical advice, were behaving like most of the rest of the population and relying on a plurality of medical knowledge.[8] This would have been difficult to arrive at in anything other than a computer-assisted medium since it depended on the cumulative association of many individual items of information, often very brief, across several repositories.

In a family which, from time to time, paid huge apothecaries' and physicians' bills, there was also a significant informal exchange of ideas and advice on managing pain, back problems, gout and stress. Members of the family were prepared to dispatch their own recipes, dispensing remedies which they had concocted themselves, and their household and kin received advice and physic. William Cecil, Lord Burghley and Sir Francis Walsingham (c.1532–1590), Elizabeth I's principal secretary, exchanged informal news and views regarding their health for many years in a lengthy correspondence that survives for the period from 1571 to 1589. They recommended particular physicians and treatment to one another, and commiserated with one another on their illnesses.[9] The QDA software has contributed to a more nuanced understanding of the use of correspondence as a medium for the exchange of medical knowledge and for understanding medical praxis. So, for example, we can determine the significance of bathing and taking the waters as part of therapeutic measures in this period by correlating the often very brief references about travelling

---

7 Now online at <http://www.rhul.ac.uk/history/research/cecils/medica/>, accessed 11 September 2007.

8 See D.N. Evenden, *Popular Medicine in Seventeenth Century England* (Bowling Green Ohio: Bowling Green State University Press, 1988), and J. Stine, 'Opening Closets: The Discovery of Household Medicine in Early Modern England'. Unpublished PhD thesis, Stanford University, California (1996).

9 See, e.g., Sir Dudley Digges, *The Compleat Ambassador: Or Two Treaties of Intended Marriage of Qu. Elizabeth of Glorious Memory; Comprised in Letters of Negotiation of Sir Francis Walsingham, Her Resident in France Together with the Answers of the Lord Burleigh [...]* (Gabriel Bedell and Thomas Collins, 1655), pp. 78, 163–5, 203. Also The National Archive, SP 12 vol. 103 no. 31 (1575); vol. 105 no. 25 (1575); vol. 126 no. 5 (1578); vol. 209 no. 83 (1588); vol. 103 nos 31, 63 (1575); vol. 190 nos 10, 37; vol. 201 no. 18 (1587); vol. 203 no. 54 (1587); vol. 205 no. 33 (1587); vol. 211 no. 36 (1588); vol. 212 nos 52, 58, 63 (1588); vol. 219 no. 46 (1588); vol. 223 no. 98 (1589); also Walsingham's letters to Burghley in British Library, Harleian MS 6992 no. 23 (1576), Harleian 6993 no. 27 (1583); Hatfield House, Salisbury Papers vol. 165 no. 86 (1581); British Library Lansdowne MS 38 nos 60, 61 (1583).

to Bath or Buxton. Put these scattered references together, however, and one is forced to the conclusion that Bath was already a recognized medical treatment centre by the second half of the sixteenth century for those who could afford to go there. Similarly, the earl and countess of Shrewsbury owned property at Buxton where they provided extensive hospitality for guests to benefit from the waters. One guest list from 1574 includes Thomas Cecil and his wife.[10] Robert Cecil's last visit to Bath is well known but details from bills and accounts indicate a number of desperate measures to get him into the baths despite his physical weakness brought on by his terminal illness. Stonemasons worked overnight to put steps in place. Bathing attendants had special clothes bought for them, and padded seats were supplied.[11] It was not his visit to Bath that was unusual, rather the amount of money that was spent whilst he was there in the attempt to keep him alive.

Although we might have found some of this material by traditional means, it would not have been possible to have reached such definitive conclusions from it. So, for example, although we might have stumbled upon some of the material relating to dentistry and dental health, or the surgical treatment of cataracts, we would not have been able to pick up the density of the incidental references to dental hygiene or concerns about eye strain.[12] It would notionally have been possible to have made some calculations regarding the family's expenditure on apothecaries or on disability aids at Bath without the use of the software. But the contextual information is essential to the interpretation of such figures, and it has been in constructing the 'context' of the medical health of the Cecil family that QDA software has radically enhanced our interpretative capacity, not to mention our ability to co-author the eventual resulting monograph.

On one level, QDA software proved to be an excellent data management tool, enabling the storage, searching and sharing of large amounts of complex data within a collaborative project. It provided a sophisticated environment for inputting and checking data. But it also provided a knowledge environment, one in which the coding structures reflected successive reiterations of our analysis of the material as it was acquired and examined from different sources, and with various linkages to other materials. It permitted us to interrogate sources in many different ways and allowed us to explore interesting hypotheses. In that sense, it was a way of creating a virtual research environment in which our essentially 'qualitative' understandings of health and illness in a historical environment could become properly understood.

---

10 G. Dynfnallt Owen (ed.), *Talbot, Dudley & Devereux Papers: 1533–1659*, Calendar of the Mss of the Most Honourable the Marquess of Bath, Preserved at Longleat (HMSO, 1980), vol. V, pp. 20–21.

11 Hatfield House, Salisbury Papers, Bills 72 (1612).

12 E.g. The National Archive, SP 12 vol. 141 no. 33 (Richard Master on Burghley's loose teeth (1580); British Library, Lansdowne vol. 101 no. 4 (Russwurin on Mrs Jane Cecil's cataracts, undated but probably from the 1570s). Apothecaries' receipts among the Hatfield papers contain many references to tooth powders, tooth picks and electuary (i.e. medicinal paste) for teeth.

Chapter 8

Stepping Back from the Trench Edge: An Archaeological Perspective on the Development of Standards for Recording and Publication

Julian D. Richards and Catherine Hardman

The development of recording and publication standards in archaeology has never been regarded as either at the cutting edge or exciting.[1] It has been seen as a worthy but dull activity. Postmodernists have been rather suspicious of it since it seemed to imply a fundamental belief in data as fact.[2] Indeed, over twenty years ago one of us spoke out against the rigid imposition of standards as potentially stultifying to intellectual enquiry.[3] However, the development of online digital resources provides the single most important reason why standards should be supported. Standards are fundamental to cross-searching and analysis of multiple data sources. Archaeological archives, if they existed at all, used to be seen as independent, self-contained entities. They were generally the by-product of a specific research project and were 'a means to an end', usually of an individual researcher. In that case the individualistic nature of recording systems and terms was not really a problem. Only in large urban centres, where the combination of results from successive small-scale

1 We are grateful to Mark Greengrass for the invitation to participate in the Virtual History and Archaeology seminar, and to the other participants for two days of stimulating discussion. This chapter originated as two contributions; the first on attempts to develop a common platform for archaeological publications (JDR), and the second on the OASIS online access to grey literature project (CSH). Both were delivered in a session linked by the GRID to the 2006 Computer Applications in Archaeology Conference, held in Fargo, North Dakota. In preparing and delivering these papers it became clear to us that what was of particular interest to an interdisciplinary audience was the relative success with which data standards had been developed in archaeology, and the question was posed as to whether this represented a fundamental difference between archaeologists and historians. This written amalgam of both papers has therefore taken the opportunity to explore this issue further.
2 A. Baines and K. Brophy, 'What's Another Word for Thesaurus? Data Standards and Classifying the Past', in P. Daly and T.L. Evans (eds), *Digital Archaeology: Bridging Method and Theory* (Routledge, 2006), p. 237.

3 J.D. Richards, 'Standardising the Record', in M.A. Cooper and J.D. Richards (eds), *Current Issues in Archaeological Computing*, British Archaeological Reports International Series, no. 271 (Oxford, 1985), pp. 93–112.

excavations could throw light on larger questions, was there a sense of interrogation of an integrated knowledge base that was greater than the sum of the individual parts, usually through an offline database.[4]

With the growth in use of the internet for the dissemination of data and results all that has changed. The potential for online delivery and re-use of datasets has been recognized and encouraged by the funding councils.[5] Moreover, rather than treating each resource as a self-contained entity with its own data structure and vocabulary it becomes possible to amalgamate resources and to undertake cross-searching. What is described as the semantic interoperability of datasets has become important, whether these are multiple datasets held on a single server or whether they are distributed across multiple physical hosts.[6] In the United States, the National Science Foundation has promoted the concept of 'cyberinfrastructure' to describe new research environments that support data storage, management, integration, mining, and visualization over the internet. Early take-up has been supported in the ecological sciences and the geosciences, through the GEONGRID.[7] There has been an exploratory workshop in archaeology but, so far, the emphasis is upon opportunity rather than delivery.[8] Elsewhere the infrastructure to support the shared analysis of research data is also described by the umbrella term 'eScience', although the best example in archaeology is provided by the Virtual Research Environment (VRE) developed for the Silchester research project, which is focussed upon a single site.[9] It is the sharing of data between projects that requires the development of shared standards. During the course of the Sheffield workshop at which the chapters in this volume were discussed, it became apparent that these were relatively well developed for some aspects of archaeology. Yet historians present found it difficult to find comparable examples from their subject area. This chapter will explore some

---

4 J. Schofield and P. Tyers, 'Towards a Computerised Archaeological Research Archive', in Cooper and Richards, *Current Issues in Archaeological Computing*, pp. 5–16.

5 J.D. Richards, 'Digital Preservation and Access', *European Journal of Archaeology*, 5 (2002): 343–66; *AHRC Research Funding Guide, 2006/7* <http://www.ahrc.ac.uk>, accessed 24 August 2007.

6 A. Austin, F. Pinto, J.D. Richards and N. Ryan, 'Joined-up Writing: an Internet Portal for Research into the Historic Environment', in G. Burenhult (ed.), *CAA 2001: Archaeological Informatics: Pushing the Envelope*, British Archaeological Reports, International Series no. 1016 (Oxford, 2002), pp. 243–51; W. Kilbride, 'The Danube in Prehistory in the Digital Age: Towards a Common Information Environment for European Archaeology', in *Archeologia e Calcolatori*, 15 (2004): 129–44.

7 <http://seek.ecoinformatics.org/>; <http://www.geongrid.org/>, both accessed 24 August 2007.

8 K. Kintigh, *The Promise and Challenge of Archaeological Data Integration. Final Report of the Workshop, Santa Barbara, California*. Unpublished report (2005); D.R. Snow, M. Gahegan, C.L. Giles et al., 'Cybertools and Archaeology', *Science* 311 (2006): 958–9.

9 A. Clarke, M. Fulford and M. Rains, 'Nothing to Hide – Online Database Publication and the Silchester Town Life Project', in M. Doerr and A. Sarris (eds), *CAA2002: The Digital Heritage of Archaeology. Computer Applications and Quantitative Methods in Archaeology, 2002* (Hellenic Ministry of Culture, 2003), pp. 401–10.

of the reasons for this. If both disciplines are to exploit the full potential of the digital age a more general acceptance of data standards is essential.

*****

We should make it clear that by 'standards' we are referring to agreed data structures and terminologies, properly collectively referred to as 'data standards', not to benchmarks for the quality of research work undertaken. Terminological standards and controlled vocabularies often develop out of typologies and classifications, of which there is a long tradition in archaeology. In this sense the nineteenth-century adoption of the Three Age System, classifying the past into three eras of Stone, Bronze and Iron, represents a fundamental data standard which underpins much later work. Most questions asked of archaeological data can be readily broken down into a combination of 'when?', 'where?' and 'what?'. A standard for the description of archaeological time is therefore crucial to the interoperability of datasets.

The Monument Inventory Data Standard (MIDAS), developed by English Heritage and its partners, provides an agreed set of period terms for the description of English sites and monuments, and has been adopted by most regional and county Historic Environment Records (HERs).[10] However, as soon as one leaves the borders of England it becomes apparent that archaeological periodicity is, in reality, culturally determined, and relative date ranges are spatially dependent. Thus, for example, most of Scotland does not have a 'Roman period', and the 'Iron Age' continues until the 'Viking period', which in Scotland is often called 'Norse'. When one leaves the British Isles the problems are magnified, and new terms such as 'Minoan', 'Mycenean' or 'Hellenic' are soon encountered. The ARENA project, which developed a prototype portal for the cross-searching of six European national or regional sites and monuments databases, found that the only solution was to attempt to map each national terminology to an absolute time scale.[11] Unfortunately, this reduced each dataset to a lowest common denominator. Searches for 'Iron Age', for example, might recover sites dated to anywhere between 1000 BC and AD 1000, depending upon the country in question. There are similar problems if one attempts to search across disciplines within one country. For instance, the term 'early medieval' has different meanings for the historian and the archaeologist. A building referred to by an archaeologist as 'post-medieval' might be described by an art historian as 'Georgian' or 'neo-classical' for instance. Nonetheless, the results from mappings between national or discipline-based terminologies will still be more useful than if there were no agreed terminologies at all.

The 'where?' question is, in principle, more easily dealt with as there are international cross-disciplinary systems for describing space, notably the use of latitude and longitude, to which national grid references can be converted. There are, however, some specific difficulties confronting projects which seek to combine

---

10 E. Lee, *MIDAS: A Manual and Data Standard for Monument Inventories*, 3rd edn (Swindon: English Heritage, 2003).

11 J. Kenny and J.D. Richards, 'Pathways to a Shared European Information Infrastructure for Cultural Heritage', *Internet Archaeology*, 18 (2005) s 4.2 <http://intarch.ac.uk/journal/issue18/kenny_index.html>, accessed 24 August 2007.

datasets collected using different coordinate systems.[12] Nonetheless, the combination of datasets using a map-based search system is one of the easiest and most visual ways of combining a number of resources, so long as they are spatially geo-referenced. The tools provided by GIS can then be used to investigate the linkages between the different data layers. However, if location has not been precisely geo-referenced then one is left with the problem of dealing with fuzzily defined polygons designed to correspond to, as it might be, a parish or township area.

The 'what?' question is the hardest to confront. There is no single subject thesaurus for archaeology, and as soon as one leaves one discipline one encounters a host of competing standards. Whilst generic library systems such as Library of Congress and Dewey Decimal subject classifications are helpful at a very general level, they are rarely specific enough for detailed searches, and they rapidly break down when they reach into specialist research areas. For categories of sites and monuments there is a well-defined standard known as the Thesaurus of Monument Types (TMT). This provides a controlled vocabulary which has been adopted by county-based records as well as the English Heritage national archaeological inventory; and it has also been adopted with slight modification for Scotland. The thesaurus has 18 top-level terms which define general functional categories of monument, such as 'defence', 'domestic' or 'industrial', and these overlie a hierarchy of approved terms, and their equivalences. These are non-exclusive terms, such that any one monument may be classified within many categories. For artefact finds there is an equivalent Archaeological Objects Thesaurus developed by the Museum Documentation Association (MDA). These however remain independent of one another, and there is currently no overarching archaeological subject thesaurus.

Thesauri of guidelines for the use of controlled vocabularies provide one of the essential building blocks by which it is possible to combine datasets sensibly. However, by themselves, they are not sufficient to allow cross-searching. It is also necessary to understand how the database fields have been defined, and here there is much more room for individual variability. Again, archaeologists have agreed standards covering the compilation and organization of 'inventories' of the archaeological and architectural heritage of England. MIDAS is a content standard that sets out what sort of information should be recorded, for instance to describe the character or location of a monument.[13] Adherence to MIDAS, and to the specific underlying wordlists, should mean that it is possible to combine the monument inventories across counties or regions and thereby to allow users to cross-search for particular categories of site. It should also allow the transfer of data between information providers, and indeed a specific XML schema (MIDAS XML) has been developed to facilitate this. This data standard indicates an appropriate mapping between database fields and the vocabulary that has been used within those fields.

---

12 I. Scollar, 'Geodetic and Cartographic Problems in Archaeological Data Bases at and within the Boundaries of some Countries', in S. Rahtz and J.D. Richards (eds), *Computer Applications and Quantitative Methods in Archaeology*, British Archaeological Reports, International Series S548 (Oxford, 1989), pp. 251–73.

13 Lee, *MIDAS*.

The Archaeology Data Service (ADS) online catalogue, ArchSearch combines a large number of data sources, drawn from local and national inventories, and allows users to cross-search over one million index records.[14] It works because the datasets which have been combined are each MIDAS compliant. ArchSearch does not include all the MIDAS fields but it uses a number of index fields which cover the 'when?', 'what?' and 'where?' questions. These fields have also been mapped to the Dublin Core metadata standard.[15] These core fields underlie the ADS catalogue and mean that it should also be interoperable with other Dublin Core metadatasets. So the metadata can be harvested using the Open Archives Initiative (OAI) protocol to allow cross-searching with resources drawn from other subject areas.[16] At this level, however, full semantic interoperability breaks down. Although information providers might agree on a Dublin Core 'subject' field, for example, different disciplines will often have qualified their usage of the Dublin Core according to discipline-specific vocabulary. That said, in general, the standards for the description of archaeological field monuments are relatively well-defined and have a long pedigree, which ultimately goes back to the field surveyors trained by the Ordnance Survey to plot antiquities on maps.

*****

The summary recording of archaeological interventions – field surveys, watching briefs and excavations, etc. – also follows quite well established practice. The OASIS project has developed an online recording form to be completed by archaeological contractors and researchers on the completion of a piece of fieldwork.[17] This records summary information which deals with the 'when?', 'where?' and 'what?' questions in accordance with a controlled vocabulary. The development and adoption of the OASIS form, which is now required by the majority of archaeologists responsible for fieldwork specifications in England, provides an interesting case study in the take-up and development of a national standard, with a combination of top-down and bottom-

---

14 ADS ArchSearch <http://ads.ahds.ac.uk/catalogue/>, accessed 24 August 2007.

15 A.P. Miller, 'Metadata for the Masses: What is It, How Can it Help Me, and How Can I Use It?', *Ariadne*, 5 (1996) <http://www.ukoln.ac.uk/ariadne/issue5/metadata-masses/>, accessed 24 August 2007; also 'The Importance of Metadata in Archaeology', in L. Dingwall, S. Exxon, V. Gaffney, S. Laflin and M. Van Leusen (eds), *CAA97: Archaeology in the Age of the Internet: Computer Applications and Quantitative Methods in Archaeology*, British Archaeological Reports, International Series S750 (Oxford: Tempus Reparatum, 1999), p. 136; A.P. Miller and D. Greenstein (eds), *Discovering Online Resources: A Practical Implementation of Dublin Core* (UKOLN/AHDS, 1997); A. Wise and P. Miller, 'Why Metadata Matters in Archaeology', *Internet Archaeology*, 2 (1997): s 8.1 <http://intarch.ac.uk/journal/issue2/wise_index.html>, accessed 24 August 2007.

16 M. Day, 'E-print Services and Long-term Access to the Record of Scholarly and Scientific Research', *Ariadne*, 28 (2001) <http://www.ariadne.ac.uk/issue28/metadata/>, accessed 24 August 2007.

17 C. Hardman and J.D. Richards, 'OASIS: Dealing with a Digital Revolution', in M. Doerr and N. Crofts in M. Doerr and A. Sarris (eds), *CAA2002: The Digital Heritage of Archaeology. Computer Applications and Quantitative Methods in Archaeology, 2002* (Hellenic Ministry of Culture, 2003) pp. 325–8.

up carrots and sticks. Again the standard has been consolidated by the development of a specific OASIS XML schema. Completed OASIS records are validated by the local archaeological authority (in the HER), and by the English Heritage National Monuments Record. They are then imported into the HER database and into the English Heritage Excavation Index, which is mapped to Dublin Core and made available by the ADS. OASIS was initially funded by the Research Support Libraries Programme, taken up by English Heritage, and is now being further developed with support from Historic Scotland and the Royal Commission on the Ancient and Historical Monuments of Scotland (RCAHMS).

However, although the OASIS record provides the minimum level of metadata required to record any archaeological intervention it does not prescribe what should be recorded beyond that. Indeed, although the AHDS Guides to Good Practice are widely regarded as providing valuable data standards for digital data recording, they do not dictate what to record, but instead suggest what metadata should be recorded in order to permit data preservation and re-use.[18] In fact, despite countless attempts to establish a single, agreed recording system for archaeological fieldwork, it currently does not exist. Most excavators use fairly standardized pro-forma to record each excavated layer and feature ('single-context recording forms') and, although most have a shared origin in the systems employed either by the former Department of Urban Archaeology (DUA) at the Museum of London, or by the former Central Excavation Unit (CEU) of English Heritage, each contracting unit has, in reality, developed its own variant. Although there is a common denominator to the fields used on most of these forms, and also overlapping vocabularies, most excavators have stuck to their own systems.

Why is this so? Part of the reason must be that there has been no good research reason for combining primary records from more than one site. There is limited utility, for example, in searching for all layers of silty clay loam with charcoal flecks across two or more excavations. However, it is possible to envisage legitimate research enquiries which are not supported by the current fragmented systems. There might be value, for example, in finding all hearths, or all storage pits. This is rarely possible at present. In the case of the digital archive derived from the Channel Tunnel infrastructure project, for example, there are currently individual archives for no fewer than 122 interventions.[19] The individual archives are the result of the recording systems employed by the contracting unit working on a specific site, whether Oxford Archaeology, Wessex Archaeology or the Museum of London Archaeological Service. Even limited cross-searching of the combined archives was made possible only by a large investment in the creation of metadata following the deposition of the archive with the ADS. In one major infrastructure project, however, an attempt has been made to create a single homogeneous archive. In archaeological fieldwork

---

18　J.D. Richards and D.J. Robinson, *Digital Archives from Excavations and Fieldwork: A Guide to Good Practice* (York: Archaeology Data Service and Oxbow Books, 2000); A. Schmidt, *Geophysical Data in Archaeology: A Guide to Good Practice* (York: Archaeology Data Service and Oxbow Books, 2002).

19　<http://ads.ahds.ac.uk/catalogue/resources.html?ctrl_2003>, accessed 24 August 2007.

undertaken at Heathrow and Stansted Airports by the consortium of contracting units known as Framework Archaeology on behalf of the British Airports Authority, a single shared recording system was devised.[20]

*****

What, then, of standardization in the publication of archaeological excavation reports? There has, in reality, been little progress here, despite a succession of working parties and user surveys that have sought to address the perceived publication crisis in British archaeology.[21] In reality, the crisis has partly come about because of two long-established but contradictory theoretical positions regarding the role of fieldwork publication. An empiricist tradition sees field data as a factual record, making the full and complete publication of site and archive a professional duty. Another view regards the report as just one possible set of recorded observations, and argues that what is important is the 'story', or interpretative synthesis, rather than the data. The idea of the excavation report as the factual and complete record of a site goes back at least as far as the nineteenth-century pioneer excavator, General Augustus Henry Lane-Fox Pitt-Rivers (1827–1900). For Pitt Rivers, publication provided an objective record of what had been excavated (and thereby destroyed) and it was the archaeologist's professional responsibility to publish in full. He practised what he preached in his own four massive reports on the excavations he conducted on his estate in Dorset.[22] On the other hand, the distinguished Egyptologist (Sir William Matthew) Flinders Petrie (1853–1942) argued that the contents of notebooks and listings of data were not publications, and that such observations must necessarily lead to conclusions and generalizations which alone were the suitable material for the public domain.[23] Notwithstanding this early plea for synthetic publication, it was Pitt-Rivers who was to have the greater influence on publication trends, even though the resulting tension between brief synthetic publication and full data presentation has periodically re-emerged. Throughout the first half of the twentieth century, publication was seen as an integral part of the excavation process. In much of the literature there was little mention of the archiving of such reports. The only effective record was full publication – the published report and the archive being regarded as one and the same thing.[24]

---

20 A. Beck, 'Intellectual Excavation and Dynamic Management Systems', in G. Lock and K. Brown (eds), *On the Theory and Practice of Archaeological Computing* Oxford University Committee for Archaeology Monographs no. 51 (Oxford: Oxford University Committee for Archaeology, 2000), pp. 73–88.

21 See, for a recent survey and summary, S. Jones, A. MacSween, S. Jeffrey et al., 'From the Ground Up. The Publication of Archaeological Reports: A User-needs Survey. A Summary', produced for the Council for British Archaeology, York and available in *Internet Archaeology* 14 (2003) <http://interarch.ac.uk/journal/issue14/puns_index.html>, accessed 24 August 2007.

22 A.L-F. Pitt-Rivers, *Excavations in Cranbourne Chase*, 4 vols (privately printed, 1887–9).

23 W.M.F. Petrie, *Methods and Aims in Archaeology* (Macmillan, 1904).

24 See S. Jones et al., 'From the Ground Up', s 2.

During the 1960s and 1970s, archaeology had to acknowledge a growing publication crisis. Against a background of large-scale building development in the UK, there was increased archaeological activity and a great deal of rescue excavation, but soaring publication costs also contributed to a resulting post-excavation and publication backlog. The Frere Report (1975) attempted to address the problem. It endorsed the traditional view that archaeologists were under an obligation to produce a full record; but it accepted that full publication was no longer practicable.[25] The report advocated a rationalization of recording and publication. Four levels of recording were held to characterize the successful completion of an excavation:[26]

- Level I – the site itself and the excavated finds;
- Level II – the site notebooks, on-site recording forms, drawings, finds records, photographs etc.;
- Level III – the processed complete archive: full illustration and description of structural, stratigraphic and artefactual/environmental data;
- Level IV – a synthetic description with supporting illustrations.

Hitherto, full Level III publication had been the norm, at least in theory. Now refined publication at Level IV was recommended, on condition that a Level III report was produced for archiving, a report that would be readily available on request. In essence, the Frere Report responded to the publication crisis by recommending a reduction in the amount of material that would go into print, coupled with an improvement in archival organization and curation. The Frere Report was the first attempt by a state heritage body to address standards of publication systematically. With hindsight it can be argued that this did not constitute a radical departure from traditional practices. All that it advocated was an uncoupling of an accepted record (known as the Level III report) from the process of formal publication (Level IV). It was a pragmatic response to the costs of formal publication and the pressures on publication outlets.[27]

Although Frere's recommendations were very influential on archaeological practice, it is a moot point whether they had much impact upon the backlog brought about by increasing numbers of large projects. Indeed, the high standard of preparation required by Level III reporting meant that in many cases *more* time was required for post-excavation work than had been allocated beforehand. A joint working party of the Council for British Archaeology (CBA) and the Department of the Environment, under the chairmanship of Barry Cunliffe, was convened to attempt to address the continuing problem. With its emphasis on the importance of an accessible archive, and on targeted research and publication, the Cunliffe Report marked a departure, both from the traditional model (with its ideal of full excavation and publication) and the Frere compromise (which had confined publication to a

---

25　S.S. Frere, *Principles of Publication in Rescue Archaeology: Report by a Working Party of the Ancient Monuments Board for England* (Committee for Rescue Archaeology, 1975), p. 2.

26　Ibid., p. 3.

27　S. Jones et al., 'From the Ground Up'.

Level III report).[28] The detailed description of the evidence was to be reduced to a summary, with detail confined to microfiche. The report had considerable impact but its implementation was problematic and, indeed, it was rejected by the CBA. With the benefit of hindsight it seems that one of the main problems was practical and stemmed from difficulties with the technology of the 1980s. No archive could be truly accessible, and the use of microfiche was universally loathed. Another difficulty was increasing theoretical debate about whether the full report actually represented a complete factual account of the site. John Barrett argued that the publication crisis extended beyond report production to the ways in which archives and reports could be used and re-used.[29] Although it may be impossible to judge an excavator's general competence from a published report, it is possible 'for the reader to undertake a critical analysis of the internal logic of the report, examining the linkages between the assumptions employed, the stated record of observations, and the interpretative account'.[30]

Ian Hodder regretted that reports had become impersonal objective accounts of data.[31] He argued that since the excavation process is interpretative from start to finish, personal factors which lead to that interpretation should, as far as possible, be written into the report rather than kept out of it. In other words, there should be *greater* integration of description and interpretation. Another perspective, criticizing the use of synthetic reports as the main format of dissemination of archaeological knowledge, was provided by Michael Shanks and Christopher Tilley.[32] They argued that such reports represented exercises in 'domination and control' by individuals seeking to impose their view of the past on their readers. It was therefore crucial to find ways to make data available to give a wider audience the opportunity to create their own interpretations.

One further committee tried to address the publication/archives problem. The 1992 report *Archaeological Publication, Archives and Collections: Towards a National Policy* was written in the context of the introduction of developer funding for archaeological excavation.[33] It also took account of those developments in theoretical thinking that reflected a move away from 'preservation by record':

---

28 B.W. Cunliffe, *The Publication of Archaeological Excavations: Report of a Joint Working Party of the Council for British Archaeology and the Department of the Environment* (Department of the Environment, 1983).

29 J. Barrett, 'The Glastonbury Lake Village: Models and Source Criticism', *Archaeological Journal*, 144 (1987): 409–23.

30 Ibid., p. 410.

31 I. Hodder, 'Writing Archaeology: Site Reports in Context', *Antiquity* 63 (1989): 268–74.

32 M. Shanks and C. Tilley, *Social Theory and Archaeology* (Cambridge: Polity Press, 1987).

33 M. Carver, H. Chapman, Cunliffe, B. et al., *Archaeological Publication, Archives and Collections: Towards a National Policy*, prepared for the Society of Antiquaries and the Museums Association, *British Archaeological News* 7/2 (1992) Supplement.

since the record is selective and therefore incomplete and post-excavation analysis must also, of necessity, be selective, the excavation report can only be a contemporary statement reflecting on aspects of the site: it cannot be an immutable and complete truth.[34]

The committee took the Cunliffe Report one stage further and recommended that dissemination should normally be in the form of a published summary report and an accessible site archive. Once more, however, the technology lagged behind and lacked the means of providing access to an archive with links between it and the summary publication. The report was effectively shelved.

In 1998 the CBA was commissioned to carry out a survey of publication user needs. Its recommendations reflected the fact that, by then, technology had moved on. Whilst their survey once more focused on reducing the scale of conventional publication, the 'PUNS Report' recommended alternative means of electronic publication and the dissemination of archival and specialist material in electronic format as a means round the practical problems. The introduction of digital technology provided an opportunity to shift away from pure synthesis towards making archaeological data accessible digitally.[35] The report recognized that there are separate user groups for different aspects of a report and suggests that multiple forms and media of dissemination should be used, as appropriate to a given project. These might include a summary account produced during the project or immediately after; a synthetic journal article or monograph; internet publication either alongside or instead of the above; and electronic availability of detailed and well-indexed structural and specialist reports. The report also concluded that all project archives should be placed on the internet.[36] The growth of electronic dissemination has also allowed some blurring of the distinction between publication and archive, with a seamless interface between the two.[37]

Although the majority of archaeological fieldwork reports follow an accepted format and implicit structure, archaeologists have resisted attempts to impose a common platform upon them. In 1999, the University of California at Los Angeles undertook a doomed attempt to introduce a digital imprint template in the United States.[38] Despite significant funding, they found it difficult to locate authors with suitable data for the project. In the USA and UK, most basic fieldwork reports are no longer published. They become instead part of the grey literature of the discipline, with one or two copies lodged in the office of the state or county archaeologist. The potential offered by the internet for the online dissemination of these reports, through projects such as OASIS, now provides – for the first time – an incentive for the standardization of their structure and format. Gray and Walford advocated

---

34   Ibid., 2.2.1.

35   V. Gaffney and S. Exon, 'From Order to Chaos: Publication, Synthesis, and the Dissemination of Data in a Digital Age', *Internet Archaeology* 6 (1999) <http://intarch.ac.uk/journal/issue6/gaffney_index.html>, accessed 24 August 2007.

36   S. Jones et al., 'From the Ground Up'.

37   J.D. Richards, 'Electronic Publication in Archaeology', in Daly and Evans (eds), *Digital Archaeology*, pp. 213–25.

38   <http://www.sscnet.ucla.edu/ioa/labs/digital/imprint/imprint.html>,   accessed   24 August 2007.

an XML-based approach to creating standard site descriptions in 1999.[39] They were followed by more recent investigations of the appropriate XML tagging for grey literature.[40] In one of these, Gail Falkingham demonstrates that, if contractors were provided with an appropriately developed XML template, then the same report might be easily published online for different audiences.

The use of XML markup begins to illustrate the potential for the semantic web for archaeology.[41] If we can agree standards for the XML encoding of reports then it will be possible to harvest structured content. In Norway, for example, the Museum Documentation project has undertaken TEI markup of antiquarian accounts by hand for many years.[42] Such manual encoding can be time-consuming and expensive but research on data mining using natural language processing, as suggested elsewhere in this volume, demonstrates the potential for automated markup of text documents.[43] Most archaeological data collected in the field is highly structured. But it would require detailed semantic mapping in order to render it truly interoperable on a cross-project basis. Imagine, for example, that each reference to each specific category of artefact was tagged. This would mean that future research could cross-search any number of integrated excavation archives looking for occurrences of pottery type X or brooch type Y. For some themes – including artefact classification – archaeology probably has sufficiently standardized typologies to provide the level of detailed ontology required for the semantic web. It is not surprising that the US Cyber-infrastructure for Archaeology workshop concluded that artefacts and animal bones offered the most promising case studies.[44] However, as noted above, it is not sufficient to have an agreed classification in order to implement meaningful cross-searching. One also needs to take account of higher-level data structures. Here the ISO draft standard for a 'Conceptual Reference Model' (CRM) developed by CIDOC – the CIDOC CRM – is seen by many as providing a way of mapping higher-level reasoning and relationships: 'The primary role of the CRM is to serve as a basis for mediation of cultural heritage information and thereby provide the semantic "glue"

---

39 J. Gray and K. Walford, 'One Good Site Deserves Another: Electronic Publishing in Field Archaeology', *Internet Archaeology*, 7 (1999) <http://intarch.ac.uk/journal/issue7/gray/gray1.html>, accessed 18 February 2008.

40 C. Meckseper and C. Warwick, 'The Publication of Archaeological Excavation Reports Using XML', *Literary and Linguistic Computing*, 18/1 (2003): 63–75; G. Falkingham, 'A Whiter Shade of Grey: A New Approach to Archaeological Grey Literature Using the XML Version of the TEI Guidelines', *Internet Archaeology*, 17 (2005) <http://intarch.ac.uk/journal/issue7/falkingham_index.html>, accessed 24 August 2007.

41 J.D. Richards, 'Archaeology, e-publication and the Semantic Web', *Antiquity* 80 (2006): 970–79.

42 J. Holman, C-E. Ore and O. Eide, 'Documenting two Histories at Once: Digging into Archaeology', in K.F. Ausserer, W. Börner, M. Goriany et al. (eds), *CAA 2003. Enter the Past: The E-way into the Four Dimensions of Cultural Heritage*, British Archaeological Reports International Series no. 1227 (Oxford: Archaeopress, 2004), pp. 221–4.

43 See above, ch. 5 (Ciravegna, Greengrass et al.).

44 K. Kintigh, *The Promise and Challenge of Archaeological Data Integration*.

needed to transform today's disparate, localised information sources into a coherent and valuable global resource.'[45]

*****

To summarize, it is apparent that standards in archaeology actually have a mixed history. In some areas, such as monument inventories, they are now quite well evolved. In others, such as excavation recording or publication formats, they have so far not been pursued with any sustained enthusiasm and have even, in some cases, been positively resisted. The situation really seems to depend upon user need. As research questions about distributions of particular types of sites of specific periods may span the boundaries of several administrative areas there are powerful research imperatives to develop standardization which will aid cross-searching. But there are also political reasons to facilitate the transfer of monument data between local and national bodies and vice versa. When one studies the evolution of data standards in these areas, they have been hard-fought for over many years, with a lot of investment in committee work, before the emergence of an approved thesaurus. There has also been a combination of take-up at the grass roots level in exchange for the obvious benefits of being able to access standard software applications, with pressure from the top to fall in line. In other areas, such as excavation recording or artefact studies, there have been neither the political pressures, not the user needs, to drive the development of standards. It is maybe only now, with the obvious advantages to be derived from cross-searching multiple project archives online, that the pressures for standardization will begin to achieve tangible results.

Similarly, looking at the study of history from the outside, it seems apparent that most computer-based projects have developed in relative isolation, and that digitization has frequently been undertaken with the aims of a specific research project in mind. It is only in recent years, perhaps partly prompted by pressures from the AHRC for the re-use of data, but also by the growing demand from users to integrate datasets, that an awareness of the need for ontologies, controlled vocabularies and agreed data structures has emerged. There is little doubt that such goals will not be easily accomplished, but they are an aim worth aspiring to.

---

45 Cited from M. Doerr and N. Crofts, 'Electronic Esperanto: The Role of the Object-orientated CIDOC Reference Model', in DS. Bearman and J. Trant (eds), *Cultural Heritage Informatics 1999: Selected Papers from ichim99* (1999) and also available at <http://cidoc.ics. forth.gr/docs/doerr_crofts_ichim99_new.pdf> accessed 24 August 2007. Cf. T. Gill, 'Building Semantic Bridges between Museums, Libraries and Archives: The CIDOC Conceptual Reference Model', *First Monday* 9/5 (2004) <http://firstmonday.org/issue9_5/gill/index. html>, accessed 24 August 2007; and S. Ross, 'Position Paper', in *Towards a Semantic Web for Heritage Resources*, DigiCULT Thematic 3 (2003): 7–11, also available at <http://digicult. info/downloads/ti3_high.pdf>, accessed 24 August 2007.

PART III
THE VIRTUAL REPRESENTATION
OF SPACE AND TIME

Chapter 9

Which? What? When? On the Virtual Representation of Time

Manfred Thaller

There are two aspects to the problem of the virtual representations of time in information systems in archaeology and history. They should not be separated. On the one hand, there is, of course, the 'application-level' question of how time should be represented in a knowledge domain, especially in one where it is always important, but very frequently only known imprecisely. On the other hand, there is a more fundamental conceptual question of the representation of time as a dimension along which to integrate separate information systems. How the latter might be developed, is currently a central concern.

I have therefore decided to examine the problem from three different starting-points. The first describes the need for an integration of humanities information systems from the point of view *research politics*. The second present a short introduction to the various *technical aspects* of representing time. The third looks at the current *interoperability of cultural heritage information systems* in general. These are three lines of argument which, when placed in different contexts, could lead to three completely different types of discourse but which, in the context of this volume, converge into a meaningful synthesis.

*****

Three starting points

1. Research politics

The concept of 'e-Humanities' has enjoyed considerable prominence of late, partly as a result of the general spreading of information technology, but partly also as the result of dedicated initiatives of national funding bodies. Whilst there is no universally accepted definition, the following formula usually meets little opposition. There is an increasingly generalized availability of information technology. This is either as a part of an intentional programme such as the various national grid or cyber-infrastructure programmes, or as a side effect of uncoordinated but co-existing programmes to make digital resources as well as digital forms of publication more easily available. As a result, so the formula goes, we are rapidly approaching a situation where digital media will become the standard medium of scholarship. Scientific research, resting on the acquisition of scientific data from a general and distributed information infrastructure, analyses this data within a grid of distributed computational resources. The results of these analyses are broadcast in a system of electronic publishing. That ensemble of digital data, analysis and publication is 'e-Science'. Its equivalent in 'e-Humanities' therefore comes about when digital media become the standard medium for the acquisition, analysis and publication of information within the humanities as well.

In some contexts, there is considerable emphasis on the effects of these changes upon the humanities disciplines. The consequences are taken for granted in some places, and are resulting in national study programmes.[1] In others, the support for this switch to a new default medium for research is regarded as a reason for a dedicated national effort for the building of an appropriate infrastructure.[2] Hence we derive the first of the three axioms on which the discussion in this chapter proceeds:

> *Axiom 1*: The value of digital information systems for the humanities will, in the coming years, therefore depend much more than so far has been the case, on the ease with which they can be integrated into these processes of research, using many different digital sources of information concurrently.

2. Technology

In the current discussions on 'metadata', most proposals for simplifying descriptions reach the conclusion that most subject areas can be served by a scheme which starts from core categories such as 'what?', 'who?', 'where?', 'when?'. They then build upon these progressively by qualifying these basic concepts into continuously more refined descriptors.[3] If we examine the 'when?' a little more closely, we should start by differentiating between four aspects of the problem of 'representing' time in humanities information systems which are frequently confused. There is (1) the philosophical question as to what time is; and (2) the computer science question as to how a specific view of time can be represented and processed. Then (3) the pragmatic question of the notation of time within a working environment is a further aspect, to which we should add (4) the question of how time should be integrated into the overall design of an information system. Let us now examine these aspects in turn.

What do we mean by time? That time – for the understanding of human communication, as well as for its implementation in artificial intelligence systems – can be understood in many different ways is well understood.[4] Such considerations are

---

1 Cf. The Dutch project, The Virtual Knowledge Studio for the Humanities and Social Sciences, an initiative of the Dutch Academy of Sciences <http://www.virtualknowledgestudio. nl/en/as>, accessed 14 April 2006.

2 On the initiative of the American Council of Learned Societies in this respect, see <http://www.acls.org/cyberinfrastructure/cyber.htm>, accessed 18 December 2007.

3 See, e.g., the core categories in the proposal for a minimalist core metadata standard at <http://dublincore.org/groups/kernel/>, accessed 18 December 2007.

4 See Georges Gurvitch, *The Spectrum of Social Time* (Dordrecht: D. Reidel, 1964), translated from the French *La multiplicité des temps sociaux* by Myrtle Korenbaum, assisted

also relevant for archaeological interpretations, as has recently been demonstrated.[5] For the purpose of this presentation, we will assume, however, that time is simply a linear, continuous dimension which can be used as a coordinate indicating the relative position of material objects and intellectual constructs.

How do we represent and process time?   The representation of time is discussed quite extensively in the literature relating to the use of GIS-based approaches to archaeological information systems.[6] Unfortunately, the varying solutions for processing temporal information are different in historical, art historical and archaeological object databases. They have largely been created in very many different projects independently of one another over the last decades, and they are rarely documented in a systematic way. Most projects, however, have arrived at a model of representing time, supported by subsets of one or more of the following properties:

1. Time is expressed as a numeric offset from some origin.
2. Historical dates are frequently, or have at the very least to allow, intervals.
3. Historical dates are frequently not unique, so precautions are made to allow for the presentation of an object or event having a number of alternative values for a date field.

Allowing for the different emphases within the context of these various projects, it would probably be quite straightforward to construct a formal model for the representation of time that, based on these assumptions, could cover the way in which time has been represented in the majority of projects. However, considerably less development work has been invested in the way in which these representations can be processed in a consistent way. Whilst there is general agreement that an archaeological, art-historical or historical database system has to provide for a way in which it is possible to enter the dates such as 'the second quarter of the third century AD' or 'the first third of the third century AD' – and many databases have implemented solutions to do just that – there is no agreement as to how a database should react if it is asked to present data objects from the first third of the third century and it encounters a data object from the second quarter of the third century. Does it display the latter on the basis that there must be some overlap between the calendar dates 201–233 and 226–250? Or does it ignore it on the grounds that less than 50 per cent of the interval 201–233 is contained in 226–250 and, at the same time, less than 50 per cent of the interval 226–250 is contained within 201–233? Does it return a non-Boolean truth value, which can be used for ordering the selected objects,

by Phillip Bosserman.

    5   Cornelius J. Holtorf, 'Towards a Chronology of Megaliths: "Understanding Monumental Time and Cultural Memory"', *Journal of European Archaeology*, 4 (1996): 119–52.

    6   See, e.g. N.W.J. Hazelton, *Integrating Time, Dynamic Modelling and Geographical Information Systems: Development of Four-dimensional GIS* (Melbourne: Melbourne University Press, 1991). More recently see the interesting unpublished Leicester MSc thesis of 2002 by Chris Green, 'An Experiment in the Creation of a Temporal GIS for Archaeology', available at <http://www.zen26819.zen.co.uk>, accessed 18 December 2007.

reflecting the degree of overlap between the two intervals? From this problem, we derive our second axiom:

> *Axiom 2*: The different, usually very poorly documented, semantics of existing databases with regard to time is a major obstacle to their future interoperability. A solution, which could take the form of a well-documented temporal class, implemented in the major programming languages, and therefore easily integrated into the usual script and command languages, is highly desirable.

What notation do we use for time?   This problem is frequently conflated with how we represent and process time although, in reality, it is completely independent from it. Whether an information system contains a field with the string 'the first third of the third century AD' or two fields with the numbers '201' and '233' is irrelevant at any level of abstraction so long as it also provides modules that apply a consistent model for processing those fields as temporal information. While all information systems can probably be reduced to this generalization, the acceptable notations actually in place vary widely, and there is little recognizable consensus in practice.

Why should this be the case? The reason is probably because the ability to process a specific notation for temporal values depends heavily on application-specific software layers. So the number of information systems which access notations like 'the first third of the third century AD' as a phrase, formulated in natural language, albeit natural language with a restricted vocabulary and syntax, is rather small.[7] What more typically happens in object databases is that the string is one of a finite number of set phrases, denoting specific temporal intervals, which are presented to the user as part of a restricted vocabulary via a pop-up selection list. There have been almost no attempts at a generalized system of notation for time and temporal intervals. The TEI assumes (essentially in section 20.4 of the TEI Guidelines) that temporal marked-up phrases are encoded by a human user for processing, assigning the components of the date phrases, expressed in natural language, to attribute values which then allow a machine to recognize a sketchy framework of an internal representation for time. They do not, however, provide a complete model for the encoding of temporal information. Some time ago, I attempted to formulate a system for documenting temporal notations.[8] Since then, however, this system has been rendered obsolete since many, particularly archaeological, forms of notation now exist which were not encompassed by it.

Generally speaking we may assume, therefore, that a completely explicit and detailed model for the internal representation of time and its processing is now much more urgent, since this is one of the basic means of providing interoperability. Notational differences, which frequently represent the implicit assumptions of the various sub-disciplines within the domains of history and pre-history, should not stand in the way of the interoperability of software systems, so long as the mappings

---

7 Such as, e.g. the modules of this author's Kleio software system, specifically developed for the processing of historical data.

8 M. Thaller, 'A Draft Proposal for the Coding of Machine Readable Sources', *Historical Social Research/Historische Sozialforschung*, 40/3 (1986): 3–46; here 12–17.

between the locally available notation schemes and the underlying internal structure are clear and unambiguous.

What is the role of time in the design of an information system?   'Time', particularly when we are discussing it in the form of 'calendar dates', is usually seen as the data type of a specific field. This is particularly so in the context of databases or annotated textual corpora, where 'time' is generally presented as a set of attributes. For these purposes, this use of time is intuitive. It becomes much less convincing, however, when the objects we are handling become more complex.

Let us start with the notion of a system administering a historical document from the middle ages, which had been written at a time which we may designate as t_0, describing an event or situation which had arisen in the past, at a time that we shall delineate as t_{-1}. To prove that this event or situation had, in fact, taken place at t_{-1}, the document in question then cites an earlier text, itself written in the past at t_{-2}, but referring to a further earlier event or situation, which had occurred at t_{-3}. We would therefore want to delineate four separate time fields for this document, viz. date-of-writing, date-of-situation, date-of-insert, date-of-inserted-situation. Would it, however, be immediately, unmistakably and automatically clear to a casual user, that this event or situation in past time – perhaps the existence of 'Bishop x' which he or she has found in this document (written, let us say, 'after 1250 and before 1300') – was actually mentioned in an inserted document, to be dated earlier? Similarly complexities occur in respect of archaeological objects. Let us imagine a temple which had been 'built' in the first century AD. Its columns, however, are part of a renovation that we have dated to the third century AD, whilst the mosaic in an attached room was laid in the second century. Meanwhile, the major part of the surviving superstructure is ascribed to a Christian remodelling of the early fifth century. This example is a hypothetical one, but such characteristics are often a practical reality. What temporal notation for such an entity would really orient a researcher who wants to discover the date to be ascribed (for example) to the surviving fragments of paint covering the walls?

To solve that problem, we have to begin with an alternative model, one that would require that each 'data-object' (that is to say, 'field' in an information system that is field-delimited, or 'tagged element' in those information systems which have the character of marked-up text) 'knows' that it belongs to a specific time. Now there are at least three intuitive (or not so intuitive) ways in which such a relationship between the information contained within a data-object and a temporal property of that information can be related:

(a) Most intuitively, we might simply establish a solution in which the temporal coordinates of a data-object are understood as the functional equivalent of a display characteristic. Just as you can assign a default font, in which the content of a specific field of a database is to be displayed, we might simply conceptualize an architecture of an IT system in which each field has an inherent 'location in time' which should be administered independently of the position of that field within the overall framework of the information system.[9]

(b) Within the ongoing discussion of markup systems the idea of a 'context' being applicable to part of a markup structure, and administered as a semi-structured database, is integral to proposed extensions of the current XML model. It has been shown that such a notion of 'context' could also be used to develop an embedded markup into an explicit temporal coordinate system, which would then be available to assign a temporal position to each individual tag.[10]

(c) The most complete proposition as to how to conceptualize and model temporal coordinate space, one in which the objects of an information system form other structures, is contained within the CIDOC *Content Reference Model* (CRM). This is mainly the brainchild of Martin Doerr at the Greek Foundation for Research and Technology (FORTH), Heraklion.[11] The CRM is a very general ontology which has been created originally for the creation of interchangeable object-descriptions of museum holdings. Being constructed along very general logical concepts, the claim of its creators is that it can be used to provide a generalized metadata model for *all* sorts of cultural heritage material. That may, indeed, be the case since the purpose of the CRM is precisely to provide a common language for heterogeneous information depositories, allowing for their integration, despite all sorts of possible semantic and structural incompatibilities. In this context, the model is particularly interesting, since it is built upon the assumption that each of the building blocks of the descriptions implies a temporal coordinate. This means that provisions exist to provide explicit time coordinates at the lowest level of conceptual granularity (solving the two problems we have just exemplified for documents and buildings). It also means, however, that there is an implicit temporal logic, which allows us to make statements about temporal co-existence and relationships, even when no explicit temporal coordinates are present. (So, for example, it is clear from the underlying ontology that the event 'destruction' implies a terminus *ante quem* for all components of an object.)

The CRM is explicitly described by its authors as a purely intellectual framework. It has been described as a format for the interchange of

---

9 This description tries to give an intuitive description of a possible solution. So far as I an aware, no implementation of this intuitive solution currently exists. I should point out, however, that the notion of connecting individual fields to a temporal location, independent of the structure within which this field exists, is far from exotic. It has a strong grounding in all information systems which handle cash transactions. See R. Elmasr and S.B. Navathe, *Fundamentals of Database Systems*, 4th edn (Boston: Pearson, 2004), pp. 767–80; note particularly the concept of attribute versioning, pp. 776-7.

10 T. Mitakos et al., 'Representing Time-dependent Information in Multidimensional XML', in D. Kalpic and V.H. Dobric (eds), *Proceedings of the 23rd International Conference on Information Technology Interfaces, Pula, Croatia, June 19-22, 2001* (Heraklion: SKEL Publications, 2001), pp. 111–16.

11 <http://cidoc.ics.forth.gr/>, accessed 24 August 2007. The best short introduction is probably M. Doerr, 'The CIDOC CRM: An Ontological Approach to Semantic Interoperability of Metadata', *AI Magazine, 24/3 (2003)*.

information between heterogeneous information architectures. One should note, however, that an RDF schema for the model already exists. In so far as RDF schemas can be considered as valid input into the abstract data model of concrete information systems, the CRM is therefore not only a conceptual framework, but a concrete data-model for such information systems. I cannot prove the point here in detail, but this effectively means that all CIDOC CRM descriptions can, in principle, be understood as valid input for native XML databases.

3. Cultural heritage information systems

Digital resources in the cultural heritage world are currently moving quickly beyond the digitization of individual objects to the systematic conversion of collections. At the University of Cologne, for example, I have implemented a project in collaboration with the *Diözesan- und Dombibliothek der Erzdiözese Köln* (The Diocesan and Cathedral Library of the Archbishopric of Cologne) where we have digitized the *complete* holdings of all medieval manuscripts in their collection.[12] This, in turn, has inspired a project for the digitization of the library of the monastery of St Gall.[13] That project has, in turn led to a proposition for a national project in Switzerland, which aims at the high-level digitization of all Swiss manuscripts.[14]. Among our other projects in Cologne, we are responsible for around four million digital objects.[15] Recently, we were also responsible for a feasibility study of the systematic digitization of all the incunabula books in German libraries (those printed before 1500).[16] In yet another project, we created the technical infrastructure for a 'German art-historical slide archive', where the basic assumption is that every German art-historical institute may use whatever hardware or software they wish, and devise whatever data-model (abstract or concrete) they find most appropriate to their purposes, secure in the knowledge that their digitized slide holdings will be preserved in a central server so long as they conform to the agreed metadata schema. Amidst this plethora of activity, illustrative of the dynamics of digitization, the Prometheus Project is the one which is most directly relevant to the subject of this chapter.[17] This is because it specifically set out to broker the different surface representations of time, mapping the controlled vocabulary expressions of temporal phraseology provided by the different individual databases onto a general internal representation of temporality, which than can be deployed for query evaluation. That this is what is happening is in no way obvious to the user. He or she simply consults a service which integrates 20 to 30 databases behind the scenes, unaware of the integrated processing environment which is following the temporality logic that has been constructed into the system.

---

12 The results are available under <http://www.ceec.uni-koeln.de>, accessed 24 August 2007.

13 <http://www.cesg.unifr.ch>, accessed 24 August 2007.

14 <http://www.codices.ch/>, accessed 24 August 2007.

15 <http://www.hki.uni-koeln.de/projekte/projekte-b.htmlm>, accessed 24 August 2007.

16 <http://inkunabeln.ub.uni-koeln.de/>, accessed 24 August 2007.

17 <http://www.prometheus-bildarchiv.de/>, accessed 24 August 2007.

Users logging on to Prometheus have access to a search engine which allows them to 'collect' slides on the internet, relevant to their research needs. These are displayed as thumbnails initially. The image can be enlarged, and augmented by the descriptive information from the database. 'Collecting' these slides means, in reality, that they are stored for the user under their name in a work-sheet which displays the thumbnails, which (once again) can be enlarged at various stages, and accompanied by their relevant descriptive information. These work-sheets can then be arranged into slide-shows, again stored under the user name of the individual concerned. Finally, these slide-shows can be loaded into a set of multiple virtual-slide projectors which then show them in the same way as more conventional slide-show presentations given by art historians, historians and archaeologists in lectures and seminars. If during the presentation a question is asked, the individual images can still be zoomed in on and, if a question challenges the memory of the presenter, the individual can still call up all the information connected to the slide in the database.

This kind of 'working environment' also exists for the other projects I have just mentioned. Looked at together, however, these digital repositories offer not just an image of the evolving pattern for the integration of resources, but also illustrate the way in which such integration encourages the shared interrogation of content. They all provide a mechanism by which the individual manuscripts or early printed texts can be integrated into other working environments. They allow the user to address the resources individually, each individual printed page or each manuscript folio, as a Digital Autonomous Cultural Object (DACO). The principle of a DACO is that it is always:

(a) functionally complete. It has 'to bring along' all the means of navigation which are necessary to get to its neighbours within the larger cultural heritage object which contains it. In the context of manuscripts that means (for example) buttons like 'Next page', 'Table of content' or 'Go to a specific page'.[18]. But the *principle* is much broader. A DACO that represented a room in the digital representation of a historical building would presumably provide the means to 'Go to the room on the left'. In other words, the generic power of a DACO is that, by addressing any component of a collection, you are able to navigate through it to any other component.

(b) unobtrusive. Anybody referencing them can be absolutely sure that the properties of the DACO will not in any way try to 'take over' the website linking to it. A DACO must be prepared, for example, to be integrated into frames or other overarching software constructions.

The projects that I have cited demonstrate two important trends which are more generally observable too. Firstly, cultural heritage projects are more and more created with an understanding that they should provide means to 'export' the objects they administer in the most flexible way. This means that they will permit other

---

18 The application of this principle which usually comes to mind first is the possibility of linking from one spot within an electronic publication where a specific source is discussed right into the electronic publication of that source itself.

systems to integrate the components they provide into diverse and growing working-environments. These environments then implement the tools to support the research processes most required and typical for a particular and specific research community. Secondly, cultural heritage systems cease to be simple information systems, which merely provide a retrieval mechanism. They are increasingly considered as deficient if they do not also offer at least some components of a digital environment to support the most usual types of analysis for a specific community. Most of them, furthermore, provide a feedback mechanism for the users, allowing them to augment the data contained within the system.[19] From these two trends, we derive our third, major axiom, viz:-

> *Axiom 3*: If these trends continue, they will make cultural-heritage information-systems coalesce. The latter will increasingly be based upon designs which are conceptually – if not technically – object-oriented in the sense that the do not provide 'records and fields' but more complex information-objects which can: (a) easily be exchanged between individual information systems; (b) provide a persistent identity to allow quoting; and (c) provide mechanisms by which their metadata can be integrated into the search-mechanisms of other systems as readily as their data can be manipulated by the tools implementing the type of work required by different research communities. These developments have advanced considerably in the cultural heritage community (archives, museums, libraries). Humanities research information systems will follow suit in due course, albeit within a more narrow compass.

Conclusion

I began by pointing out that I would look at the problem I have posed by examining it from three very different angles. Those three approaches have produced three axioms which, at first glance, seem to be unrelated to one another. I hope now to be able to show that they actually converge. I do so in a sequence of eight points:

1. Looking at the world of cultural heritage information systems we have seen that they show a clear tendency towards, on the one hand, systems which are built around exchangeable content-objects and, on the other hand, working environments, implementing the typical tools of analysis within a specific research community.

2. Such working environments represent exactly the 'analysis' phase in the process by which digital media became the 'standard medium for the acquisition, analysis and distribution' of scientific information in the concept of 'e-Science'. The same processes are at work in the evolution of 'e-Humanities'.

3. The observable development, as well as the goals of current research policies, favour a re-conceptualization of Humanities information systems

---

19 See J.A. Inman et al. (eds), *Electronic Collaboration in the Humanities: Issues and Options* (Mahwah, NJ: Lawrence Erlbaum Associates, 2004) on some dimensions of this.

as collections of recursive information objects which can easily be readily exchanged between individual working-environments/information-systems.

4. This process of exchanging (persistent) information-objects (which represent long-term knowledge) with (transient) information systems (which represent a specific state of the art in their processing) will be less problematic, the finer the granularity of the information in the exchangeable information-object.

5. The granularity of the information-objects can be refined by making the individual elements of information attached to the object independent from a technical point of view.

6. As time provides a conceptual reference-system for virtually all other types of system, solutions which allow its representation and processing in a way which cuts across all types of objects and processing frameworks would be a major step forward.

7. To do this, a concise formalism for an internal representation and processing-logic needs to be developed.

8. A model for the relationship between time and these humanities 'information-objects' is provided by the CIDOC CRM. It will require, however, a good deal of further development.

If this had been a text in a computer science manual, it would end with the following statement: 'To demonstrate that what we have described here for the concept of "time" can also, step-by-step, be derived for "space" is left as an exercise for the reader' ...

Chapter 10

In the Kingdom of the Blind: Visualization and E-Science in Archaeology, the Arts and Humanities

Vincent Gaffney

Arts, e-Science and the grid

It seems appropriate to start this chapter with a bold assertion that, in the tradition of academic statements, is only variably correct![1] The use of computer-based technologies within the arts and humanities, including those used for visualization, appear to have become, along with taxes and death, a fact of life. This does not deny the valued activities of gifted individuals who can, and do, labour long and hard to provide significant scholarly works. However, it is undeniable that the creation and organization of large data sets, the desire for enhanced accessibility to data held in disparate locations and the increasing complexity of our theoretical and methodological aspirations inevitably push us towards greater use of technology and a reliance on interdisciplinary teams to facilitate their use. Despite this, the arts and humanities community has largely remained aloof from the recent development of large-scale, ubiquitous technologies, with the notable exception of those that permit resource discovery. Significantly, even these applications may be opaque to academics whose use is limited to the large internet search engines.

Consequently, it remains a fact that the emergence of (for example) grid technologies in other disciplines has not had the impact one might have expected on the arts and humanities. Such reticence has not been the consequence of a lack of data within the arts, as has occasionally been suggested, nor should this be taken as indicative that humanistic enquiry is not amenable to such research. It is, however, true that successful grid applications within disciplines, including particle physics, are linked to the ability of researchers to agree methodologies that, to some extent, permit a 'mechanistic' worldview that is amenable to such analysis. These methodologies have also been supported by massive levels of funding in a relatively

1 I would like to thank the following for their comments and suggestions when writing this paper – Paul Hatton, Meg Watters, Andy Howard, Keith Challis, Dr Henry Chapman, Ben Gearey, Helen Goodchild, Simon Fitch, Dr Ken Thomson, Dr Mark Jolly, Dr Lorna Hughes, Dr Stuart Dunn, Dr Roger White, Helen Gaffney, Professor Bob Stone, Dr Eugene Ch'ng.

homogeneous technology infrastructure.[2] The scale of such networks can be almost overwhelming. A visit to the live map of the Particle Physics Grid data brokerage site at Imperial College provides an ample demonstration of the scale of such networks, although this is not recommended for arts researchers of a nervous disposition or those prone to suspicion of every aspect of globalization.[3]

Such large-scale data management and analytical systems are not commonplace, or perhaps even existent, in the arts. Yet it is still true that arts research is neither so chaotic nor anarchic that it is impossible to demonstrate the value, at least, of e-Science applications to our disciplines. Arts e-Research activities can be broken down, in general terms (see Figure 10.1) and one suspects that most arts researchers would be comfortable with the assertion of one or more of these general themes as being central to their own work. Furthermore, the extent of analytical methodologies implemented within arts analysis can also be assessed through the taxonomy of computational methods produced as part of the AHDS Projects and Method databases.[4]

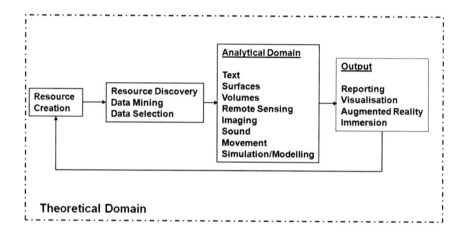

Figure 10.1   Primary activities in e-Science

From this it seems reasonable to suggest that, actually, the use of powerful technologies may be more prevalent than is usually believed, and that the strategic consideration of how these technologies support individual disciplines, how their existence manipulates and formulates academic agendas, and how such agendas are likely to develop over time, must be a priority.

---

2   <http://www.gridpp.ac.uk/portal/>. All urls in this chapter accessed on 21 September 2007.

3   <http://gridportal.hep.ph.ic.ac.uk/rtm/applet.html>.

4   <http://www.ahds.ac.uk/about/projects/pmdb-extension/index.htm#documents>.

Visualization and the arts

This chapter is primarily concerned with one aspect of this process – visualization. Visualization is a particularly interesting process. As a technical operation visualization carries the implication of being, in most senses, a final act within a larger process that has involved the collection, selection and manipulation of data in some manner (although any process may be iterative). It therefore carries with it considerable theoretical or methodological baggage. Indeed (intellectually) the act of visualization is a highly emotive act (certainly within archaeology) and there has been considerable debate as to the legitimacy of visualization as an isolated output.[5] Despite this, and with due cognisance of the value of other sensory experiences available to individuals, it remains true that visualization is a critical faculty or skill that enables human groups to order and comprehend their world either as direct sensory experience or, through technical or artistic visual aids, as an indirect proxy of wider experience.

The emphasis on or (perhaps) the fetishization of visual experience in contemporary western society should not come as a great surprise. Whilst we cannot claim actually to see more than other societies, past or present, the range of sources for visual experience has increased, and visual technology is at the centre of a society in which dazzling imagery is ubiquitous and pervades everyday life. We currently live within a society where we can daily experience the depths of the sea, or even space exploration, through screens wider than our fields of vision, and where our children can fight global or gang wars with disturbing verisimilitude.[6] On occasions, we appear close to Jean Baudrillard's 'precession of simulacra', where the realities we create may appear more real-than-real, to the extent that they can be engaged directly by the observer or exist without any prior basis in reality.[7] Whether or not our children believe in the violence they consume, it sometimes appears that media representations of historical events and archaeology in particular, seem particularly open to virtual representation and, perhaps, misrepresentation. By definition, our reality is usually a degraded image of an original that has eroded or rotted away. We interpret residual or even proxy evidence to produce a new reality and the impact that a reconstruction may have on the observer is inevitably more real than the heap of rocks and lines of postholes that we encounter daily on archaeological sites, or the dry, detailed footnotes of a historical text.

It is not surprising that within many British universities the central role of these technologies is such that imaging and visualization are seen to be enabling, cross-cutting disciplinary boundaries. At my own university – Birmingham – the Institute of Archaeology and Antiquity maintains an interdisciplinary research laboratory, the

---

5 S. Exon, V. Gaffney, P. Yorston and A, Woodward, *Stonehenge Landscapes: Journeys through Real-and-Imagined Worlds* (Oxford: Archaeopress, 2001); M. Gillings, 'Virtual Archaeologies and the Hyperreal: Or, What Does it Mean to Describe Something as Virtually-Real?', in P. Fisher and D. Unwin (eds), *Virtual Reality in Geography* (Taylor and Francis, 2002), pp. 17–34; D.W. Wheatley and M. Gillings, *Spatial Technology and Archaeology: The Archaeological Applications of GIS* (Taylor and Francis, 2002).

6 <http://www.sciencemuseum.org.uk/imax/index.asp>; <http://www.totalwar.com/>.

7 J. Baudrillard, *Simulations* (New York: Semiotext(e), 1983).

'HP Visual and Spatial Technology Centre', with responsibility to provide a central visualization resource and to disseminate the use of visualization technologies across the university.[8] Institutionally, the University of Birmingham Strategic Plan pointedly accepts imaging as

> a research discipline in its own right [which is] inherently multi-disciplinary, drawing on physics to understand the underpinning physical processes; on mathematics, statistics and signal processing to derive principled solutions; and on computer science and engineering to construct working algorithms and devices. It is also pervasive as an important investigative tool in many academic disciplines, including Arts, Sciences, Medicine and Business.[9]

So there we have it: imaging must be important!

This, of course, is a simplistic statement but such observations do draw out a number of specific characteristics of visualization that are relevant to archaeology and the historical disciplines. The first relates to the descriptive procedures underlying visualization. These are tangible assets but they may relate to the implementation of a Cartesian network, a statistical model or some other mathematical descriptor. Allied to this is the chosen vehicle for implementation. In sensory terms output may range from relatively simple map displays through to complex immersive stereo solutions; it might also include integrated sensory capacities including haptic environments. However, the key concern here is the existence of a potential link with some physical reality. Following this, the concept of visualization being an investigative tool is also central to the perceived value of these technologies, and here academics may have significant concerns with the application of visualization.

In this context, we might consider the example of a digital model of a Wild Goat style cup created from an original in the Museum of the Institute of Archaeology at Birmingham.[10] The cup itself is a relatively simple stemmed vessel and of interest mainly because of the suggestion that the painted design might indicate that the vessel was a skeuomorph whose metal prototype possessed incised angular designs that were repeated in paint on the clay copy. Some time ago, this cup was scanned and rendered with an image of the surface design. This model was used, with the surface of the design raised, to create a casting in metal, but the digital model was also rendered haptically to permit the user to view the digital model either as metal or clay and to feel, through a relatively clumsy wand, the different surface renderings: relatively rough for the clay model and relatively smooth for the metal version (see Plates 18a and 18b). Aside from the apparent veracity of the scanned surface the significance of the exercise was not so much the ingenuity of permitting visitors to touch, virtually, an object that would otherwise have only been experienced through the glass of a museum case; rather it was the fact that the visitor experienced an enhanced act of interpretation. It may be that there never was a metal original of the stemmed cup and its representation (digital or physical), remains an act of

---

8   <http://www.iaa.bham.ac.uk/Computing/HP_VISTA/HPindex.htm>.
9   <http://www3.cs.bham.ac.uk/crni/>.
10 <http://www.iaa.bham.ac.uk/research/opening/main.htm>.

subtle imagination. The experience of interpretation is therefore a central role of visualization rather than the simple representation of any particular reality.

In terms of technological application, this may appear reasonably obvious but there is another aspect of visualization in historical disciplines that must be considered, and which is particularly relevant to my own area of research in landscape. The environment itself is a physical and viewable research asset that requires incorporation within interpretative schema. Imbued as it is with meaning, we now study our physical and natural context in its own right and appreciate the ability of landscapes to manipulate human action as a consequence merely of its existence.

Archaeologically this leads to something of a paradox in respect of how we view space, as few studies retain significant elements of direct analysis of space, preferring instead contextual narratives. In some instances, this position has led to considerable difficulties in relation to the primacy of personal reading of individual landscapes.[11] Irrespective of this particular debate, the management, as opposed to the interpretation, of space and its visualization has to be a technical issue and some of the technical aspects of the work have, to some extent, passed out of the hands of landscape archaeologists, and this process continues with the rapid advance in data capture and analytical technologies

There is an important point to be made here with respect to landscape. The significance of the new technologies is not simply that of computational power. The application of the continuous measurement and analysis of space and the extension of the analytical sphere to virtually every part of a landscape may be equally significant. One can also predict that, over the next five years or so, the emergent technologies for 3D landscape scanning from ground or air-base platforms will further transform our capacity for control of space, filling the gap between ground-based geophysics and traditional aerial photography through the reproduction of the surface of the landscape in an almost seamless fashion.[12] However, powerful as these technologies are, the description of space is not interpretation, and infinitely finessing the resolution of data cannot satisfy our disciplinary aspirations to explain the past.

Visualization of time is a case in point. It is an important observation that, despite chronologies being the very stuff of archaeology, archaeologists are not always well-equipped to study temporal change. Archaeological chronologies are frequently characterized by poor resolution, particularly over the medium temporal scales – i.e. we understand gross chronologies quite well, but frequently cannot distinguish change within shorter periods. These shorter periods are, it is true, a narrow definition of time, however, one which is particularly constraining in relation to the study of landscapes.[13] Personal time, as implied by the movement of an individual through time/space and landscape, can in fact be modelled within parameters. This does not

---

11 A. Fleming, 'Phenomenology and the Megaliths of Wales: A Dreaming too Far?', *Oxford Journal of Archaeology*, 18/2 (1999): 119–26.

12 <http://www.iaa.bham.ac.uk/bufau/services/3Dscan/Lidar.htm> and <http://www.iaa. bham.ac.uk/bufau/projects/weoley%20castle/laser.htm>.

13 C. Gosden, *Social Being and Time* (Oxford: Blackwell, 1994).

deny the complexity of landscape and environmental change, but many characteristics of personal movement; associated time and perception of place remain achievable. When this is appreciated, we can begin to construct a link between space, time, landscape perception and an enhanced role for computational cartography within an interpretative archaeology.

Unfortunately, whilst time is implicit within the study of space (and therefore landscape), our technology of choice, GIS (Geographic Information Systems), currently contribute relatively little to temporal discourse. For this we must turn to the converging spatial technologies that also have a real potential for greater immersion, specifically virtual or augmented realities, to provide an enhanced sensuousness of experience and incorporate approximations of time/space movement. Whilst also highly situated, these technologies provide interpretative schema that can merge archaeometry with ideational models. A model's spatiality, computationally derived, provides a definable relationship with empirical reality, whilst their digital location permits powerful and imaginative spatial manipulation.

The work of the Birmingham computational group on the Stonehenge Landscape provides an example of what can be achieved through digital cartography.[14] This study was aimed at an analysis of funerary and ritual monuments within the area of Stonehenge. This is a relatively small study area – approximately 40 by 40 kilometres – but incorporating c. 1200 Neolithic or Bronze Age funerary and ritual monuments, including cursuses and henge enclosures built on a landscape scale. The monument complexes around Stonehenge often appear unique in their scale and intensity but their analysis is a commonplace problem in terms of landscape. Having emerged over millennia, the landscape is a four-dimensional puzzle in which spatial relations of monuments (in Cartesian terms) must be merged with archaeological time (interpretative periods – Neolithic, Bronze Age) and personal time (measured by the scale of monuments). Interpretational significance is situated both in the past through the, presumed, liturgical and social significance of the monuments and the present, where our personal appreciation of the surviving landscape or situation of a monument must be gauged and represented. The archaeological problems of landscape are therefore quantitative, semi-quantitative and qualitative in nature. To represent this in any sense has been a challenge and the final publication provided primary data digitally alongside descriptive statistics, static and animated representations of GIS, 'bubbleworlds' and audio description embedded within the digital landscape (see Plate 19). The result is as much a research environment as a publication – one that does not represent a final product but may be returned to, infinitely, within the digital environment.

These latter points are particularly significant given that one characteristic of the phenomenological school is the tendency to believe that a landscape can be experienced simply by physical presence. Whilst one would not denigrate any experience of the landscape, one has to be honest and suggest that many publications demonstrate a partial experience of a desperately partial archaeological database. Seeing (hearing or smelling!) a landscape is not seeing the past, or even our limited

---

14 Exon et al., *Stonehenge Landscapes*; cf. <http://www.arch-ant.bham.ac.uk/research/computing/SHBarrows/home.htm>.

knowledge of that unknowable past. Once again, experiencing interpretation is becoming *the* challenge of landscape research.

The role of visualization, or imagination, is therefore increasing as a methodological tool of consequence. Perhaps nothing demonstrates this more dramatically than the Birmingham project on the Palaeolandscapes of the Southern North Sea.[15] This project seeks to explore the land inundated by the sea during the last great period of global warming. Between the end of the last glacial maximum and c. 6,000 BC an area larger than England was lost to the sea. This great plain was probably the heartland of the Mesolithic populations of north-western Europe. Man lived and walked the rivers and valleys of this country and the hills and the plains have since been lost beneath a remorseless onslaught of water. Water drowned the land, which was remodelled by eustatic movement and sediment deposition to the point that we can barely trace the outline of this vast landscape.

A research team in Birmingham, funded by the Aggregates Levy Sustainability Fund, is currently mapping more than 23,000 km^2 of this landscape using three-dimensional seismic data collected for the purposes of oil and gas exploration and provided by Petroleum Geo-Services (PGS). This is an archaeo-geophysical survey the size of the whole of Wales and to date the results have been little less than staggering. Using this data we have begun to trace, and even to name, the rivers, hills and valleys that have been lost to mankind for more than eight millennia (See Plate 20). Yet, whilst we work on the lost lands of the North Sea, analysing vast amounts of data and using some of the most sophisticated imaging hardwares and softwares currently available to archaeologists, this country is fundamentally imaginary.

Where next?

The intellectual freedom that arts and humanities research projects necessarily demand, and the range of legitimate research routes towards providing provisional research conclusions, both require flexibility and the imaginative use of available technologies. However, whilst flexibility and imagination are desirable qualities in general, the intellectual and technological landscape relating to visualization looks to have more in common with the Wild West rather than the Arcadian backdrop often more suitable for a considered national research strategy. So we should conclude with an appropriate statement on the practice and principles regarding ICT development in the arts and humanities. We should note that the number of groups that are currently involved in large-scale e-Science programmes within the arts is relatively small, nationally and internationally. It is unlikely that any one specific group among them will establish complete competence across the range of technologies likely to be used, or be able to provide appropriate resource for all potential projects. However, it is critical that the United Kingdom possesses and develops the potential of existing expertise. Integrative technologies, most notably the Access Grid, perhaps linked with virtual network computing, will be central to creating distributed research groups. Powerful low-latency networks such as UKLIGHT, with near-seamless computing capabilities, may become central to the development of distributed

---

15 <http://www.iaa.bham.ac.uk/research/fieldwork_research_themes/projects/North_Sea_Palaeolandscapes/index.htm>.

research programmes dealing with significant shared datasets.[16] Reception of past or contemporary landscapes and environments is a central theme to many disciplines and the remit of one current AHRC-directed research programme.[17] On that basis, 'augmented-reality' and 'wearable' technologies (ones which interpret the landscape to the viewer in real space and time), capable of integrating real data, interpretative overlays and incorporating the real world, should be pursued as a matter of priority.

Although volume datasets are always likely to require serious computing solutions, big is not always best. We should also explore the potential of 'serious gaming' technologies to provide the facility for low-cost development environments as well as large-scale distributed systems for larger modelling and rendering exercises.[18] The creation of more sensuous environments incorporating human movement remains a serious challenge. Integration with monuments, dress and reception studies, particularly in classics or ancient history, probably demands high-quality photorealistic representation. The capacity for immersive replication of human movement is likely to become significant over time and appropriate data capture facilities and rendering capacity will follow from this.

I think it equally appropriate to highlight a number of strategic issues. It is essential that technology is adopted on our terms. Even if the technology is shared, our requirements are not those of other disciplines. We must avoid, for instance, the situation relating to archaeological science, the responsibility for which was devolved to the Natural Environment Research Council (NERC).[19] We must avoid the position where arts technology development is judged not only by external reviewers but perhaps also on the basis of research rules which are not applicable to archaeology. External disciplines have advice to offer but they cannot be allowed to determine the particular research agendas of archaeologists and historians. As a group we have to seek for levels of funding that allow appropriately for infrastructural development. There has been a tendency in the past for 'big science' rather than the arts to control dedicated computational facilities. If we do not have appropriate funding, then we will fail to establish an appropriate pool of expertise within our disciplines and our research agendas will suffer as a consequence. With the possible demise of the Science Research Infrastructure Fund, it is difficult to see where future substantial capital funding may come from even, if one suspects, the arts never benefited sufficiently from the SRIF scheme in the past.[20] The nature of modelling behaviour is such that we require resources capable of modelling exponentially expanding datasets and the complexities of human action. In areas where we touch the physical sciences, most notably in relation to landscape, environment, geomorphology and topography, we need parity for our research with physical geography, geology and the social sciences. Whether the level of funding required to provide a successful base for grid development among the arts and humanities communities will ever be available must, however, remain an open question. At the very least, we can be

---

16 <http://www.uklight.ac.uk/>.
17 <http://www.ahrc.ac.uk/apply/research/sfi/ahrcsi/landscape_environment.asp>.
18 <http://www.applyseriousgames.com/>.
19 <http://www.nerc.ac.uk/funding/sbarchaeology/strategy.shtml>.
20 <http://www.hefce.ac.uk/research/srif/>.

confident about the significance of our activity in arts visualization. Its contribution to the tourist economy alone means that there is a good case to argue for more substantial investment on national macro-economic grounds.[21] We are part of a larger visualization market that feeds into the cultural economy.

HP VISTA, the centre to which I am currently attached, is probably one of the better-equipped visualization facilities run by an arts and humanities research group in the UK, but it was founded with virtually no input from direct arts funding. This might be regarded as a positive achievement (in that we have attracted substantial alternative funding) but the truth is that we are compromised in our research potential by the lack of adequate funding through arts and humanities sources. It is difficult to see how that situation will change in the short or medium term. So we must acknowledge that visualization is a challenge for the arts and humanities community. This is not simply because visualization is technically complex or even because it is expensive. Rather, it reflects the fact that so much of our visual content is itself contentious. However, we cannot side-step tensions over the interpretations of visualization since these are doubtless part of the multi-vocal debates that are central to academic exploration. In such situations, sophisticated visualization may well be the most appropriate route to investigate such phenomena. It follows from this, however, that if we do accept that complex visualization is an integral part of our research strategy, there can be no half-measures in providing the resources to develop it. Whilst it is good to share, and we have much to learn from other disciplines in relation to specific technologies, we must accept responsibility for the relevance of visualization technologies to the arts, and the implementation of those technologies. The responsibility is ours. We should not expect cheap or quick fixes. We must hope that the national research funding bodies, in particular the AHRC, recognize this ineluctable fact.

---

21 <http://www.dfes.gov.uk/skillsdialoguereports/docs/tourism.pdf>.

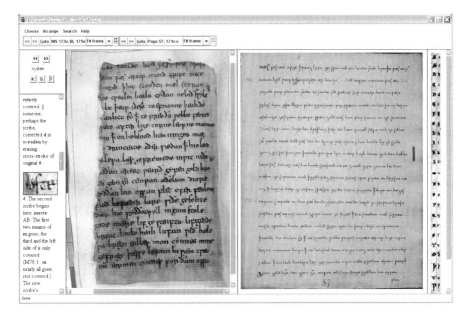

Plate 1   A sample electronic facsimile from *The Electronic Beowulf,* edited by
         Kevin Kiernan (2000), showing a folio from British Library, Cotton
         MS. Vitellius A.xv, together with shots of the manuscript under
         special lighting conditions, with the relevant section of one of the
         eighteenth-century transcripts of *Beowulf* prepared for the Danish
         antiquary Thorkelin

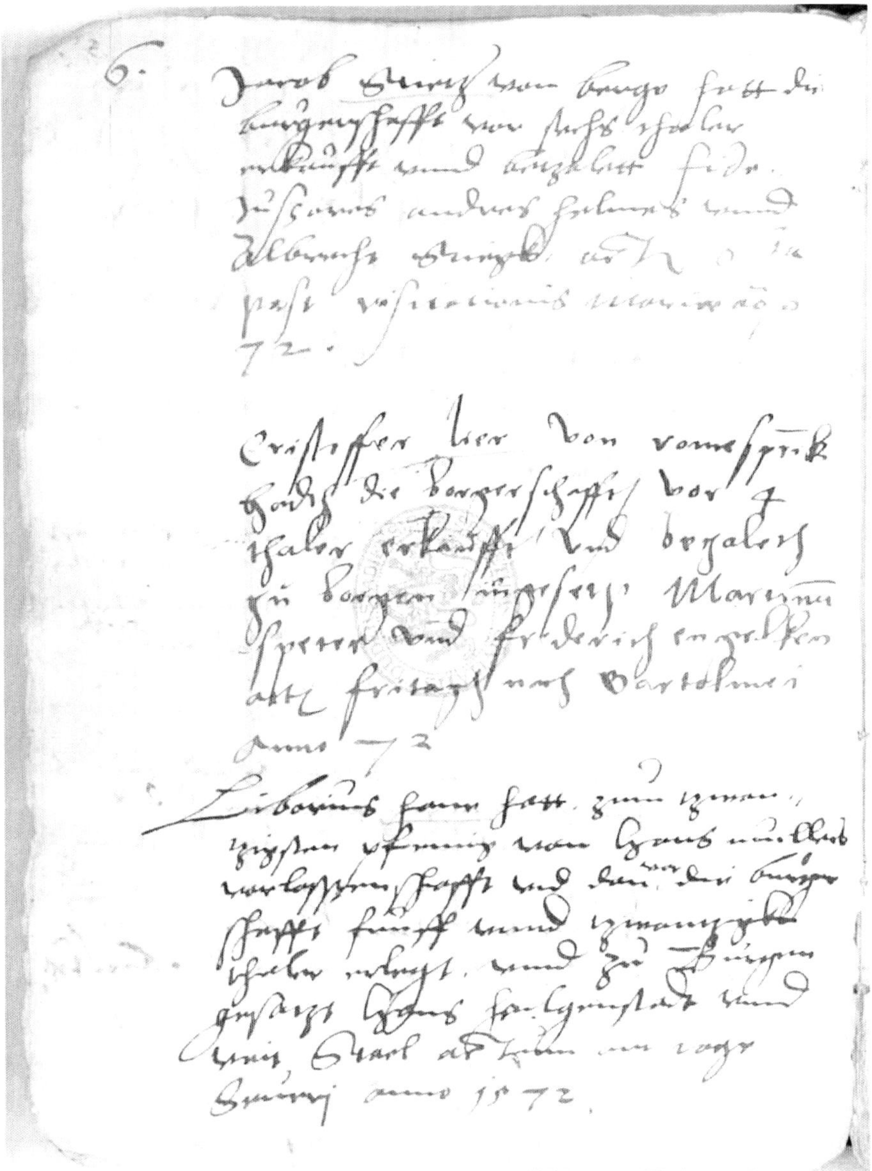

Plate 3 Facsimile record of admissions of burgesses in the German town of Duderstadt, 1572, from the Duderstadt archive <http://www.archive.geschichte.mpg.de/duderstadt/dud-e.htm>

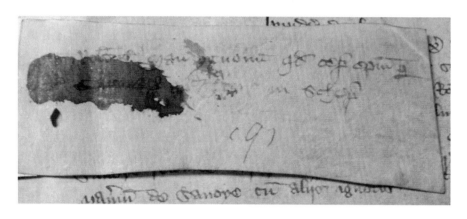

Plate 4   Informal note of the confession of Robert Man to participation in the killing of the Archbishop of Canterbury during the Peasants' Revolt in 1381: The National Archives, KB 9/43 m. 9

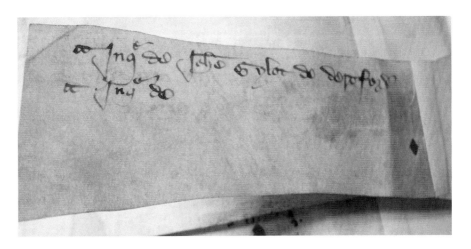

Plate 5   Note made during a commission against the rebels of 1381 to investigate John Gyllot of Dartford: The National Archives, KB 9/43 m. 9d

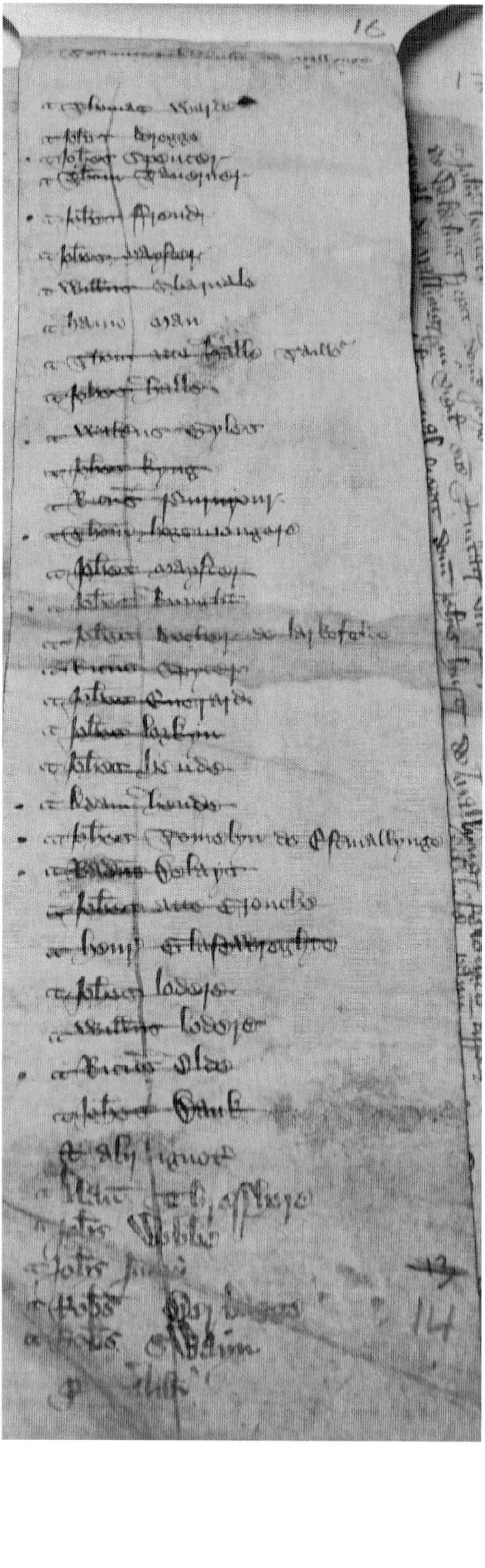

Plate 6   List of names made during the interrogation of tenants of the Abbess of Malling concerning their involvement in the rising of 1381: The National Archives, KB 9/43 m. 14

Details of stolen goods added

*Indictment against John Leg of
Birling added at the last minute*

*Names of tenants of Abbess of Malling accused
of attacking her added from membrane 14*

**Plate 7   Indictment from Larkfield hundred in Kent: The National Archives,
KB 9/43 m. 15**

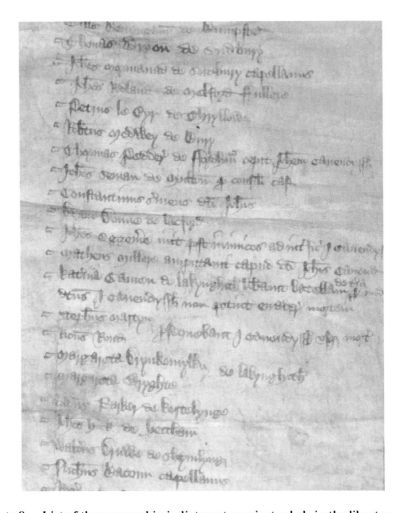

Plate 8 List of those named in indictments against rebels in the liberty of St Edmund retained by Thomas Morreaux: The National Archives, KB 9/166/1 m. 2

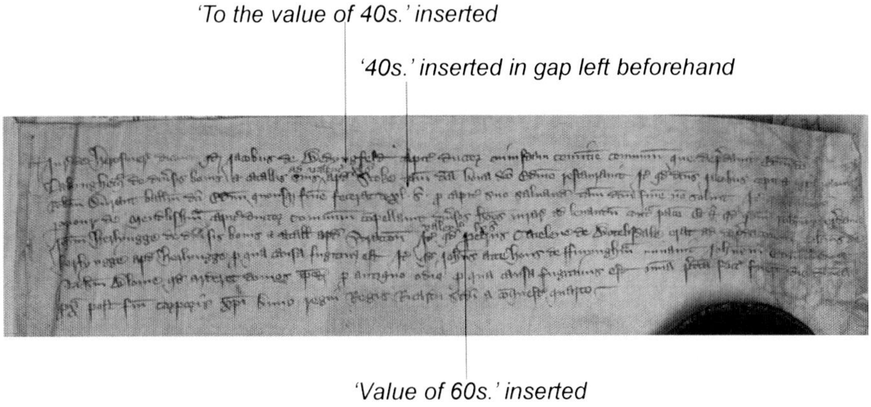

'To the value of 40s.' inserted

'40s.' inserted in gap left beforehand

'Value of 60s.' inserted

Plate 9   Indictment by jurors of Hartismere Hundred, Suffolk, showing late addition of information about value of goods stolen by rebels: The National Archives, KB 9/166/1 m. 5

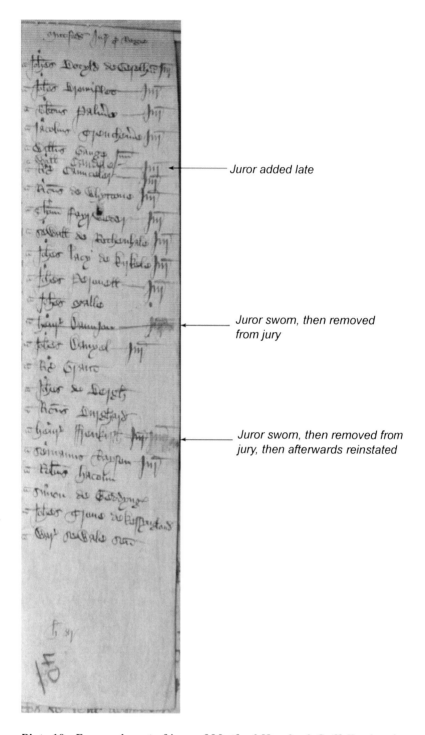

Juror added late

Juror sworn, then removed from jury

Juror sworn, then removed from jury, then afterwards reinstated

Plate 10 Empanelment of jury of Mutford Hundred, Suffolk, showing apparent manipulation of the membership of the jury: The National Archives, KB 9/166/1 m. 40

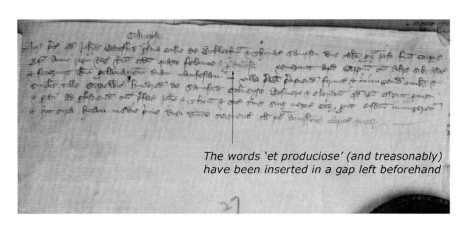

The words 'et produciose' (and treasonably) have been inserted in a gap left beforehand

Plate 11   Indictment from Colneis Hundred in Suffolk: The National Archives, KB 9/166/1/ m. 27

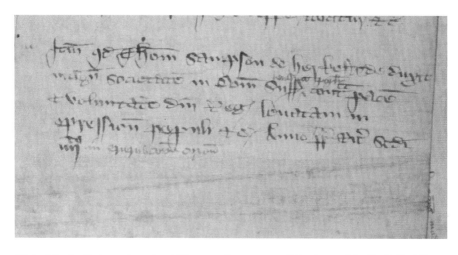

Plate 12 Indictment against Thomas Sampson of Harkstead in Suffolk: The
National Archives, KB 9/166/1 m. 31

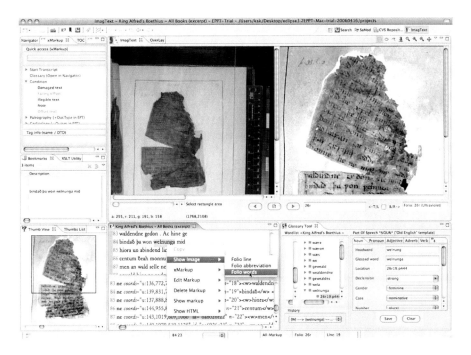

Plate 13   The Image-text perspective in EPPT

Morgan James Sworn States - I lived at Pillgwenlly some time ago - I lived there, last Saturday I was employed at the Coal pit near the Fleur de lis - I ditch the teams at the bottom of the Pit - I am a Labourer - I some time ago enrolled myself a Chartist at Newport. I attended some of their public meetings - I recollect attending a public meeting at Blackwood on Whitsun Monday. I knew John Frost - I know his person well - I know a person of the name of Jones who is usually called Jones the Watchmaker of Pontypool - those two persons were present at the meeting at Blackwood they both addressed the people that were assembled there on the subject of the Charter - Afterwards saw them at another meeting held at Dukes Town above Abbacury - it was after the meeting at the Blackwood - Frost and Jones were both present and addressed the meeting at Dukes Town on the subject of the Charter - they urged the people to have the Charter to have it in a quiet way if they could and if they could not have it in a quiet way have it they would - they say they will have it - they told the meeting that they were men enough in Dukes Town to take the Charter by force - there were present at Dukes Town a good many thousand - I know the men had come in every direction to the meeting - I saw them marching in different other places the men were going there from all parts - I heard them bid the men to be ready and lend their hands when they were called - this was as said by Frost and Jones - the men then made motions with their hands clapped their hands and said "we will, "we will" - I heard the men desired to be prepared with arms that it was lawful for every one to carry arms - I dont know that this was said by Jones and Frost - I have heard Frost & Jones tell them that . every man had a right to carry arms In consequence of something I heard I left my work and came home on last Saturday week - I got home at Pillgwenlly about 12 o'Clock at night - after I got to Pillgwenlly I came up to the Town of Newport - I saw a person of the name of Jenkin Morgan at Newport - he lives at Pillgwenlly - he told me he was a Chartist - I have met him at Some of the Chartist Lodges he asked me then how the Chartists got on up the Hills - I

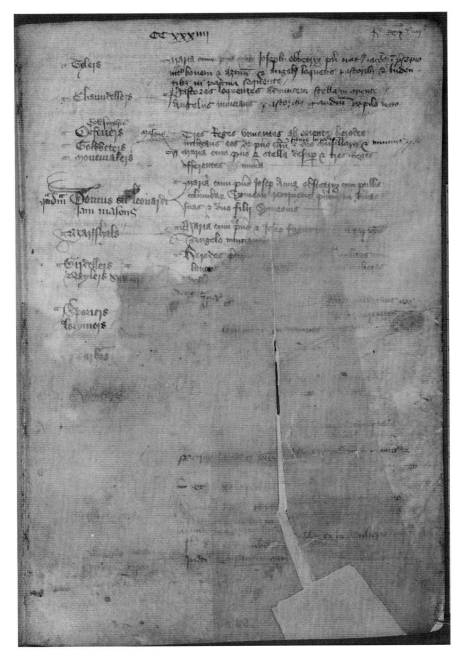

Plate 15   York City Archives, A/Y Memorandum Book, fol. 253r, showing water damage

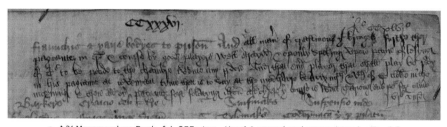

a. A/Y Memorandum Book, fol. 255r, top. Hand A erased and overwritten by Hand C

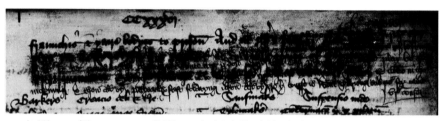

b. UV scan of the same area, slightly manipulated: Hand A beginning to emerge from erasure

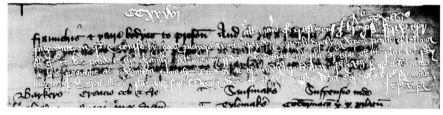

c. UV further manipulated, and overlaid with inverse (in white) of Hand C

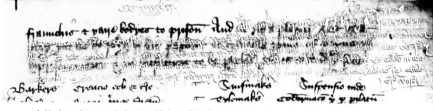

d. Underwriting copied using 'Select Color' procedure and pasted onto clean background

Plate 16 York City Archives A/Y Memorandum Book: Stages in the restoration of erased and overwritten portion on fol. 255r

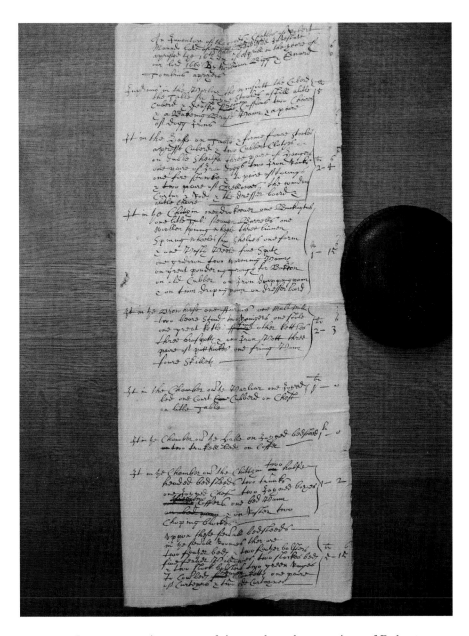

Plate 17   Post-mortem inventory of the goods and possessions of Robert
Maund dated 1660 (Oxfordshire Record Office – PEC 46/2/26)

Plate 18a Original wild goat cup

Plate 18b Digitally scanned cup

Beaker Distribution

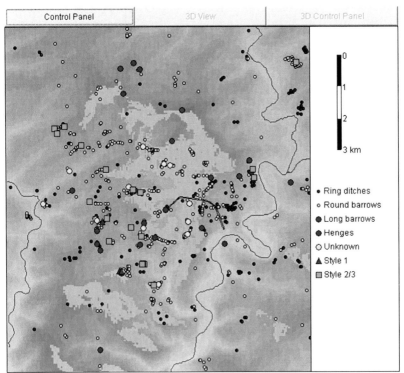

Plate 19   Viewshed and monument distribution from *Stonehenge Landscapes*

Plate 20   Opacity rendered time-slice of a Holocene river channel beneath
            the North Sea. <www.iaa.bham.ac.uk/research/fieldwork_research_
            themes/projects/North_Sea_Palaeolandscapes/index.htm>

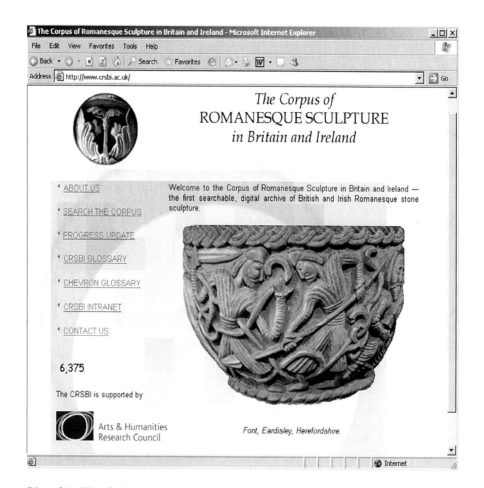

The Corpus of Romanesque Sculpture in Britain and Ireland - Microsoft Internet Explorer

File   Edit   View   Favorites   Tools   Help

Back   Search   Favorites

Address http://www.crsbi.ac.uk/

The Corpus of ROMANESQUE SCULPTURE in Britain and Ireland

‹ ABOUT US

‹ SEARCH THE CORPUS

‹ PROGRESS UPDATE

‹ CRSBI GLOSSARY

‹ CHEVRON GLOSSARY

‹ CRSBI INTRANET

‹ CONTACT US

6,375

The CRSBI is supported by

Arts & Humanities
Research Council

Welcome to the Corpus of Romanesque Sculpture in Britain and Ireland — the first searchable, digital archive of British and Irish Romanesque stone sculpture.

Font, Eardisley, Herefordshire.

Internet

Plate 21   The CRSBI website, April 2006. A screenshot of the home page showing the font at Eardisley, Hertfordshire

Plate 22　Beakheads decorating the chancel arch of St Mary Magdalene's
　　　　　Church at Tortington, Sussex, c.1140

Plate 23 All Saints Church, Buncton, Sussex. Figure carved on the north impost of the chancel arch prior to the November 2004 damage

Chapter 11

Using Geographical Information Systems to Explore Space and Time in the Humanities

Ian Gregory

Introduction

Geographical Information Systems (GIS) represent and store data in a computer in a way that explicitly incorporates a spatial reference for every item of data.[1] From a software perspective they can be thought of as spatial database management systems. GIS originated in the earth sciences but has spread through the social sciences to become increasingly prevalent in the humanities. History and archaeology have been at the forefront of this but it is spreading into other disciplines including English literature, linguistics, religious studies, anthropology, art and music.[2] The use of GIS is leading to a reawakening of our understanding of the importance of space and, beyond this, geography in the humanities. A major and common criticism of GIS is that while it is good at handling space it has no explicit concept of time.[3] This is certainly true at a database level. At a conceptual level, too, GIS is more than capable of providing an integrated approach to handling space and time together, as this chapter seeks to demonstrate. It has long been argued by many authors that truly to comprehend any human phenomenon requires an understanding of both its spatial and temporal aspects.[4] To date, however, this has proved highly problematic

1 I would like to thank the Leverhulme Trust for their assistance in writing this paper under Early Career Fellowship ECF/40115.

2 For history, see I.N. Gregory, *A Place in History: A Guide to Using GIS in Historical Research* (Oxford: Oxbow, 2003); I.N. Gregory and P.S. Ell, *Historical GIS: Technologies, Methodologies and Scholarship* (Cambridge: Cambridge University Press, 2006); A.K. Knowles (ed.), *Past Time, Past Place: GIS for History* (Redlands, CA: ESRI Press, 2002). For archaeology, see K.L. Wescott and R.J. Brandon (eds), *Practical Applications of GIS for Archaeologists: A Predictive Modeling Toolkit* (Taylor and Francis, 2000); D. Wheatley and M. Gillings, *Spatial Technology and Archaeology* (Taylor and Francis, 2002).

3 G. Langran, *Time in Geographic Information Systems* (Taylor and Francis, 1992); D.J. Peuquet 'It's About Time: A Conceptual Framework for the Representation of Temporal Dynamics in Geographic Information Systems', *Annals of the Association of American Geographers* 84 (1994): 441–61.

4 R.A. Butlin, *Historical Geography: Through the Gates of Space and Time* (Edward Arnold, 1993); R.A. Dodgson, *Society in Time and Space: A Geographical Perspective on*

in the humanities. A major reason for this is simply the complexity of handling large datasets that contain both a spatial and a temporal component.

Space and time are concepts that we understand intuitively until we start thinking about them. Then they become complex and difficult.[5] For this reason this chapter discusses the importance of space, of time, and of handling them together in academic research. It then provides a brief review of studies that have used space and time in a GIS environment in historical research. It shows that GIS has much to offer to studies of this type, as it can provide a comprehensive description of *what* happened, *where* and *when*. This in turn can challenge existing historical orthodoxies and potentially lead to new explanations being developed.

Space and GIS

Figure 11.1 shows the classic view of how GIS represents the world. The basic unit of storage within a GIS, analogous to a database table, is the layer. A layer combines two types of data. On the one hand there is attribute data which may be thought of as conventional data such as text, statistics, images, or multimedia formats. This is combined with spatial data which says where each item of attribute data is located. It does this using one of four types of graphic primitives: a point, a line, a polygon (which represents an area or zone), or a pixel. In each case these are represented using one or more coordinate pairs that give the location of the feature on the Earth's surface using coordinate systems such as the British National Grid, Universal Transverse Mercator (UTM), or latitude and longitude. Thus the GIS knows that polygon 3 in Figure 11.1 is owned by 'A. Elliot' and has a value of £5,025. In the same way it is able to select all areas that are worth less than £2,000 and show where they are.

This combination of spatial and attribute data makes GIS unique. The spatial data is, however, a very limited model. It is based on two very crude quantitative ways of representing space. The first, *absolute space*, uses coordinates and Euclidean geometry to allow straight-line distances to be calculated between two points, and bearings to be calculated between two lines. It is based on the assumption that space is uniform in all directions and from all locations. Thus it assumes that all features are located on an isotropic surface or uniform plane. The second, *relative space*, uses topology to show where different features are located in relation to each other using connectivity. Topology allows GIS to understand that one polygon is adjacent to another, or that one line connects to another line. Its best-known implementation is the London Underground map, a model of space that has no concept of distance or bearings.

Change (Cambridge: Cambridge University Press, 1998); J. Langton, 'Systems Approach to Change in Human Geography', *Progress in Geography*, 4 (1972): 123–78; D. Massey, 'Space-time, "Science" and the Relationship between Physical Geography and Human Geography', *Transactions of the Institute of British Geographers* 24 ns (1999): 261–76; D. Massey, *For Space* (Sage, 2005); R.D. Sack, 'A Concept of Physical Space in Geography', *Geographical Analysis*, 5 (1973): 16–34; R.D. Sack, 'Chronology and Spatial Analysis', *Annals of the Association of American Geographers*, 64 (1974): 439–52.

5 W.H. Newton-Smith, 'Space, Time and Space-time: A Philosopher's View', in R. Flood and M. Lockwood (eds), *The Nature of Time* (Oxford: Basil Blackwell, 1986): 22–35.

Spatial data

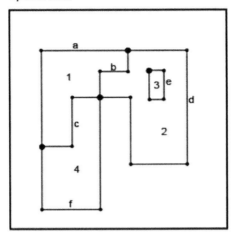

Attribute data

Polygon id	Parcel no.	Owner	Value (£)
1	437	A. Elliott	2201
2	617	J. Sutcliffe	1432
3	133	A. Elliott	5025
4	991	A. Smith	1692

Figure 11.1   The GIS data model

Although these two concepts are very simple they allow the GIS to make a number of statements about the real world that conventional databases cannot make. We have already identified three of these: it allows data to be discovered, managed and integrated, using location; it allows the geographies of the past to be visualized; and it enables analytic methodologies that explore the spatial patterns found within datasets.[6] At its simplest level using space to discover and manage data involves querying a layer of data to discover where certain features are and what other features are near them. Multiple layers can be brought together to ask more complex queries such as 'are features on one layer found near to features on another layer?'. Spatial data can also be used as a tool for resource discovery over the internet to find items or datasets that refer to a certain location or whose location intersects with another item or dataset. This idea is used by many projects including the International Dunhuang Project, the Perseus Project, and the Alexandria Digital Library (ADL).[7]

---

6 I.N. Gregory, K.K. Kemp and R. Mostern, 'Geographic Information and Historical Research: Current Progress and Future Directions', *History and Computing*, 13 (2001): 7–21.

7 For the Dunhuang Project, see <http://idp.bl.uk/>, accessed 10 January 2008; The Perseus Project, see <http://www.perseus.tufts.edu/>, accessed 10 January 2008; the

Each of these exploits location to allow a user to search for records from, in the first instance, a database of archaeological records from the Silk Road, in the second a digital library of texts from Egypt in the third millennium BC to nineteenth-century London, and in the third from maps and other records that have evolved from the map library of the University of California Santa Barbara's Davidson Library.

Visualization usually involves the creation of maps of data. This in turn has led to the creation of a number of 'historical atlases' such as The Atlas of the Great Irish Famine, or The Atlas of Mortality in Victorian England & Wales.[8] There are also more complex forms of visualization such as virtual worlds that attempt to recreate past landscapes that no longer exists. A good example of this is Trevor Harris's (2002) recreation of the landscape around Moundsville, West Virginia circa 2500 BP.[9]

Spatial analysis is concerned with any analysis that makes explicit use of where the items under study are located. It can involve quantitative or qualitative studies at a number of scales. Examples in the historical arena include Benjamin Ray's (2002) study of the Salem witchcraft trials, in which he uses court transcripts and other contemporary documents to study the spatial patterns of where people accused of being witches lived and how this related to where those who accused them lived.[10] This is a qualitative study of a single village. On the quantitative side, Amy Hillier undertook a study of mortgage availability in 1930s Philadelphia to investigate the phenomenon of 'redlining'.[11] Alastair Pearson and Peter Collier, for their part, completed a study of how agricultural productivity related to landownership and occupancy in a parish in south Wales in the mid-nineteenth century.[12]

These uses of space are undoubtedly useful and have already enhanced our understanding of a wide range of historical issues. But they are based on very crude

---

Alexandria Digital Library, see <http://www.alexandria.ucsb.edu/>, accessed 10 January 2008. Cf. D.M. Smith, G. Crane and J. Rydberg-Cox, 'The Perseus Project: A Digital Library for the Humanities', *Literary and Linguistic Computing*, 15 (2000): 15–25; M.F. Goodchild, 'The Alexandria Digital Library Project: Review, assessment, and prospects', *D-Lib Magazine*, 10/5 (2004) <http://www.dlib.org>, accessed 10 January 2007; L.L. Hill and G. Janee, 'The Alexandria Digital Library Project: Metadata Development and Use', in D.I. Hillmann and E.L. Westbrooks (eds), *Metadata in Practice* (Chicago: American Library Association, 2004), pp. 117–38.

8 L. Kennedy, P.S. Ell, E.M. Crawford and L.A. Clarkson, *Mapping the Great Irish Famine: An Atlas of the Famine Years* (Dublin: Four Courts Press, 1999); R.I. Woods and N. Shelton, *An Atlas of Victorian Mortality* (Liverpool: Liverpool University Press, 1997).

9 T. Harris, 'GIS and Archaeology', in A.K. Knowles (ed.), *Past Time, Past Place: GIS for History* (Redlands, CA: ESRI Press, 2002), pp. 131–43.

10 B.C. Ray, 'Teaching the Salem Witchcraft Trials', in Knowles (ed.), *Past Time, Past Place*, pp. 19–33.

11 A.E. Hillier, 'Redlining in Philadelphia', in Knowles (ed.), *Past Time, Past Place*, pp. 79–93; A.E. Hillier, 'Spatial Analysis of Historical Redlining: A Methodological Exploration', *Journal of Housing Research*, 14 (2003): 137–67.

12 A.W. Pearson and P. Collier, 'The Integration and Analysis of Historical and Environmental Data Using a Geographical Information System: Landownership and Agricultural Productivity in Pembrokeshire c. 1850', *Agricultural History Review* 46 (1998): 162–76; also 'Agricultural History with GIS', in Knowles (ed.), *Past Time, Past Place*, pp. 105–16.

models of space based around two possible algebraic representations: either distances and bearings across Euclidean space, or topological connectivity. In reality space is a complex and cultural concept that relies heavily on human perception. It is a subject that has recently attracted new interest among human geographers who argue that even in their discipline space has been neglected. Doreen Massey identifies three roles that space can play in academic study.[13] Firstly and most obviously, space allows people and places to interact, but it also limits that interaction. Secondly, having space allows different things to happen in different ways in different places because it allows us to study many different places rather than one homogeneous whole. Thirdly, she argues that space is something that is always evolving. As the relations between the places and people located in space change so space itself is changed.

Within GIS in the humanities, space can thus be considered at technical, methodological and conceptual levels. At the technical level it allows statements to be made about the distances, angles, and connectively within and between datasets. At the methodological level this allows data to be managed, visualized and analysed in ways that stress spatial relationships. At a more conceptual level it means that when using GIS in the humanities a researcher should think closely about how individuals and places interact over space, how different places behave in different ways, and that space is not a static concept but is something that changes and re-invents itself.

Time and GIS

Time underlies many of the concepts expressed above. The time that it takes to cross space clearly has a major impact on how people and places interact. If we are interested in multiple places then we need time to tell the different stories of how they have developed differently, and if we do not wish space to be static then time is required to provide its dynamism.[14]

The basic GIS data model has no concept of time. As can be seen from Figure 11.1, GIS provides a cross-section over space at a set point in time. Approaches to adding time to this model have been proposed.[15] Mainstream GIS software increasingly provides functionality to allow such things as vehicle tracking and animated maps to be produced. This is, however, only very limited temporal functionality. Time can be handled without these in two different ways. Firstly, it can be treated as an attribute so that features such as points can have a start and end date, and this can be used to allow them to move from one location to another. Secondly, time can be handled spatially by comparing a layer from one date with layers at different dates.[16] So, simply because GIS has little or no functionality that is explicitly temporal does not mean that time cannot be handled within GIS.

---

13 Massey, *For Space*.

14 Ibid.

15 See, for example, M. Wachowicz, *Object-Orientated Design for Temporal GIS* (Taylor and Francis, 1999).

16 Gregory, *A Place in History*.

Like space, time is also a complex and subjective concept. At least three different ways of conceptualizing time can be identified. In the first, time flows continuously in one direction from the infinite past to the infinite future. To help to conceive of this, time can be containerized into fixed intervals such as days, weeks, months and years, or into more flexible and subjective units such as periods, ages, dynasties and eras. This can lead to oddities such as the fact that two events can occur in the same week but in different years. There are also oddities concerned with how eras are defined in different places. This may be down to the use of different calendars, or due to the fact that the Civil War period in the United States, for example, was two centuries later than the Civil War period in England. Time is also not necessarily a linear flow. It can be conceived of as something that flows cyclically. For example, we may be interested in how things vary with times of day, days of the week or with seasons. Like space, time is a complex concept and we need to be able to take the crude representations of them that occur in databases, such as date fields or the names of eras, and interpret these in the more subjective, culturally specific and complex ways.

Towards an integrated handling of space and time

There are clearly both similarities and differences in the ways that space and time can be conceptualized. The major difference is that time can be considered as being one-dimensional and flowing in a single direction, while space can be considered as two- or sometimes three-dimensional and can flow in any direction. Within this there are points in both time and space; we talk about distances in time and space, and we containerize time and space. In time this is done using fixed intervals such as months and years that correspond to spatial areas such as grid squares or administrative units. We also have vaguer periods of time, such as 'the Victorian era', and these correspond to vaguer spatial areas such as 'the industrial north-east of England'.

The problem is that while space and time can be conceptualized as being similar, most studies in the humanities focus on either time or space but rarely on both of them together. A good example of the very different interpretations that this can produce is provided by William Cronon's (1991) study of the development of Chicago and the American West through the nineteenth century.[17] He contrasts two different theories about how an area develops from wilderness to urban/industrial, one of which was put forward by Frederick Jackson Turner (a historian) and the other advanced by Johann von Thunen (an agricultural economist). Turner had argued that development in American frontier areas

> begins with the Indian and the hunter; it goes on to tell of the disintegration of savagery by the entrance of the trader, the pathfinder of civilization; we read the annals of the pastoral stage in ranch life; the exploitation of the soil by the raising of unrotated crops of corn

---

17 W. Cronon, *Nature's Metropolis: Chicago and the Great West* (New York: W.W. Norton, 1991).

and wheat in sparsely settled farming communities; the intensive culture of denser farm settlement; and finally the manufacturing organization with city and factory system.[18]

In other words the wilderness would develop over time from 'Indians and hunters' to traders, then to cattle ranching, extensive agriculture, intensive agriculture, to finally reach the 'city and the factory'. Von Thunen, by contrast, was interested in patterns of agricultural land use in Europe. He argued that given a single city on a completely flat and uniform plane, patterns of agriculture would develop according to the costs of transport from the country to market in the city. This would result in agriculture forming concentric rings around the city. Nearest the city would be a ring of intensive agriculture, such as diary and orchards, whose products were expensive to transport. The second ring would be less intensive agriculture which in von Thunen's time typically meant timber and firewood, which was bulky and expensive to transport. Next there would be extensive agriculture, and then the fourth and final ring would be livestock farming based on ranching. Beyond this would be wilderness, as it would not be economic to transport goods to market from beyond a certain distance. He went on to consider how features such as lines of improved transport, variations in soil fertility, and smaller settlements would distort, but not fundamentally change, this pattern.

These two theories were advanced by two nineteenth-century authors, one in North America and the other in Europe. Neither is believed to have been in contact with the other. Turner's theory has time but no space, and charts the developments that an area will go through as it develops from wilderness to city. There is no possibility of it taking a different route as there are no other places in which that route can be taken. Von Thunen, on the other hand, puts forward a theory that has space but no time. There is no way of explaining why the city was located where it was in the first place and why this dominated other smaller settlements. There is no explanation of how the land use patterns developed over time, or the process that they would go through in response to a change in the system such as the development of a new transport route. The most interesting thing about these two theories, as Cronon points out, is that they are basically the same. In each case there is a progression from the wilderness to the city through increasingly intensive agriculture. In spite of this, however, the two theories remain irreconcilable. Turner has only one place and von Thunen has only one time. Turner's story at least implies that we must inevitably arrive in an urban/industrial present, while von Thunen presents a timeless model on a two-dimensional plane where space is simply understood in terms of transport costs.

To attempt to a fuller and more flexible understanding of a phenomenon such as this requires a combined understanding of space and time. Doreen Massey argues this from her perspective as a geographer.[19] She argues that interpreting an individual place at a specific point in time requires an understanding of the chronology of how the place developed. This provides a single story or example of its origins and thus

---

18 Turner (1920), cited in ibid., p. 31.

19 Massey, 'Space-time, 'Science' and the Relationship between Physical Geography and Human Geography'.

of how a process can operate. To gain a fuller understanding, however, requires multiple stories giving a variety of examples of how places develop and processes operate. Time thus provides the story of how a particular place or phenomenon evolved without which it is impossible to understand the processes driving this evolution. Space is important because without space there can be only one story, with the risk that this implies that this story is inevitable and will inevitably occur in the same way in different places. Space provides the ability to tell multiple stories of how places or phenomenon evolve to become what they are at the present. Thus

> space could be imagined as the sphere of the existence of multiplicity, of the possibility of the existence of difference. Such a space is the sphere in which distinct stories coexist, meet up, affect each other, come into conflict or co-operate. This space is not static, not a cross-section through time; it is disrupted, active and generative.[20]

Only by acknowledging space can it be acknowledged that different places can behave differently, and thus 'we could imagine space as a simultaneity of stories-so-far'.[21]

Space and time in historical GIS

From the argument so far it should be clear that when using GIS in the humanities our objective should be to make full use of all three components of the data: the attribute, the spatial and the temporal, such that different stories can be told about how different places have behaved differently at different times. This section presents a review of how effectively this has been done to date in the humanities, concentrating in particular on history.

A highly effective use of space and time in historical research is presented by Geoff Cunfer's work on the dust storms on the American Great Plains.[22] He claims that it has traditionally been argued that dust storms were caused by insensitive agricultural practices driven by free-market capitalism. This led in particular to the over-ploughing of unsuitable soils causing the destruction of topsoils which then blew away in high winds. Cunfer asserts that this explanation was based on detailed case studies of only two counties in the centre of the Dust Bowl region during the New Deal period, the peak time for dust storms. To test whether the explanation really holds good, Cunfer presents a much broader analysis in both its spatial and temporal extent. He investigated all 280 counties in the Great Plains using annual data over a period from the late nineteenth century to the late twentieth century. His dataset includes variables such as soil type, proportion of the land under the plough, rainfall and temperature, all of which are interpolated onto a county framework. Using GIS's data manipulation and visualization abilities, he demonstrates that dust

---

20 Ibid., p. 274.
21 Massey, *For Space*, p. 9.
22 G. Cunfer, *On the Great Plains: Agriculture and Environment* (College Station: TX A&M University Press, 2005); G. Cunfer, 'Causes of the Dust Bowl' in A.K. Knowles (ed.), *Past Time, Past Place: GIS for History* (Redlands, CA: ESRI Press, 2002), pp. 93–104.

storms prior to the Dust Bowl period were far more common than had previously been acknowledged, and that the link between agriculture and dust storms was not particularly convincing. Instead he argues that a drought caused by low rainfall and high temperatures in the mid-1930s seems to have been a far more significant factor than insensitive agriculture in causing the Dust Bowl. His analysis is highly effective in challenging the traditional explanation of the Dust Bowl. Where his analysis is less effective is in that although it shows that there appears to be a relationship over space and time between drought and dust storms, it does not show how this operated in any detail. This is perhaps an inevitable consequence of his broad-brush approach, which is highly effective at portraying bigger patterns and thus challenging conventional explanations, but is less effective at developing its own detailed explanations. It does, however, clearly illustrate the dangers of assuming that an explanation developed for a restricted location over a short period of time (in this case the story of two counties in the centre of the Dust Bowl region in the 1930s) can be applied more generally.

In a further example of an analysis that also uses space and time in a GIS environment, Etan Diamond and David Bodenhamer examined the city of Indianapolis in the 1950s. They wanted to test the orthodox theory that in this period mainline Protestant churches left downtown areas as their congregations moved to the suburbs,[23] driven by what is termed 'white-flight'. It is conventionally argued that this left downtowns as areas with large African-American populations where the shortage of churches led to social problems. Diamond and Bodenhamer claim that there is little evidence to substantiate this idea. They took the locations of churches in Indianapolis in 1950 and 1960 and compared changes in their locations with the changing ethnic makeup of Indianapolis during the same two periods. They found that only a small number of churches had actually moved, but that the ones that had generally moved from inner-city areas with large African-American populations to white suburbs. Thus, while there was some evidence for churches relocating in response to population changes, this was not as widespread as might have been expected. The analysis was very simple since it was based on two snapshots for one city. To be more convincing a larger temporal range would have to be used for a larger number of cities. Nevertheless, this paper again suggests that by explicitly incorporating space and time into an analysis it becomes possible to present some intriguing challenges to well-established historical orthodoxies.

The census and related sources (such as vital registration statistics) should provide key resources for understanding change over space and time as they are published for well-defined geographical units at regular intervals, usually every decade. In many countries they have been taken for around two hundred years. To date, these sources have not been well used to understand long-term spatio-temporal change as the boundaries of the geographical units used change at regular intervals, meaning that it is almost impossible to compare one census with the next without resorting to massive levels of aggregation. A set of techniques that can be used within GIS known as *areal interpolation* allows this to be resolved. This is based on allocating data from one set of boundaries onto a second set based on the degree of intersection

---

23 E. Diamond and D. Bodenhamer, 'Investigating White-flight in Indianapolis: A GIS Approach', *History and Computing*, 13 (2001): 25–44.

between the two.[24] To date, the full potential of this has yet to be demonstrated but there are some studies that show their potential. One, for example, compares two temporal snapshots for London.[25] The investigators wanted to compare patterns of poverty in Victorian London with modern mortality patterns. To do this, they used Charles Booth's survey of poverty in late nineteenth-century London with 1991 mortality patterns. They show that the most poverty-stricken parts of London a century ago still have high rates of poverty and mortality. They claim that this shows that the characteristics of areas have remained stable over time and thus that the characteristics of an area have a strong impact on the mortality characteristics of the people who live there. In a similar national-level analysis Gregory et al. (2001) used four time-slices rather than two to look at changing patterns of poverty in England and Wales through the twentieth century. They took the data on infant mortality, overcrowded housing and unskilled workers from the 1890s, 1930s, 1950s and 1990s, and explored how the patterns of these variables change once all of the data have been interpolated onto 1890s registration districts. The results suggested that the inequality between the areas containing best- and worst-off sections of the population appears to have risen over the century for all three of these variables. To be more convincing this analysis requires more time-slices in order to demonstrate how the patterns have changed in more detail.

More recently the potential for using this kind of technique with a variety of spatial analysis techniques has been explored. A primarily methodological study based on the period of the Irish Potato Famine in the late 1840s examined the censuses from 1841 to 1881 to see how population changed as a result of the Famine.[26] It came to two interesting conclusions: firstly, that although the famine was worst in the west as previously identified, the Irish Midlands continued to lose population for at least as long as the west and perhaps longer. Secondly, it was found that although Skibereen in the south of Ireland is often used as a case study for the famine, its characteristics were far from typical.

These studies show that using GIS does have a clear potential to improve our understanding of the past by explicitly incorporating space and time. In particular it is able to challenge whether the lessons learned from detailed studies conducted on small areas are robust when these are tested for broader areas and longer time periods.

Conclusions

Although researchers have long argued for the importance of understanding space and time together, the complexity of their data has severely hampered their ability to

24 I.N. Gregory and P.S. Ell, 'Breaking the Boundaries: Integrating 200 Years of the Census Using GIS', *Journal of the Royal Statistical Society*, Series A, 168 (2005), 419–37.

25 D. Dorling, R. Mitchell, M. Shaw et al., 'The Ghost of Christmas Past: Health Effects of Poverty in London in 1896 and 1991', *British Medical Journal*, 321 (2000): 1547–51.

26 I.N. Gregory and P.S. Ell, 'Analysing Spatio-temporal Change Using National Historical GISs: Population Change during and after the Great Irish Famine', *Historical Methods*, 38 (2005): 149–67.

do this. This has frequently meant that they have ignored one or other of space and time, or explored them both together for a relatively small study area and hoped that the conclusions that were drawn from this were more broadly applicable. Although the basic GIS data model does not explicitly incorporate time, the use of GIS does allow a significant improvement in our ability to handle the spatial and temporal components of data together. This in turn has the potential to provide new insights into our understanding of change over space and time, particularly through its ability to integrate different layers of data and to visualize their changing locations in space. At an intellectual level this provides exciting new opportunities to both revisit traditional orthodoxies and to conduct new research that could not previously be undertaken. In terms of challenging orthodoxies, it is clear from the work of Cunfer, and Diamond and Bodenhamer that, in both cases, previous researchers have performed in-depth studies on relatively small locations and time periods. The conclusions from these have then been applied to much wider areas and times but this has often been done inappropriately and led to erroneous, or at best over-simplistic, conclusions. GIS has the potential to challenge this by performing much broader analyses that cover a far wider spatial area with more temporal depth. These can test whether the patterns that the orthodoxy predicts are actually found in the wider data. The conclusion from these early studies is that they frequently do not. Where GIS studies of this type are perhaps limited is that due to their nature they are inevitably less detailed than the types of study that they challenge, so their ability to present their own explanation is somewhat limited. The census-based studies described above show the potential of using GIS to perform completely new work to improve our understanding of space and time. These are still somewhat limited by the techniques and data that they use, but there is clearly the potential to develop new insights into long-term change in society from studies of this type even though the sources used have been extensively researched for many years.

At present we are still in the early stages of using GIS in history and more broadly across the humanities. Studies so far have shown potential but there is clearly much work that remains to be done. To assist in this development, a variety of further developments need to take place.

In an ideal world GIS software would provide a better explicit handling of time. This is frequently called for but is in some ways a red herring. GIS software developers do not regard the academic humanities community as a major market and are unlikely to do so in the future. They are responding to calls for a better handling of time in their data models, but this tends to focus on subjects such as real-time monitoring of the locations of vehicles within a transport fleet, or simple analyses of point patterns to help local government agencies deal with issues such as crime or graffiti. The extent to which these are relevant to humanities researchers is debatable but it seems foolish to limit the academic agenda to applying tools developed for a very different set of purposes. Developing our own software in the humanities is fraught with risks and does not have a high success rate. As a result, making imaginative use of existing tools and adapting them to the needs of humanities research seems likely to be the most effective way of making progress.

Intellectually, there are also many challenges that remain to be overcome. Our understanding of exactly how an improved handling of space and time can aid our knowledge of disciplines across the humanities is still limited, although, as this chapter describes, there has been significant progress in this area. Much of the progress made has been in the more quantitative elements of the discipline. This is largely a legacy of the roots of GIS but, as the Salem witchcraft case study demonstrates, there is no clear reason why this should remain the case.[27] We can expect the ability of GIS to handle large volumes of textual, image and multimedia data to lead to significant improvements in change over space and time from qualitative sources. GIS has shown its ability to challenge orthodoxies by exploring whether the patterns they predict exist over broad spatial areas and long periods of time. It has been less successful in suggesting theories to explain the patterns that it identifies and describes. The extent to which the software can do this remains to be proven but it is clear that it does provide a useful tool in aiding our understanding of time and space in the humanities.

---

27 Ray, 'Teaching the Salem Witchcraft Trials'.

Chapter 12

Spatial Technologies in Archaeology in the Twenty-first Century

Paul Cripps

Let us begin with a bold assertion: the use of digital spatial technologies in archaeology in the twenty-first century can now be considered the norm rather than the exception. This reflects the wider adoption of such technologies by society at large and also the importance given to spatial information by the archaeological community, for whom site plans, stratigraphic matrices, maps and section drawings are the building-blocks of archaeological interpretation. Spatial technologies are here being considered in the broadest sense – as digital systems which create or manipulate spatial data. They include two-dimensional drawing and mapping applications, fully-fledged GIS applications such as, for example, AutoDesk Map,[1] ArcGIS,[2] GRASS[3] or MapInfo,[4] and also truly three-dimensional applications such as, for example, AutoCAD,[5] Maya,[6] Fledermaus,[7] Vue Infinite[8] and 3D Studio[9] or Viz.[10] Many devices used by archaeologists also create spatial data. These include geophysical or geochemical survey instruments, GPS and Total Stations used for topographic and other forms of survey, airborne survey systems such as LiDAR (Light Detection and Ranging), and also satellite-mounted sensors. This broad definition even takes in onboard navigation devices and PDAs or mobile phones equipped with location-based services. Combined with the rise in availability of affordable, high-quality, global-positioning devices and developments in internet technologies allowing spatial data to be transmitted across the World Wide Web (even to mobile devices), the impact

---

1 The GIS-enabled version of AutoCAD from AutoDesk <http://www.autodesk.com/map3d>. All urls accessed August 2007, unless otherwise specified.

2 A family of related GIS applications from the Environmental Systems Research Institute (ESRI) <http://www.esri.com/>.

3 An open-source GIS application <http://grass.itc.it/index.php>.

4 A GIS application from MapInfo Corporation M<http://www.mapinfo.com>.

5 Leading industrial CAD application from Autodesk <http://www.autodesk.com/autocad>.

6 A 3D modelling package now owned by AutoDesk <http://www.autodesk.com/maya>.

7 A powerful 3D visualization application from IVS 3D <http://www.ivs3d.com/products/fledermaus/>, accessed July 2006.

8 A powerful 3D modelling package from Eon Software <http://www.e-onsoftware.com/products/vue/vue_5_infinite/>.

9 A 3D modelling package from AutoDesk <http://www.autodesk.com/3dsmax>.

10 A basic 3D modelling package from AutoDesk <http://www.autodesk.com/viz>.

of these various technologies has been felt in many contexts, including research, management and the dissemination of archaeological information.

Associated with this development, we are also witnessing an increasing demand within the sector for people with appropriate skills in spatial technologies. Commercial units, public sector bodies and research institutes all employ staff in this area and universities are increasingly providing training to meet this need. While some roles require specialist computing skills first and foremost, the key point to emphasize is that many practitioners are archaeologists with training in spatial technologies, essential where the main focus of the post is archaeology. As such, there are specialist postgraduate degree courses in archaeological geomatics and archaeological computing at a number of universities, and those that do not offer such courses are looking to incorporate some aspects of spatial technologies into, for example, their research skills units by collaborating with other departments or individuals within their institutions or further afield. Furthermore, a number of research centres have emerged in the field of spatial technologies applied to archaeology including the Centre for Advanced Spatial Analysis at University College London, the Vista Centre at the University of Birmingham and the Archaeological Computing Research Group at the University of Southampton. A number of other universities have practitioners whose research is also within this area. Oxford University even have a spin-off company (OxfordArchDigital), realizing research outputs in working environments, and there are other spatial data and archaeological IT consultancies doing the same. There is also a significant specialist literature now widely available in this domain.[11]

Funds are increasingly being made available for archaeological applications of spatial technologies, with PhD schemes such as that offered by the AHRC (Arts and Humanities Research Council) now more open to archaeological science and funding streams such as those managed by organizations such as EPOCH (Excellence in Processing Open Cultural Heritage) also available.[12] Digital spatial technologies have, in short, come of age.

Digital spatial technologies and research

The growing corpus of research using spatial technologies is evident in a number of archaeological domains. In landscape archaeology, for example, GIS has become an essential part of many projects, initially for data management and cartographic output but also increasingly for analysis of one kind or another. Resources such as the Digimap service provided by EdiNA[13] give students and researchers access to vast repositories of digital map data, whilst access to high-power computing facilities allows practitioners to undertake novel research using this data. Within this area, 'archaeological visibility analysis' has particularly benefited from the application

---

11 G. Lock (ed.), *Beyond the Map: Archaeology and Spatial Technologies* (Amsterdam: IOS Press, 2000); D.W. Wheatley and M. Gillings, *Spatial Technology and Archaeology: The Archaeological Applications of GIS* (Taylor and Francis, 2002).

12 European Research Network <http://www.epoch-net.org/>.

13 <http://edina.ac.uk/digimap/>.

of spatial technologies. Methodological approaches such as Cumulative Viewshed Analysis (Wheatley[14]), Probabilistic Viewshed Analysis (Fisher[15]) and Total Viewshed Analysis (Llobera[16]) have built upon the basic line-of-sight function to provide novel approaches to archaeological questions using the concept of visibility. From the initial viewshed, representing all positive lines of sight from a location, it is possible to build cumulative viewsheds and test for the relative significance of their visual envelopes for each site location. Such probabilistic viewshed evaluation attempts to account for the relative uncertainty of the calculation, whilst the total viewshed calculation provides the background visual characteristics of a landscape against which any particular viewshed can be compared for significance. This area of research demonstrates how a fairly simple calculation (the 'line-of-sight vector calculation') has, over time, been developed into a more sophisticated way of understanding archaeological situations.

Other GIS-based projects within the field of landscape studies include that of 'historic landscape characterization' (HLC) which provides a GIS-based methodology for characterizing landscape in a structured manner.[17] HLC projects are ongoing or completed for large parts of the country. Once completed, the outputs are then typically incorporated into site management record (SMR)/heritage environment (HER) management systems such as HBSMR[18] used to manage the cultural heritage resource and to inform the planning process. Research projects such as the Stonehenge Landscapes project have also used GIS as a means to coming to novel understandings of the particular landscape in question.[19] At the same time they have used digital technologies to present results in conjunction with traditional publications. Not only has the GIS database become central to the underlying analysis but the cross-platform, user-controllable Java applets distributed with the publication now also

---

14 D. Wheatley, 'Cumulative Viewshed Analysis: A GIS-based Method for Investigating Intervisibility and Its Archaeological Application', in G. Lock and Z. Stancic (eds), *Archaeology and Geographic Information Systems: A European Perspective* (Taylor and Francis, 1995), pp. 171–86.

15 P.F. Fisher, 'First Experiments in Viewshed Uncertainty: Simulating Fuzzy Viewsheds', *Photogrammetric Engineering and Remote Sensing*, 58 (1992): 345–52.

16 M. Llobera, 'Extending GIS-based Visual Analysis: The Concept of Visualscapes', *International Journal of Geographical Information Science*, 17 (2003): 25–48.

17 G.J. Fairclough, G. Lambrick and A. McNab, *Yesterday's World, Tomorrow's Landscape – The English Heritage Historic Landscape Project 1992–94* (English Heritage, 1999); G.J. Fairclough, G. Lambrick and D. Hopkins, 'Historic Landscape Characterisation in England and a Hampshire Case Study', in G.J. Fairclough, S. Rippon and D. Bull (eds), *Europe's Cultural Landscape: Archaeologists and the Management of Change*, Europae Archaeologie Consilium Occasional Paper 2 (EAC, 2002); G.J. Fairclough, 'The Long Chain: Archaeology, Historical Characterization and Time Depth in the Landscape', in H. Palang and G. Fry (eds), *Landscape Interfaces: Cultural Heritage in Changing Landscapes* (Dordrecht: Kluwer Academic Publishers, 2003), pp. 295–318.

18 Historic Buildings, Sites and Monuments Record (HBSMR), an integrated GIS enabled SMR/HER management system by exeGesIS SDM Ltd <http://www.esdm.co.uk>.

19 S. Exon, W. Gaffney, A. Woodward and R. Yorston, *Stonehenge Landscapes: Journeys through Real and Imagined Worlds* (Oxford: Archaeopress, 2000).

provide readers with the option of pursuing their own independent investigations of the data.

So, moving away from purely Cartesian approaches to space, it is also possible to use network-based approaches to model a particular variable or variables representing some relationship other than Euclidean distance between two locations. Such approaches have been applied successfully to (for example) Roman transport networks. Indeed, site catchment analysis and the analysis of territories associated with particular sites can use purely geometric variables such as Euclidean distance to/from a site and also be subjected to more complex trend surfaces reflecting (for instance) energy expended, access to transport routes, proximity or cost-distance to other locations, visual characteristics or other properties or combinations of properties of the space being studied. These still need to be put into a research context but the days of applying simplistic functional models to the distant past should be behind us. However, not all the functionality in GIS applications will be equally and always applicable. The idea of defining territories in prehistory using Thiessen polygons (a purely geometric function of space) can, for example, now be seen as fundamentally flawed, given what we now understand of perceptions of space in prehistory, with paths and places being of importance rather than territories per se. Having said this, the construction of such polygons may fit a particular model of some past phenomena; the technique should simply be understood and applied appropriately.

The impact of such pieces of work has been significant; associated methodologies and their derivatives are now used in other archaeological projects and the outputs of such projects, such as sensitivity maps, are used to inform cultural heritage management decisions beyond the initial research contexts. This is not to comment either way on the validity or otherwise of individual approaches, simply to say that GIS applications are becoming central to the process of undertaking archaeological research.

Truly three-dimensional applications have primarily been used as tools to produce views of spatial data, either still-rendered images, animated sequences or interactive environments. These have become familiar through the reconstructions presented on television programmes and interactive booths which have become popular in display contexts. There has been a good deal of discussion about the production and consumption of such digital images and virtual worlds, the central issues being those of the 'realism' that is implied by the results and the 'uncertainty' that is hidden from the casual observer. Nevertheless, three-dimensional technologies have made an impact on the archaeological discipline, predominantly in the dissemination of ideas but increasingly as a reflexive part of the digital reconstruction process and for analytical purposes.

The use of digital spatial technologies in archaeology remains, however, problematic. Firstly, in a post-processual world of phenomenological archaeology – one which stresses the embodied personal experience of an archaeological landscape or artefact – how do we reconcile the essentially generalizing methodologies of GIS with such perspectives that are based on something more individual? If we are interested in understanding human experience from the point of view of individual human actors, is there not a conflict between this and such computer-based techniques? There is undoubtedly a serious issue here, but it is probably not insoluble. Improvements in GIS methodologies to incorporate new perspectives on time and space can provide a reflexive and interpretative environment which can also be 'experienced'. To emphasize the point, let us highlight some recent and ongoing work in the field of landscape and architectural studies that in novel ways bridges the apparent theoretical divide between the claims of phenomenological archaeology and the practices of digital spatial technologies.

Vision, perception and temporality

At issue is our human sense of vision and perception. Its experiential and subjective nature has been widely documented. A phenomenological approach to archaeological vision and perception has been to walk around the landscape, taking down observations which can later be built into an experiential narrative from which interpretations of the archaeology can then be deduced.[20] In the field of digital spatial technologies this has traditionally been tackled using GIS-based visibility analysis, the simplest form of which is a binary surface representing areas visible and not visible on a terrain model from an observer location. The most obvious criticism of such analyses focuses on the way in which they privilege vision over other senses. In addition, they are based on an abstract mathematical model of space and fail to account for the experiential nature of being in the world. The presence or absence of a line-of-sight vector between two locations may not adequately represent the visual experience of an observer. Having said this, the concept of lines of sight is not a new one and has been used for centuries as a means to quantify the visual characteristics of landscape, the only difference now being the speed with which such vectors can be calculated. If we accept that such abstractions are both necessary and useful, rather than dismissing applications of spatial technologies in favour of more humanistic approaches (such as narrative), we can aim to improve the nature of these abstractions and develop new methodologies which fuse the benefits of both schools of thought. A number of publications have attempted to provide GIS-based analysis with a firmer footing in archaeological theory.[21]

In the same way as it is possible to see the shift from purely geometrically derived territories calculated as part of territorial analyses towards territories based on cost surfaces, there is a similar shift in visibility analyses. If we accept that our purely mathematical model of space may affect our analysis, why not deliberately introduce variables to represent potential errors which can be changed in a controlled manner to study their effects? The notion of incorporating variables representing error into functions and then repeating the function many times to produce a distribution of

20 E.g. J. Thomas, *Understanding the Neolithic* (Routledge, 1999).

21 M. Gillings and G.T. Goodrick, 'Sensuous and Reflexive GIS: Exploring Visualisation and VRML', *Internet Archaeology*, 1 (1996) <http://intarch.ac.uk/journal/issue1/gillings_index.html> (accessed February 2006); M. Gillings and D.W. Wheatley, 'Seeing is not Believing: Unresolved Issues in Archaeological Visibility Analysis', in B. Slapsak (ed.), *On the Good Use of Geographic Information Systems in Archaeological Landscape Studies* (COST Action G2: European Union: EUR19708, 2001), pp. 25–36.

results rather than a single result is a process called probabilistic modelling and can be found in use in most scientific disciplines today. Such 'fuzzy' approaches to data allow us to compensate (within controlled parameters) for the apparent clarity of results produced by digital systems. In the case of visibility analysis, the viewshed is no longer represented by areas of visible and invisible with hard edges between them, but rather by a continuous distribution of visual sensitivity across the study area.[22] This remains an approximation but it can be seen to be a *better* approximation since the edge of a view is rarely a clear-cut line and the accuracy of the viewshed area is always uncertain.[23]

So we can use simulation techniques to provide better approximations of the kind of view afforded a person placed within the study area. We can calculate probabilistic viewsheds across the landscape from various locations to see how patterns of visibility and intervisibility change. We can even use statistical approaches to compare these viewsheds with the total viewshed for an area to test for significance. What this does not do is give us an understanding of landscape from the point of view of an active agent. Humans rarely stand still for extended periods of time and the calculation of viewsheds from fixed locations infers that there is something significant about that location. In many places the presence of a site is often used – such as, for example the comparative work on the barrow distributions around Avebury and Stonehenge or the extensive work in the Stonehenge environs.[24] In prehistory, where it has often been argued that routes and movement are of importance, we need to develop new methodologies (on the basis of existing ones) which are capable of answering such questions. One such approach has been the development of dynamic viewsheds, where viewsheds are calculated not from fixed locations, but from intervals along a hypothetical pathway.[25] These viewsheds can be composited into a sequence representing change in a visual envelope through time. This approach provides us with an analysis which approximates more closely that of a dynamic human actor, engaged with their environment, rather than an analysis of relationships to, from and between supposedly significant places in a world devoid of people.

A further, significant criticism of GIS spatial technologies has been the bald terrain models which have been deployed, ones lacking in any kind of terrain or upstanding features. Whilst it is possible at broader scales to incorporate vegetation or anthropomorphic features as extrusions directly into terrain models used for analysis, this is of limited use, especially in those applications where a truly three-dimensional approach is required. So, for example, it is impossible to study the megaliths themselves at Stonehenge using a 2.5D GIS-based approach; a truly 3D approach is required. Indeed, whilst it is applicable to many landscape contexts,

---

22 Fisher, 'First Experiments in Viewshed Uncertainty: Simulating Fuzzy Viewsheds'.

23 P.F. Fisher, 'First Experiments in Viewshed Uncertainty: The Accuracy of the Viewshed Area', *Photogrammetric Engineering and Remote Sensing*, 57 (1991): 1321–7.

24 Wheatley, 'Cumulative Viewshed Analysis'; Exon et al., *Stonehenge Landscapes: Journeys through Real and Imagined Worlds*.

25 P.J. Cripps, 'Pathways through the Avebury Landscape: A Study of Spatial Relationships Associated with the Beckhampton Avenue, Avebury, Wilts', unpublished MSc dissertation, University of Southampton, 2001 <http://www.soton.ac.uk/~pjc196/files/CrippsPJ_MSc2001_LoQuality.pdf>, accessed July 2006.

such an approach is wholly unsuited to architectural spaces in general. Research is ongoing within the Archaeological Computing Research Group at Southampton and elsewhere to develop new tools within existing spatial technologies to facilitate such analysis using truly three-dimensional applications such as 3D Studio and the notion of ray-casting as an analogue for GIS-based viewshed calculations.[26]

Such approaches can also help to resolve the lack of temporality inherent in GIS. Whereas two-dimensional GIS affords a static, map-based view of the world, three-dimensional technologies embody a sense of time in that objects placed within such environments can be made to move and to interact. The best approximation for temporality in GIS is dependent on the notion of time-slices, whereby a phenomenon can be viewed relative to a timescale with fixed intervals (i.e. a series of distinct states of being, with associated time attributes). Such an approximation can be useful, as in the case of dynamic viewshed calculations, population models and other forms of trend surface modelling, but it further restricts the potential for other parameters of analysis. Can games engines be customized for such interactive purposes? The optimizations found in such technologies mean that, whilst not specifically designed for archaeological research, they are effectively highly efficient real-time spatial data visualization applications, incorporating advanced visualization features such as High Dynamic Range lighting (until recently the preserve of highly specialist applications and requiring vast computer resources). Furthermore, data can be captured upon the experience of such simulations, using the computer base model as a data capture and analytical tool in addition to a visualization tool and interface.

Data

Improvements in measurement do not directly correlate, of course, with improvements in the data to be analysed.[27] So we should never sacrifice measurement to analysis and visualization. That said, the availability of data at increased resolutions can provide new opportunities for research. A relevant example is provided by airborne LiDAR, a system which uses a laser scanner fitted to an aircraft to produce high-resolution terrain models. Early GIS-based work made use of very crude elevation models which were often the prime determinant factor in any results, representing the terrain using square blocks measuring some 50 m². Currently, the most common terrain model in use is the Ordnance Survey LandForm DTM which has a horizontal resolution of 10 m and stated vertical error of the order of 2.5 m.[28] Given these parameters, it is easy to see why the terrain model has had a limited impact on subsequent visibility analyses for archaeological purposes, since small features remain invisible. LiDAR, on the other hand, is of a much higher horizontal resolution (1–2 m) and has a much more controlled vertical error (typically of the order of ±20 cm or even less in some

---

26 See, e.g. G.P. Earl, 'Texture Viewsheds: Spatial Summaries of Built Archaeological Spaces Derived from Global Light Mapping', *Proceedings of the 11th International Conference on Virtual Systems and Multimedia* (Ghent: VSMM, 2005).

27 Cf. above, Chapter 10.

28 OS Landform technical specifications: <http://www.ordnancesurvey.co.uk/oswebsite/products/landformprofile/techinfo.html>, accessed July 2006.

circumstances). As such, small landscape features are clearly visible and the error inherent in the terrain model has a lesser effect on any visibility analyses conducted. Already, LiDAR data has been used on a number of archaeological projects to great effect, for example by the Aerial Survey Team at English Heritage in collaboration with Cambridge University, to identify new archaeological features in the Stonehenge Landscape.[29] This was undertaken using traditional means of analysis: hill-shading the elevation data, and then transcribing features of interest using a top-down view in CAD, as is typically done with aerial photograph interpretation. Tentative work on the same data but using three-dimensional techniques raised the possibility that there are even more features to be transcribed and validated.[30] Techniques used for the analysis of rock-art on the megaliths at Stonehenge were applied to the LiDAR data, it being simply another form of surface data. In the same way that laser-scan data from the surface of megaliths is more useful for detecting surface features than a vertical photograph of the same area, LiDAR data (treated as three-dimensional data) has more potential for morphometric analysis than if it is reduced to a two-dimensional elevation model in GIS or similar applications. As such, we should be aware that new ways of working with such data sets may be beneficial and that the development of new techniques in this field is vital if archaeologists are to be able to ask the kinds of questions of the data they would like to ask.

Information systems

Finally, digital spatial technologies need to be placed in the context of information systems. Spatial data is like any other data, handled by information systems of one kind or another. This is where the lines of distinction become blurred, since there is considerable overlap between research into space, time and text in the humanities. Developments in the fields of textual processing, ontologies and markup are vital to the ongoing development of digital spatial technologies. Using ontologically aware middleware to interface between data warehouses and client applications, it should be possible to ask complex archaeological questions of our shared information resources. This would include any combination of spatial and temporal operators as well as language-independent concept matches rather than simple string-pattern matches. Furthermore, the adoption of standard formats such as MIDAS XML, which incorporates a spatial component, allows for the packaging and sharing of spatial and related data independent of source and target system data structures, further removing barriers to research.[31] This is dependent, however, on information passed as text in XML formats using standard transmission technologies such as Hypertext Transfer Protocol (HTTP). Indeed, spatial information can now be viewed as text using the

---

29 R.H. Bewley, S.P. Crutchley and C.A. Shell. 'New Light on an Ancient Landscape: LiDAR Survey in the Stonehenge World Heritage Site', *Antiquity*,79 (2005): 636–47.

30 Personal communication from Alistair Carty, director of Archaeoptics Ltd, a commercial laser-scanning bureau and collaborator on the Stonehenge laser-scan project <http://www.stonehengelaserscan.org/>, accessed July 2006.

31 An XML schema for cultural heritage information <http://heritage-standards.org>, accessed July 2006.

SVG (Scalable Vector Graphics) format, a standard XML (i.e. text) format for spatial data or as WKT (Well Known Text), a simple text-based representation of geometries. So there is a convergence of technologies. There will always be a place for dedicated applications in specialist tasks, such as the creation of three-dimensional models or analysis of spatial data, but increasingly the functionality available through such systems is being made available through lightweight technologies designed for the World Wide Web. This gives much greater access to spatial information and the tools needed to manipulate it. There are now many examples of this as more and more SMRs and HERs as well as national resources such as CanMap and PastMap have become available over the internet.[32] Many such resources use proprietary server technologies to process requests for spatial data and return data in a format suitable to be rendered in a web browser; commercial GIS packages, however, offer web-server components as extensions to their main applications but there are also open-source resources available.

In fact, the provision of open APIs (Advanced Programming Interfaces) to web-based applications is now growing. GoogleMaps and YahooMaps (among others) offer mapping applications which have published APIs to allow users to write their own mapping applications based on the technology Already there are third-party mobile phone versions (for example, Google's Mobile GoogleMaps) and many institutions now routinely use these services to provide visitors with relevant location information. It may be that the mapping developments of these in the context of the Semantic Web or what is being referred to as Web2.0 will have considerable potential for archaeological purposes. RSS feeds are already used, for example, to supply updates to information, including geographical and other datasets via 'enclosures'. For projects with disparate teams, such feeds can be used to keep everyone up-to-date whilst collaborative environments such as the Wiki can be used to engage in discussion. Server technologies allow data to be stored centrally and accessed by any permitted device or user remotely, with metadata facilitating information retrieval and AJAX providing editing tools over the web.[33] Another aspect of the Web2.0 is the concept of web services which can be used to provide access to data or even undertake tasks such as to augment or validate datasets including spatial datasets, automatically checking and updating before delivering an enriched dataset and an XML metadata file containing a list of updates. These are not, of course, dedicated spatial technologies, but they are part of the broader framework of digital systems which the research community is adopting and spatial data can be created, stored, repurposed, repackaged, enriched and disseminated through them in the same way as other data.

---

32 Canmap – a portal site bringing together a number of resources for Scotland, including Canmore: <http://jura.rcahms.gov.uk/PASTMAP/start.jsp>, accessed July 2006. Pastmap – an online presence for the national archaeological record provided by the Royal Commission on the Ancient and Historical Monuments of Scotland: <http://www.rcahms.gov.uk/>, accessed July 2006.

33 Asynchronous JavaScript and XML; a technology for providing a more interactive web experience.

Conclusions

Digital spatial technologies have become an integral part of the archaeological discipline. Replacing manually produced pie-charts, stuck to hand-drawn maps, site plans are now largely 'born digital' within a Total Station Theodolite or GPS with statistical distributions overlain using GIS. Theoretically speaking, there is an outstanding agenda to reconcile such computer-based approaches with strands of current archaeological theory relating to space, time and perception. But nothing in the theoretical conception of computer-based spatial technologies precludes its being applied alongside more humanistic approaches. It requires, however, a degree of lateral thinking to marry rigorous computer-based, scientific investigation with the kinds of current archaeological discourses which have followed previous functionalist and processual archaeological theoretical approaches, many of which were intrinsically reliant upon implicit cultural assumptions. A myriad metrics about a landscape are redundant unless they are accompanied by meaningful interpretations – and the latter can readily take into account recent developments in landscape phenomenology. If spending time in a landscape in order to understand it more thoroughly is useful, then so too is the creation of digital resources in order to interpret it. The experience derived from the construction of such digital environments may well be an equivalent phenomenology that has its own importance.[34]

Spatial technologies have developed considerably over the last few years alongside increased computing power, availability and software development. Two- and three- dimensional technologies are becoming fused. There is a cross-fertilization of ideas between users of different systems. Line-of-sight vectors or hill-shading in GIS, for example, have become light rays and movable light sources in 3D Studio, whilst 3D Studio outputs from three-dimensional applications are subjected to traditional forms of image analysis and quantification. But such technologies are no substitute for thought. More measurement and observation will only bring results when subjected to interpretation. New and emerging spatial technologies, albeit no automatic panacea, provide important tools for such interpretation. We now have robust, useable standards for spatial data and systems capable of working with and taking advantage of these standards. It is possible to deliver spatial data and even provide tools for working with such data over the World Wide Web with little associated cost to the end-user. Perhaps most importantly, there are rising skill-levels among archaeologists capable of making use of digital spatial technologies, for whom they afford tremendous potential for new research, enhanced cultural resource management and the dissemination of their results.

---

34 P. Cripps, G. Earl and D.W. Wheatley, 'A Dwelling Place in Bits', in V.O. Jorge, J.M. Cardoso, A.M. Vale, G.L. Velho and L.S. Periera (eds), *Journal of Iberian Archaeology*, vol. 8 (Porto: Adecap, 2006).

PART IV
THE VIRTUAL REPRESENTATION
OF HISTORICAL OBJECTS
AND EVENTS

Chapter 13

Digital Artefacts:
Possibilities and Purpose

David Arnold

There are many potential purposes for creating and using digital representations of cultural artefacts and indeed there are many forms that such digital artefacts can take. But a digital representation of an artefact is a representation of certain relevant characteristics of the artefact. It is not the original and complete artefact, nor even a metonymy or *simulacrum* of the complete artefact. It is only a representation of some 'relevant characteristics'. The definition of what is relevant depends upon the purposes of creating the artefact. In principle, therefore, there may be as many digital representations of a single artefact as there are purposes leading to their creation, each being targeted at a different purpose or combination of purposes. In practice there are usually reasons for wanting to capture characteristics required for many purposes, only some of which may be understood or appreciated before the exercise of capturing the data is undertaken. These reasons may vary from pragmatic aspects such as the cost of undertaking data capture to the intrinsic logistics in the process of recording being undertaken. So, at one extreme, data capture for archaeologists is typically a unique opportunity since the act of investigating a particular site actually destroys much of the evidence. Hopefully, this is not so much the case for data capture from individual artefacts although, in many fields, the act of digitization may involve some risk of wear and tear, ranging from handling fragile objects to digitizing material where extended exposure to strong light is undesirable.

For these reasons, therefore, we should first consider a typical range of purposes for digitization of cultural heritage objects, and what the relevant characteristics for those purposes might be. Two broad ranges of purposes can be identified:

- applications concerned with documentation and analysis for use by cultural heritage professionals
- applications with a component of dissemination to the 'general public', or at least that fraction of the public who have a potential interest in the artefacts.

These need to be analysed further.

Relevant characteristics for applications of digital artefacts

There are, of course, many ways of classifying cultural artefacts, depending upon the analysis to be undertaken. Alonzo Addison, for example, divides them by means of the digital capture technologies which created them in the first place, viz:[1]

Visual	Still/video cameras, colour scanners
Dimensional	3D scanning, photogrammetry (remote-sensing technology in which geometric properties of objects are determined from photographic images), digital surveying (employing electronic distance measuring devices (EDM) linked to a total station), ground-penetration radar systems (GPR)
Locational	Global Positioning Systems (GPS) sensors
Environmental	Thermal registration, acoustic measurement systems, Carbon-14 (radio-carbon dating)

For the purposes of this chapter we will consider the categories of data which might be required to support applications in each of the two broad categories of purposes that we have identified: documentation and analysis, and dissemination to the public.

Documentation and analysis

The objective of documentation is clear: it is to catalogue and record the evidence of a site or the contents of a collection. But there are many potential objectives to an analysis of the documentation. It might be, for example, one or more of the following:

*   dating and classification by comparison with other artefacts;
*   interpreting the authorship and cultural origins of a digitized illuminated manuscript;
*   monitoring deterioration by comparison with the earlier state of the real artefact;
*   analysing the substrata hidden by the final layers of paint in an old master;
*   analysing a statue's composition and structure and the processes used in creating it;
*   understanding the use of colour in the context of historic lighting conditions.

---

1 Reproduced from A.C. Addison, 'Beyond Digital Recording: A Shared Portal to the World's Heritage', paper presented at the International Workshop on Recording, Modeling and Visualization of Cultural Heritage, Ascona, Switzerland, 22–27 May 2005; first published in 'The Vanishing Virtual', in T. Kvan and Y. Kalay (eds), *New Heritage: Beyond Verisimilitude, Conference on Cultural Heritage and New Media* (Faculty of Architecture, University of Hong Kong, 2006), pp. 36–48; also published in F. Niccolucci (ed.), *Digital Applications for Tangible Cultural Heritage*, volume 2: *Report on the State of the Union Policies: Practices and Developments in Europe* (Budapest: Archaeolinga, 2007), pp. 15–26.

This is an illustrative rather than an exhaustive set. All of these applications have been attempted using a digital representation of artefacts. The characteristics of their analysis are different in each case. Some of the 'applications' are still speculative, or only implemented in demonstrations and case studies. The experience of their creation suggests that there is an asymmetric relationship between data collection and analysis. Where considerations of data usability have been properly considered, rather different conclusions emerge about the set of characteristics that need to be included in the digital artefact. The first consideration is obvious, but it is all too often naively overlooked. Any analysis is supported by data which is recorded. If it has not been recorded, analysis cannot follow. This is a statement of the obvious, but is surprisingly often overlooked, especially if the individual conducting the analysis does not understand the computational processes involved.

How can we best generalize about the considerations which practitioners need to bear in mind when approaching these issues of documentation and analysis? It is clearly important for application to undertake a good analysis of its own individual data requirements. But the following is presented as a characterization of the essential sub-areas about which decisions are required – a checklist (as it were) of issues which need to have been addressed in any such analysis:

1. Shape, size and position

In considering these issues, accuracy of recording is the most obvious domain on which an initial set of decisions has to be made. Interpolation can, of course, be used subsequently to enhance apparent accuracy at a later stage. But artefacts may have worn or been damaged over time, and interpolation makes assumptions about the continuity of data. So interpolation techniques are potentially suspect as a way of enhancing datasets of cultural artefacts if accurate representation is a key objective. A less obvious consideration is the dimensionality of the data recorded. Should one record the 3D surface of an oil painting, for example, including thickness of paint? How are such surfaces recorded or derived? There are many mathematical techniques used for defining surfaces and fitting them to a set of points. Devices have been proposed which combine point sampling with surface estimation in real time. They then verify the surface estimates in critical areas by taking additional samples. If there is a high degree of confidence in the mathematical accuracy of the surface definitions then we can have more confidence when intermediate data points are calculated. Wherever position is recorded, and by whatever method (including manual methods), the issue of accuracy remains paramount. But there are many ways of expressing accuracy. Many elements determine whether data is accurate or not. Some factors are characteristic of the recording equipment. The equipment's performance may be influenced by the circumstances of data recording (extremes of temperature, light levels, etc.). As technology improves there are increasingly conscious decisions to be made about the degrees of accuracy at which it is useful to record the artefact. Sample spacing is another aspect of accuracy – accurately recorded point samples across a surface will only generate an accurate surface if the density of sampling is sufficiently high. For many artefacts accuracy is measured in terms of the context of the object – the degree of its contiguousness to other objects. Recording such contexts brings another set of potential technologies into play, particularly if context is to be recorded on a geographic scale (for example, GPS and its variants). Considering how to record the shape, size and position of cultural objects is clearly crucial to their digitization; but it is easy to overlook the complexity of the issues that need consideration.

2. Colour and light properties

Colour, and colour perception, is a science in its own right. Many factors influence the perception of colour and recording base colours has been a challenge underestimated by virtually every amateur photographer since colour film was invented. Distinctions in the usefulness of colour information relate to the way data is collected – primarily the degree of care taken to relate colour to base colours by taking into account lighting conditions. This may involve recording colour under controlled conditions – for example using a light studio to record light properties of an artefact.[2] But this is only possible where either the artefact can be moved, or the normal position is in an internal space where light can be controlled. The other approach normally adopted is to record reference-colour information under the same lighting conditions. Other factors which may influence the recording of colour include some or all of the following:

- natural light behaviour; such as shadows and reflection;
- materials, such as translucency and colour bleeding;
- environmental, such as bright sunshine or wet materials;
- artificial light sources – recording under different illumination spectra (or multiple spectra).[3]

The careful use of reference colour charts in the recording process can alleviate some of these issues, but others still remain. The extreme example is probably the difficulties encountered in modelling jewellery. Colour information is, of course, unusable without a proper recording of the relationship between colour information and positional data.

3. Internal structure of an object

Applications monitoring the conditions of an artefact require some recording of the appropriate physical characteristics and comparison over time. Positional and colour information will inform some analyses, but in other circumstances, for example when recording data on internal flaws in a jewel, structural information will be required.

---

2 T. Hawkins, J. Cohen and P. Debevec. 'A Photometric Approach to Digitizing Cultural Artifacts', in *2nd International Symposium on Virtual Reality, Archaeology, and Cultural Heritage (VAST)* (Glyfada; 2001) <http://www.debevec.org/Research/LS2/hawkins_debevec_VAST2001.pdf>, accessed 20 September 2007.

3 See various papers given at the International Workshop on Recording, Modeling and Visualization of Cultural Heritage, 22–27 May 2005, Centro Stefano Franscini, Monte Verità, Ascona.

For other analyses different internal structural data may be needed: for example, information on the sub-structure of a painting may be used to understand the artist's creative process or detect earlier, now covered, works.

4. Other material properties

The list of other properties that might need recording is as long as the list of applications but density and weight, chemical composition, moisture content and structural characteristics are some examples. Some of these will be carried out with samples of like materials since the process of determining their characteristics may be destructive.

5. Informational content of the artefact.

The physical characteristics of a digital artefact are important but only a small part of the significance of an object. The first additional information to be considered is the informational content of the artefact itself. The most obvious example of this might be an illustrated manuscript – both work of art and an object containing explicit information. Other examples might be the component images in a picture or scenes in a film (ignoring for a moment the film's soundtrack). A classic example of this is the film shot in Norwich by planners seeking to identify areas for development of traffic systems in the 1950s – the film's content shows most of the streets of central Norwich, illustrating snippets of everyday life in the city and a fascinatingly rich source of information on the architectural state and physical condition of the city, frozen at a known 'point' in time.

Depending on the applications of the digital artefact this informational content may be more important than the digitized physical representation. At one end of the spectrum a printed book is a cultural artefact but an individual copy in digital form (for example, of the first edition) may have fewer applications than a representation of its linguistic content independent of appearance.

Dissemination to the public

Public dissemination needs to be based on the appropriate underlying historic information, so the considerations identified in the previous section on the nature of informational content remain relevant. The issues here are more to do with the delivery mechanisms and the implications for the version of an artefact to be delivered. Here the decisions on data collection may be driven by different considerations. Some may be taken (and often regretted) at data collection time; others will be driven by imperatives about how to derive suitable internet objects from data collected for more scholastic and curatorial purposes. For example, a museum might decide to digitize artefacts for use as part of a web presence, and increasingly there are systems showing 3D artefacts on the web. The complexities of delivering these objects to the client's browser have evolved enormously over the last few years and technology is moving fast in this area. Issues such as the size of data files, model representation and associated software for displaying the models, bandwidth assumed in delivery, watermarking and copyright protection technologies will influence the content of the online collection. However for the purposes of this paper we will assume that these decisions can be subsumed as subsets under the variations presented in the previous section, coupled with a different set of decisions about how to abstract suitable representations for use in public communication from the datasets generated as part of the assembly of a digital collection. These depend on whether it is a question of 'tangible' or 'intangible' heritage that is to be disseminated, and what metadata standards are adopted.

'Tangible' v. 'intangible' heritage

Artefacts of historic or cultural significance have knowledge and information associated with them that complete the picture of their significance. Of themselves, they may be impoverished without that additional context of the knowledge of their production, use, history, ownership, etc. Some of this will be known fact, some deduction, and some will be cultural interpretation. Many culturally significant artefacts have religious or nationalistic contexts, each of which may produce valid culturally based interpretations. All of these may be correct and significant but they may be conflicting. The contextual information can be regarded as an inextricable part of the artefact, and as such the artefact itself becomes uncertain. The cultural components of such information may be delineated as 'intangible heritage'.

In addition, there are cultural artefacts which are intrinsically intangible heritage – stories, music, performance, dance are all examples. In some cases there will be physical artefacts associated with the intangible heritage – manuscripts, etc. In other cases, associated with myths for example, there may be tangible heritage which is, in fact, interpretation of the intangible. The line between tangible and intangible is inexorably blurred, and inevitably, even where artefacts are considered purely tangible, linkage to other, non-tangible, information becomes a requirement. However, the essential characteristic of intangible heritage is that there is a degree of uncertainty because interpretation has been used which will be to a greater or lesser extent subjective. This linkage to other data is just one example of the metadata which is required for many aspects of digital artefacts.

Metadata

Metadata may be defined as 'data about data'. There have been significant efforts to define metadata formats for cultural heritage. Some of these are formal standards (for example, CIDOC-CRM); others (for example, the London Charter) are emerging principles which can be reflected in formal standards.[4] In the present context this metadata exists at a number of levels:

1. Data concerned with the provenance of an individual artefact. This includes the producer; the methods of capture; the conditions at the time of capture;

---

4 See ch. 14, below.

information on the settings used for equipment; perhaps on the algorithms used (for example, for stitching partial scans), etc. There may also be items of legal interest connected to the artefact (owner, copyright status, fee for re-use etc.). See for example Addison, 2006, reproduced here in Table 13.1 which shows the proposed metadata fields to be associated with virtual heritage.

2. External links may be needed to data which is part of the same collection (for example, data about a collection, linked data recorded at the same time, in the same season, by the same collector).

3. Metadata about the provenance of hierarchical artefacts. For example, a city reconstruction may use information on fragments of masonry collected at one time; on the archaeological records; on materials' properties; on artefacts collected from this and other sites; on typical design styles from the period; etc. Each subsection of the reconstruction may have different creators, and these may be different from the authors of the stories about its environment.

4. Relationship to data collected elsewhere, which might include previously recorded data about the same item; structural properties reflecting an analysis of comparable material samples; a discussion of the evidence behind the analysis of historic lighting materials, flame properties; etc.

Important considerations for those creating and using digital artefacts

Given the proliferation of digital artefact creation and utilization, it is worth offering a checklist of three fundamental issues which need to be decided before making a start:

1. Which underlying format of 3D models is best suited to the application?

A 3D model is a collection of all the geometric and visual data listed above (under 'documentation and analysis'). The issue of model representation is particularly significant because a model in one representation will not necessarily be simple to convert to a different format. The most obvious example of this is the contrast between image-based modelling and rendering, and models represented by their geometric boundary mapped with colour textures. Boundary representations of artefacts have been used extensively to describe a 3D object as a collection of surfaces and their properties. Such models have origins in other fields – notably Computer Aided Design (CAD), where they are used to describe an object in terms suitable for manufacturing it. Two classes of approach are now used to create such models – modelling using some sort of modelling package and capture from range scans. Between these two approaches lie systems which seek to generate models from images.

Generating realistic images of objects represented in these sorts of format has been a challenge for at least the last forty years. Methods which take into account (progressively) hidden surfaces, diffuse colour, shadows, specular reflection, participating media (smoke, etc.), radiosity, and so on have gradually improved the images of artificial objects, but as yet have not quite captured a truly life-like sense of their actual appearance. More recently the technique of image-based modelling and rendering has been developed and used with cultural artefacts in some live applications. So, at the National Palace Museum, Taiwan, high-quality digital artefacts arc displaycd alongside their physical counterparts in order to show details that could not otherwise be viewed by the museum visitor.[5] One example is a carved olive stone the carving details of which could only otherwise be shown in the museum by placing a large magnifying glass next to the artefact in its display case. Another artefact consists of 21 concentric spheres carved from a single piece of ivory; an image-based model is available in which each layer of the carving can be peeled away to show the underlying one.

Image-based modelling is undertaken very differently. The models are captured by photographing the object from 'all' directions, lit by known source or sources. This generates a potentially large number of images from marginally different directions and intermediate views are then created by interpolating between the images. In the basic method the boundary representation of an object is not derived (although for some objects – and this is only possible in certain instances – image-processing techniques can be used to generate the model.

Philosophically, the starting point for boundary-representation modelling is different from that of image-based modelling. For the former, the initial target is structural and geometrical accuracy, 'decorated' with colour information, then finally computing a life-like image by understanding how light would behave in the modelled environment. In contrast, for image-based modelling the original objective is to produce images that are truly 'life-like'. The starting point here, therefore, is to record the actual images and then to try to compute more information about the underlying geometry that must be present for the images to have been generated.

Determining the type of 3D object to be represented also involves making decisions about the need (or not) to capture the object's internal structure. This might require additional consideration of a number of issues, each of which generates further potential layers of metadata on top of those that we have already considered:

1. Whether surface textures are sufficiently distinct to represent the object visually or whether volumetric information is needed in order to be able to show characteristics such as translucency.
2. Other information which could be held as surfaces but which are connected to internal structure rather than surface geometry (e.g. the underlying structure of cracks).

2. What metadata format(s) and encodings should be adopted?

Given the costs of developing collections of digital artefacts, and the need for the results to remain usable over the long term, it is important to consider both the logical and physical formats in which the artefacts will be documented and stored. Much of

---

5 See the museum's website at <http://www.npm.gov.tw/index.htm>, accessed September 2007. The examples cited in the text are not, in fact, currently available online through the website, but they can be viewed in situ at the museum.

the tasks of planning long-term archives of digital objects has been undertaken from the perspectives of the digital libraries community. The management of collections of 3D cultural heritage objects is at an earlier stage and there remains significant debate about whether the approaches adopted for digital libraries are in fact suitable for the related, but different, domain of cultural artefacts.

In the digital libraries area, the Dublin Core Metadata Initiative (DCMI) has been strongly influential. This is an 'open forum engaged in the development of interoperable online metadata standards that support a broad range of purposes and business models'.[6] The Metadata Encoding and Transmission Standard (METS) is strongly linked to this Dublin Core framework and has been developed as an initiative of the Digital Library Federation.[7] The Dublin Core approaches are increasingly moving towards the museums area and are the adopted basis for the work of the MICHAEL project, which began in 2004 involving the development of a multi-lingual portal for sharing information on museum collections in the UK, France and Italy. It has recently been extended to incorporate another nine European countries.[8]

In parallel with these developments, and starting from the perspective of the documenting of historic, cultural heritage artefacts in museums, the CIDOC-CRM initiative has recently reached ISO standard.[9] It establishes guidelines for the exchange of information between cultural heritage institutions. In simple terms this can be defined as the curated knowledge of museums. The work is based on the work of ICOM – the International Council of Museums. This approach has been adopted by a number of other projects and is the basis of the ontological work included in the EPOCH Common Infrastructure.[10] It is to be hoped that the evolution of these initiatives will harmonize their approaches at least to the extent of ensuring interoperability. As a first step towards such harmonization, it is worth noting that it is expected to be possible to map the concepts included in the UNESCO world heritage site's proposed provenances for digital models into these other formats.

3. How do we ensure long-term archive preservation and access to digital objects?

The concerns for any potential creator or adopter of digital cultural artefacts here must cover the ability to guarantee their long-term curation, their physical security,

---

6 See glossary.

7 See glossary.

8 The Multilingual Inventory of Cultural Heritage in Europe (MICHAEL). The project website is at <http://www.michael-culture.org/>, accessed September 2007. See R. Caffo, 'MICHAEL Project: Towards a Trans-European Portal of Culture', in V. Cappellini and J. Hemsley (eds), *Electronic Imaging & the Visual Arts, EVA 2006 Florence Conference Proceeding* (Bologna: Pitagora Editrice , 2006), pp. 48–50.

9 [ISO, 2006] ISO FDIS 21127 (Information and documentation). It is formally described as a 'reference ontology for the interchange of cultural heritage information' – see <http://www.iso.org/iso/en/CatalogueDetailPage.CatalogueDetail?CSNUMBER=34424&scopelist=PROGRAMME>, accessed September 2007.

10 The European Research Network of Excellence in Open Cultural Heritage (EPOCH) – <http://www.epoch-net.org/>, accessed September 2007.

and their functioning accessibility in the long term. Part of the answer to these will be the developments of standardized metadata. However, two other aspects are worth noting. Firstly, the physical media of the computer age have a tendency to become obsolete in very short time-frames. CD materials are widely quoted as having a reliable shelf-life of around 15 years – substantially less than the lifetime of most of the artefacts we are trying to record digitally. A sound policy of moving onto new storage media is therefore an essential part of the process of using digital artefacts and unfortunately computer scientists are notoriously deficient here. Secondly, long-term access must also rely on being able to identify the digital model. This identification must also be linked to the copyright, IPR and licensing processes. Two initiatives have been started in the area of the long-term identification of digital objects – the Digital Object Identifier (a standard maintained by ISO) and the Persistent Identifier (a standard formulated and maintained by the DSMI working group) – the former being the one that is under active current development.[11]

Re-purposing cultural artefact data

Having built a digital object there is an obvious and appropriate desire to re-use the effort invested in any appropriate context. This will inevitably mean that its use will extend to applications that were not envisaged at the time the data was collected. Two challenges are commonly faced. The easier of these is when the application that has been created cannot cope with the detail and volume of data that has been digitized. This is the common situation, especially when artefacts digitized for scholastic documentation are to be used in web applications, including online publication. Here there are many approaches which reflect development work by computer scientists over many years. Almost every year there are new papers on mesh simplification at the annual SIGGRAPH conference.[12] Cultural heritage professionals would not normally expect to be working on these details, but they need to understand the nature of the data manipulations being undertaken. Some methods are irreversible, so once the data has been simplified it will remain in that form in the new environment, and reconstitution may distort the original. This is of course only the case if the original artefact has not been properly archived or is not available for other (for example, legal) reasons. This has the effect of making the simplified model both misrepresent the original and protect it against unscrupulous exploitation. There are rather different processes that are designed to compress data in various formats for transmission over networks. These methods were typically used when the internet bandwidth was not fast enough to send the full dataset in its original format. Methods can be either 'loss-less' or 'lossy': after compression at one end of the transmission, the subsequent reconstitution either reinstates the original exactly ('loss-less), or does something 'good enough' for the application in question ('lossy').

---

11 See glossary.
12 See glossary.

The second case of repurposing data is where the initial dataset needs to be repurposed with additional information added. This might occur, for example, because the accuracy of digitization was unsuitable for the higher-performance printers and displays that have since become available. In this case, smoother images may be produced by interpolation of the original data, but this data is almost inevitably an invention that cannot be more accurate than the original data, although it gives the impression of higher-quality images. A related issue here is where the original digital artefacts are to be used in an application which attempts to reconstruct their 'original' state. Examples here would be reconstituting a pot from existing sherds, or rebuilding a castle digitally from the records of the ruins. In these applications we are some way from having the intelligent tools to assist cultural heritage professionals with their reconstruction. Most commonly these applications are undertaken using general-purpose modellers (such as Maya or 3D Studio Max) and the reconstructions are effectively created by hand.

In the longer term we need modelling tools that use the evidence of the recorded artefacts and act as intelligent assistants. For example, in the case of pottery reconstruction, an assistant who understood the likely styles and the generic properties of pots of a similar age might be able to guide the modeller with suggestions as to which piece fits most appropriately where. There have been experiments with this kind of tool but they have not extended beyond the equivalent for architectural styles. In addition, the potential for coupling multiple sources (for example, archaeological evidence, historic maps and photographs or paintings) has yet to be satisfactorily harnessed.

Conclusions

We have seen many different aspects of the creation and use of digital artefacts. It is inevitable that such artefacts will find their place in the range of techniques for historical documentation and analysis over time. We are in a potentially dangerous situation at present, in which the tools are immature but there are many potential benefits in the short term of taking up the challenge. These benefits address both scholarly research and dissemination to the public, capitalizing on the public's undoubted interest in the past. During this phase it is very important for cultural heritage professionals to continue the long traditions of curatorship and caution, but their participation in the search for appropriate tools and processes is also essential if the technologies are to evolve to achieve their potential. In the meantime the pioneers in the use of digital artefacts in historic research need to remain aware of the limitations of current technologies and the restrictions on their applicability.

Table 13.1   Proposed Virtual Heritage Metadata ('World Heritage Metadata Structure')

Type	o.	Data Encoding/Format
What	i.	HeritageID (a superset of existing WorldHeritageID)
	ii.	Title/brief description
	iii.	Heritage type/classification (e.g. cultural: archaeological ...)
	iv.	Heritage time period (e.g. geologic or historic time)
Why	v.	Purpose (why recorded/produced)
How	vi.	Recording device parameters (type, sample rate, precision ...)
	vii.	Secondary device(s) (data manipulation)
Whom	viii.	Submitter and date of submission
	ix.	Environmental conditions
	x.	Rights given/withheld
	xi.	Author/copyright holder
	xii.	Sponsor/funder/client
Date	xiii.	Date (of recording, manipulation)
Where	xiv.	Location (latitude/longitude and compass direction if applicable)

Source: Reproduced from A.C. Addison, 'Beyond Digital Recording: A Shared Portal to the World's Heritage', paper presented at the International Workshop on Recording, Modeling and Visualization of Cultural Heritage, Ascona, Switzerland, 22–27 May 2005; first published in A.C. Addison, 'The Vanishing Virtual', in T. Kvan and Y. Kalay (eds), *New Heritage: Beyond Verisimilitude, Conference on Cultural Heritage and New Media* (Faculty of Architecture, University of Hong Kong, 2006), pp. 36–48.

Chapter 14

'Oh, to make boards to speak! There is a task!' Towards a Poetics of Paradata

Richard Beacham

One of the major challenges that the digital age, and in particular the advent of 3D modelling, has thrust upon us, is the reconciliation of what we see with what we know, or believe we know. Or, as it is frequently expressed these days: How do we think with things; how do we get them to talk to us? How do we communicate the meanings of visualizations that we have not yet ourselves learned fully how to 'read'? Of course, the art of the theatre has, almost from its inception, exemplified a related issue, since of the various expressive media it employs (images, movement, space, sound, time, enacted actions) language is only one, and indeed not always the most prominent or 'communicative'. That is one of the reasons why in the work of the Visualisation Lab (formerly at Warwick, now at King's London) the research and 3D modelling of historic theatre spaces and stage settings has always intrigued and challenged us. Here the medium of visualization is attempting to communicate understanding about another quintessentially 'visual' medium.

As it happens, the theatre too faced problems at a crucial point in its history not unlike those which continue to confront us in our own medium: the relationship between images and meanings, and the vexed question of the 'role' and status of language and words in communicating those visually embodied meanings. In the case of our own British theatre, a crisis of sorts was reached early in the seventeenth century, and was embodied in the two collaborators turned fierce antagonists: the playwright Ben Jonson, and the architect and scenic artist Inigo Jones. Jones was introducing through the medium of the Stuart Masque the first perspective stage settings in Britain. Perspective is another major challenge to the systems of visualization which we render onto out computer screens, and Jones wrought it onto his experimental picture-frame stages at Whitehall Palace, to delight and amaze his regal audience, while antagonizing and demoralizing Ben Jonson, who vainly (in both senses) championed the primacy of the Word. It all reached a crisis in 1611 when Jonson wrote a scathing poem, castigating both the medium and its master, that maker of 'shows, shows, mighty shows, the Eloquence of Masques! What need of prose / Or Verse, or Sense to express Immortall you?'

By contrast, in a curiously modern-sounding formulation, Jones himself described his own revolutionary scenic creations as 'nothing else but pictures with light and motion' (*Tempe Restored*, 1632). And indeed, Jonson himself, observing one of Jones's 'virtual models' described the production in words that might almost encapsulate the challenge we latter-day modellers ('trying to keep up with the Joneses ...') face when trying to capture virtually, the fleeing, now-vanished objects of our investigations: 'only the envy was that it lasted not still, or, now it is past, cannot by imagination much less description, be recovered to a part of that spirit it had in the gliding by' (*Masque of Hymen*, 1606).

Our own address to the challenge takes the form not of a scathing satirical diatribe, but a more moderate (if less poetical) document, 'The London Charter'.

Starting points

The London Charter initiative seeks to establish what is required for 3D visualization to be, and to be seen to be, as intellectually rigorous and robust as any other research method. The initiative has to be seen in the context of what has become a constant burning issue in 3D visualization circles: 'transparency'. Transparency is crucial if 3D visualization is to 'mature' as a research method and acquire widespread acceptance within subject communities. In particular, it must be possible for those communities to evaluate the choice of a given visualization method, and how it has been applied in a particular case, without having to rely exclusively on the 'authority claims' of the author. A very significant amount of work has been done in this area, and there is now an extensive bibliography on this and related issues. There had been a number of previous initiatives in the field. They included:

- the establishment of the CAA Virtual Archaeology Special Interest Group (VASIG), which first met in Sweden in 2001;[1]
- the founding of the Cultural Virtual Reality Organization (CVRO) launched at the Virginia Association of Science Teachers (VAST) in November 2000 (and which now appears to be inactive);
- the publication of the AHDS Guide on creating and using virtual reality;[2]
- the publication of the AHDS 'CAD' guide.[3]

In July 2005, the Visualisation Lab at King's College London began a project called 'Making Space'. Its objective was to investigate 'a methodology for tracking and documenting the cognitive process in 3D visualisation-based research', funded by the ICT Strategy Projects scheme of the AHRC. Drew Baker proposed the term 'paradata' to denote the intellectual capital generated during research, and highlighted that a great deal of the information essential for the understanding and evaluation of 3D visualization methods and outcomes is currently being lost. The project subsequently

---

    1   The Computer Methods and Quantitative Methods in Archaeology website is at <http://caa.leidenuniv.nl/>, accessed 20 September 2007.

    2   K. Fernie and J. Richards (eds), *Creating and Using Virtual Reality* (Oxford: Oxbow, 2003).

    3   H. Eiteljorg II, K. Fernie, J. Huggett et al., *AHDS CAD Guide to Good Practice* (AHDS, 2002). Available online at <http://ads.ahds.ac.uk/project/goodguides/cad/>, accessed 20 September 2007.

convened a Symposium and Expert Seminar at the British Academy and the Centre for Computing in the Humanities at King's College London in February 2006.[4] Over a two-day symposium, fifty delegates debated various approaches to the issue of transparency and, on the third day, a smaller group of experts produced the first 'discussion document' phase of the draft London Charter. In the Spring of 2006, we then presented it at an EPOCH/EVA conference in Florence. It is now published and in the public domain, in the process of being formally adopted as good practice by several European countries, welcomed by UNESCO, and being shaped by the experience of those who have adopted it.[5]

The nature of the Charter

The Charter is inevitably indebted to previous work in this area, not least the recommendations of the CAD Guide. But it is not discipline-specific (i.e. not just for archaeologists). It is intended for the broad range of Arts, humanities and cultural heritage disciplines using 3D visualization for research and dissemination. It follows the format and style of the ICOMOS Ename Charter.[6] The latter is an international initiative by heritage organizations who were concerned to develop an international standard for the interpretation of heritage materials. Its first draft was formulated in 2002 and it was designed to ensure that the issues of authenticity, intellectual integrity, social responsibility and respect for the cultural significance and context of the artefacts in question were clearly defined. The ICOMOS Charter, now in its sixth draft, provides a ready-to-hand language for cultural heritage artefacts, which facilitates its ease of recognition within cultural heritage milieux. It adopts a wide definition of the term 'cultural heritage', viewing it as

> encompassing all domains of human activity which are concerned with the understanding
> of communication of material and intellectual culture. Such domains include, but are not
> limited to, museums, art galleries, heritage sites, interpretative centres, cultural heritage
> research institutes, arts and humanities subjects within higher education institutions, the
> broader educational sector, and tourism.

Aims of the London Charter

The objective is to establish the London Charter as an EU and international benchmark. The initiative does not aim to make radical new proposals. Rather, it seeks to consolidate the major principles which have been published by diverse authors, but not yet fully taken up by the community. That is why the idea of a 'charter' seemed appropriate. It is also why it is important that it should emerge from, and evolve through, discussions within the target communities.

---

4   The event was jointly sponsored by the AHRC ICT Methods Network and the EU Network of Excellence EPOCH (Excellence in Processing Open Cultural Heritage) <http://www.epoch-net.org/>, accessed 20 September 2007.

5   <http://www.londoncharter.org/>.

6   See <http://www.enamecharter.org/index.html>, accessed 20 September 2007.

We recognized at an early stage that a document that aspires to be a charter should address more than the single issue of transparency. Other issues were also identified: those which address the more fundamental imperatives underlying the 'presentational aspects' of transparency. Tackling these at the level of 'principle' rather than 'pragmatics' required us to think through the disciplinary contexts of the Charter, and resolve the issues concerning 'aims', 'methods' and 'sources' which are the subject of the first three 'principles' of the draft.

The first principle with which we were concerned was that of its disciplinary contexts. As the Symposium of February 2006 proceeded, it became increasingly clear to those present that, while we aspired to create a charter which would be 'valid across all domains in which 3D visualisation can be applied to cultural heritage', different subject areas nevertheless differed very greatly in their understandings of what research is, and therefore what research methods such as 3D visualization ought to achieve. This prescribed strict limits upon the level of detail that a cross-subject document can entertain. So the draft recommends that, while 'subject areas should ... adopt and build upon the principles established by this Charter' (para. 1) they should also 'develop more detailed principles, standards, recommendations and guidelines to ensure that use of 3D visualisation coheres with the aims, objectives and methods of their domain' (para. 1.1).

The second principle revolved around the need to ensure cohesion between aims and methods. The Charter recognizes that '3D visualisation methods and outcomes can be used to address a wide range of research and communication aims' (para. 2). But we also wanted to establish that it is only one method among many and that 'it should not be assumed that 3D visualisation is the most appropriate method of addressing *all* research or communication aims' (para. 2.1). This is to ensure that, in serious contexts, it is not used simply because it is available, or because it has a 'wow' factor. Instead, the draft proposes that '3D visualisation should not normally be used when other methods would be more appropriate or effective'. We also wanted to ensure that the full range of 3D visualization options should be considered and that no single approach (for example, 'photo-realism' or 'real-time navigation') should be considered a 'default' expectation, but rather that each visualization method 'should be carefully evaluated to identify which is the most likely to address each given aim' (para. 2.3).

The third principle makes a statement about the nature and integrity of sources. This arose, in particular, out of a presentation by Daniel Pletinckx in February 2006, in which he demonstrated how important it was to assess carefully the sources that we use when undertaking visualization, and to pay attention to aesthetic and ideological factors that condition our visual sources in particular. The draft proposes a definition of 'sources' as 'all information, digital and non-digital, considered during, or directly influencing, the creation of the 3D visualisation outcomes' (para. 3.1) and recommends that 'in order to ensure the intellectual integrity of 3D visualisation methods and outcomes, relevant sources should be identified and evaluated in a structured way'.

These, then, form the first three principles which underlie the 'transparency requirements' which are the focus of its fourth paragraph. Here, the draft recommends that 'sufficient information should be provided to allow 3D visualisation methods and outcomes to be understood and evaluated appropriately in relation to the contexts in which they are used and disseminated' (para. 4). This 'transparency requirements' section is, however, worth examining in further detail since it lies at the heart of the objectives of the Charter. It proposes that 'it should be made clear what kind and status of information the 3D visualisation represents. The nature and degree of factual uncertainty of an hypothetical reconstruction, for instance, should be communicated' (para. 4.1). It also recognizes (para 4.2) that

> the type and quantity of transparency information will vary depending on the aims and type of 3D visualisation method and outcome being used, as well as the type and level of knowledge, understanding and expectations of its anticipated users. Transparency information requirements may therefore differ from project to project, or at different phases within a project.

The transparency requirements of 3D visualization projects may differ from those of other projects because of 'the high occurrence of dependency relations within 3D models', which means that, if the process and its outcomes are to be evaluated by those outside the project, 'it may be necessary to disseminate documentation of the interpretative decisions made in the course of a 3D visualisation process' (para. 4.5). A dependency relationship is defined as a dependent relationship between the properties of elements within 3D models such that a change in one property will necessitate change in the dependent properties. So, for instance, a change in the height of a door will necessitate a corresponding change in the height of the door-frame. A further point that emerged from the February 2006 Symposium was that 'the level of documentation required regarding 3D visualisation when used as a research method will vary depending on how widely and well that method is understood within the relevant communities; novel methods will require more explanation' (para. 4.6).

There then follow some corollaries, which currently form the subject of Principles 5 to 8, viz.

5. Documentation

'The process and outcomes of 3D visualisation creation should be sufficiently documented to enable the creation of accurate transparency records, potential reuse of the research conducted and its outcomes in new contexts, enhanced resource discovery and accessibility, and to promote understanding beyond the original subject community.'

6. Standards

This is the least-developed section of the draft Charter. It was felt that, as a cross-subject and long-term document, the Charter was not the place to espouse a particular standard (such as CIDOC-CRM). It was also recognized that we will only be able to begin to develop appropriate ontologies and choose appropriate standards as we improve our understanding of what it is we are doing when we use 3D visualization methods and outcomes, and how we are doing it, and that this would require further research. Consequently, the first draft simply proposes that 'appropriate standards and ontologies should be identified, at subject community level, systematically to document 3D visualisation methods and outcomes to be documented, to enable optimum inter- and intra-subject and domain interoperability and comparability'.

7. Sustainability

The draft notes that '3D visualisation outcomes pertaining to cultural heritage ... constitute, in themselves, a growing part of our intellectual, social, economic and cultural heritage' and that 'if this heritage is not to be squandered, strategies to ensure its long-term sustainability should be planned and implemented'. It also points out that 'a partial, 2-dimensional record of a 3D visualisation output should be preferred to an absence of record'. The specific recommendations contained in the draft are a first draft, and bound to be debated further.

8. Accessibility

It is evident that we have to continue to make the case for technologically expensive work in the arts and humanities – to explain its value and value for money. It is the case that the majority of research in cultural heritage (broadly defined) is publicly funded. Many 3D visualization outputs have, however, the potential to be 're-purposed'. So it is incumbent upon us to consider whether our work might have a value beyond our own immediate uses. Hence Principle 8 states that 'consideration should be given to the ways in which the outcomes of 3D visualisation work could contribute to the wider study, understanding, interpretation and management of cultural heritage assets'. 3D visualization clearly has important roles to play in 'enhancing access to cultural heritage [that is] not otherwise accessible for health and safety, disability, economic, political, or environmental reasons, or because the object of the visualisation is lost, endangered, dispersed, or has been restored or reconstructed' (para. 8.2).

There is also a 'soft' political as well as an idealistic dimension to the sections that seek to establish that '3D visualisation permits types and degrees of access not otherwise possible, including the study of change over time, magnification, modification, virtual object manipulation, multi-layered embedded data and information, instantaneous global distribution, with consequent expanded curatorial possibilities' (para. 8.3). But there may also be potential *economic* benefits to both the research/education and tourism/interpretation sectors from increased communication and collaboration with each other, which are good enough reasons, perhaps, to include them in the Charter.

Guide documents

The Charter is designed to establish 'principles' which are focused, such that they have an impact, but sufficiently 'abstract' that its principles remain current as methods and technologies evolve. Therefore, although more specific recommendations (for example, about technologies, standards, methodologies, etc.) are necessary, they belong in a different kind of document and, in particular, subject-specific Guides. The importance of subject perspective is enshrined as a principle in the Charter (para 1.1):

> Specialist subject communities will need to develop more detailed principles, standards, recommendations and guidelines to ensure that use of 3D visualisation coheres with the aims, objectives and methods of their domain.

Subject Guides might help, for example, to develop consensus around:

- visual conventions;
- technical approaches for different methods.

We want to try to allow the Charter initiative to provide the impetus for a series of such Guides, to be developed within different subject areas, and a series of case studies designed to test the implementation of compliance with the principles of the Charter. This case study process has already begun. A number of case studies are already under way to investigate what kinds of paradata could/should be recorded (and how) for 3D visualization projects. It has been suggested that in order to do this we may first need systematically to observe how we reflect upon, choose and communicate 'traditional' research methods. This would help us to build up a profile of what kinds of methodological and processual information is considered necessary to document other research methods, and to base our recommendations on comparability with established academic standards. In addition to benefiting from such examples, it could enable us to make persuasive arguments to 'traditional' scholars about the validity of 3D visualization methods in terms that they would more readily understand. It is envisaged that, like the ICOMOS Charter, the London Charter will be revised in response to consultation within the various subject communities for which it has direct relevance. It will thus become an instrument that will stimulate debate on key issues and, in its various versions, come to act as a de facto standard without over-elaborate institutional support.

Postscript: A meeting of the London Charter International Advisory Board took place at the end of November 2007 in Brighton. This meeting prepared for publication the authoritative Second Draft of the Charter, and put in place an action plan for seeking endorsement for the Charter internationally. A formal report of the meeting, detailing discussions, decisions and outcomes, is published on the London Charter website <http://www.londoncharter.org>, accessed 11 February 2008.

This work is being taken forward by Dr Hugh Denard, Associate Director of the King's College London Visualization Lab. Dr Denard contributed greatly to the development of material included in this chapter for which the author is most grateful.

Chapter 15

Electronic Corpora of Artefacts: The Example of the *Corpus of Romanesque Sculpture in Britain and Ireland*

Anna Bentkowska-Kafel

Corpus scholarship

Published, multi-volume corpora are commonplace in many academic disciplines. In visual culture studies, and the history of art in particular, some corpora have established such a trusted reputation that it is enough to refer to the *Corpus Rubenianum Ludwig Burchard*, the *Corpus van verluchte Handschriften* or the *Corpus Vitrearum Medii Aevi*, to give just a few examples, to call upon the highest standards of scholarship within the respective fields and subjects.[1] In the field of the historiography of medieval sculpture, notable examples of corpora include the *Corpus della scultura altomedievale* (1959–) which covers pre-Romanesque sculpture in Italy, organized by region; the *Corpus of Anglo-Saxon Stone Sculpture in England* (1984–); organized by county; and the *Corpus of Romanesque Sculpture in American Collections* (1979–), which covers large-scale sculpture in wood and stone from various sites in Western Europe. The latter, two-volume corpus includes

All URLs active at the time of writing, April 2006. Revised December, 2007. I wish to thank Tim Ayers, Ron Baxter, Sophie Church, Hazel Gardiner, Rima M. Greenland, Sandy Heslop, Tom Russo, Malcolm Thurlby and Rita Wood for their help in the preparation of this paper. The Minutes of the *CRSBI* Committee Meetings 1988–2006 have been an invaluable source of information about the project's early history and more recent developments. The permission granted by the *CRSBI* Committee to cite from the minutes is also gratefully acknowledged

1 *Corpus Rubenianum Ludwig Burchard*, an illustrated catalogue *raisonné* of the work of Peter Paul Rubens based on the material assembled by the late Dr Ludwig Burchard in 27 parts. The project is sponsored by the City of Antwerp and edited by the Nationaal Centrum voor de Plastische Kunsten in de XVIde en XVIIde Eeuw; various publishers, from 1968. *Corpus van verluchte Handschriften uit de Nederlanden* (a corpus of Netherlandish illuminated manuscripts) (Louvain: Uitgeverij Peeters, since 1985). The *Corpus Vitrearum Medii Aevi* <http://www.cvma.ac.uk> is an international research project dedicated to the publication of medieval stained glass. It was founded in 1949; 65 volumes have been published since 1979.

short description and at least one photograph per entry.[2] It is hoped that a comparable reputation will eventually be bestowed upon the *Corpus of Romanesque Sculpture in Britain and Ireland* (*CRSBI*) which shares similarities with the corpora just listed, and modifies the format to the digital environment.

The *CRSBI* is a British Academy research project hosted by the Courtauld Institute of Art in London.[3] It is an evolving electronic archive of stone sculpture from the period c.1066–c.1200. Over 5,000 sites featuring Romanesque sculpture have been identified, and some 6,000 predicted, of which some 70 per cent have been recorded by volunteer fieldworkers. Over 1,000 reports have been published online on the project website. The reports vary in scope and range from a description of a single object illustrated with a handful of images to a book-length entry for Ely Cathedral.

It was one of the earliest projects in the field to have not only envisaged computerization of its material but also to have made this objective its primary goal: it is believed that the project was the first British Academy research project to be conceived as a digital resource. At the very first meeting of the *CRSBI* Committee on 19 July 1988 it was agreed that the form of catalogue entries should be designed 'with *the criterion of suitability for the computer in mind*'; equally, that the glossary of terms should be compiled to suit this purpose (this would today be referred to as an authority list). The project was to develop a database for the use of fieldworkers, as well as published books: 'One aim was the production of a comprehensive archive in the form of a computerised database ... It was possible to envisage a range of different publications, from fully illustrated catalogues to annotated handlists.'[4] Digital outputs and methods were subsequently investigated throughout the course of the project. In 1991 the project's Committee 'recalled that the creation of a text/ image database was the project's first priority'.[5] Following a number of software trials initiated by Seamus Ross of the British Academy,[6] the possibility of making the *Corpus* accessible over the internet was investigated in the summer of 1995 (however, at that time the Courtauld Institute of Art, where the project had moved

---

2 *Corpus della scultura altomedievale* (Spoleto: Centro italiano di studi sull'alto Medioevo, 1959–); R. Cramp (ed.), *The Corpus of Anglo-Saxon Stone Sculpture in England*, published for the British Academy by Oxford University Press, 1984–; W. Cahn and L. Seidel (eds), *Romanesque Sculpture in American Collections* (New York: B. Franklin, Turnhout: Brepols, 1979 and c.1999).

3 *The Corpus of Romanesque Sculpture in Britain and Ireland* started in 1988. It has benefited from support and contributions from many institutions and individuals. See the project's website <http://www.crsbi.ac.uk> for information about the project history, progress, its funding bodies, staff and voluntary contributors.

4 The British Academy Corpus of Romanesque Sculpture in the British Isles, *Minutes of the First Meeting of the Committee*, 19 July 1988, p. 3.

5 The British Academy Corpus of Romanesque Sculpture in Britain and Ireland, *Minutes of the Meeting of the Committee*, 19 March 1991, p. 3.

6 For the early development of the system see S. Ross, 'Designing a Tool for Research in Disciplines Using Multimedia Data: The Romanesque Sculpture Processor', in F. Bocchi and P. Denley (eds), *Storia e multimedia*, proceedings of the Seventh International Congress of the Association for History and Computing (Bologna: Manchester University Press, 1994), pp. 629–35.

from the British Academy, had no internet access, as *CRSBI* records show).[7] The suggestion of 'storing text in a hypertext format *in anticipation of it becoming available on the Internet*' was put forward in November 1995.[8] Shortly after this the project began to benefit from collaboration on technical development with the Centre for Computing in the Humanities (CCH) at King's College London. A Microsoft Access relational database application was subsequently developed in conjunction with an XML model for *Corpus* site entries. The Access application was, and still is, the prime means of linking text and image data as well as functioning as an essential management tool for the project's editors. Since the launch of the project's website (<http://www.crsbi.ac.uk>) in 2001, the *Corpus* has published solely online (Plate 21). The project's website originally introduced the *Corpus* as 'the first fully searchable database of British and Irish Romanesque stone sculpture'. In April 2004 the wording was changed to read 'the first digital archive' of Romanesque sculpture, thus reflecting the semantic shift in the understanding of multi-functionality of electronic resources of this kind. The idea of books and other paper publications has been left at the discretion of individual contributors.

A corpus is, however, more than a publication format. A corpus implies not only completeness of the material it presents, but also an exhaustive and up-to-date presentation of scholarly interpretation of the subject.[9] Some of the corpora listed above have been referred to, understandably, but often incorrectly, as inventories. The American *Corpus* is introduced as a volume which 'inventories' the material preserved in American museums.[10] An inventory usually aims to provide an exhaustive listing of all items within a collection and to give their location; this makes old inventories of artefacts an invaluable source of information about, among other things, the social history of collecting, matters of patronage and artistic taste, as well as techniques and economics of art. However, an inventory provides, if at all, only a brief description of objects listed. It does not consider earlier research, and is rarely illustrated. As those who have tried to research an extinct collection through its historic inventories would confirm, descriptive limitations, both textual and visual, may make the study incomplete and unreliable.

In the preface to the first volume of the *Corpus of Anglo-Saxon Stone Sculpture*, published in 1984, George Zarnecki emphasized the need for 'a comprehensive catalogue, both descriptive and visual, of every surviving example of sculpture'.[11] From its inception in 1988, the aim of the *Corpus of Romanesque Sculpture in Britain and Ireland* has been the very same need to record *all* Romanesque stone sculpture executed between the middle of the eleventh and the end of the twelfth centuries that has

---

7 The Corpus of Romanesque Sculpture in Britain and Ireland, *Minutes of the Committee Meeting*, 17 May 1995, p. 4.

8 The Corpus of Romanesque Sculpture in Britain and Ireland, *Minutes of the Committee Meeting*, 6 November 1995, p. 3.

9 See the generic definition of 'corpus *n.* (3.)' in the *Oxford English Dictionary* (<http://dictionary.oed.com>): 'A body or complete collection of writings *or the like*; the whole body of literature on any subject.'

10 Cahn and Seidel (eds), *Romanesque Sculpture in American Collections*, p. vii.

11 Cramp (ed.), *Corpus of Anglo-Saxon Stone Sculpture*, vol. 1, *County Durham and Northumberland* (Oxford: Oxford University Press, 1984), p. 7.

survived in the British Isles and in Ireland. Romanesque sculpture in Britain constitutes a complex artistic phenomenon. English sculpture is characterized by a strong Normal influence from mainland Europe as well as a rich Anglo-Saxon local heritage. After 1120, distinctive formal features became common, such as the chevron (zigzag) ornament and beakheads, i.e. imaginary creatures that decorate arches of doorways and chancels (Plate 22). Figurative sculpture and narrative schemes are also a twelfth-century development. Romanesque sculpture decorated not only churches, but also secular buildings, such as keeps and castles. The Herefordshire and Northamptonshire schools are renowned for the exquisite quality of their sculpture. Subject to different influences and under generally less affluent patronage, Irish, Scottish and Welsh sculpture developed in a different manner, and some forms persisted longer than in England. The dissolution of the monasteries by Henry VIII, and the Civil War resulted in irreparable damage to this medieval heritage.

Some 5,000 sites, predominantly churches, featuring Romanesque sculpture have been identified; another 1,000 are predicted. Romanesque sculpture remains *in situ* either in its original setting or reused as part of later features. It can also be found *ex situ*, moved to new locations, in churches and cemeteries, as well as museums and private houses. The definitive number of sites is difficult to determine; it fluctuates as the recording progresses. Previously unknown sculpture has been discovered, recorded and photographed by the project fieldworkers for the first time. Individual pieces have been found in the most unusual locations, sometimes put to a new use, for example as a garden feature or other ornament. Sculpture, especially that sited externally, is exposed to weathering, pollution and other damage. Sadly, on occasion it is vandalized. The church of All Saints in Buncton, Sussex is an example (November 2004).[12] The figure of the so-called Sheela Na Gig, or a female 'exhibitionist' on the north impost of the chancel arch had been recorded in March 1997, prior to the damage, by the project investigator, Kathryn A. Morrison (Plate 23). The *CRSBI* is playing an important role, through its routine fieldwork, in drawing attention to the significance of the Romanesque heritage, as well as through direct actions that had been undertaken on a number of occasions to alert the custodians of sculpture and the general public alike to the issues in its conservation and preservation. The project raises awareness and enables knowledge of this medieval heritage not only through fieldwork, but also through research activities, professional and private contacts and in particular through the project website which supports an ever-growing network of users.[13] For its community of users, the *Corpus* is a reliable and informative source for medieval sculpture. This group views the resource not as a surrogate for real sculpture (as frequent criticism of digital resources has it) but as an incentive to visit its sites, and as a means of monitoring any deterioration of the original materials, thus supporting conservation.

---

12 See <http://www.crsbi.ac.uk/crsbi/frsxsites.html>; J. Harding: The Sheela-Na-Gig Project, <http://www.sheelanagig.org/index.htm>, http://www.sheelanagig.org/ SheelaBuncton.htm>.

13 The site meter installed on the *CRSBI* website in November 2004 provides statistics which indicate that those using the website for two or more hours per visit come mainly from academic institutions. The website has on average 200 visitors per week.

Interdisciplinary corpus scholarship

The defining impact that the *CRSBI* is likely to have on what has been termed 'corpus scholarship' is interdisciplinary. In recent decades, corpus scholarship has been informed by methodological and theoretical developments in linguistics. In linguistics, corpora 'were originally engaged mostly in providing detailed descriptions of linguistic phenomena, and corpus-based computations were primarily concerned with practical applications'; this was 'coupled with ... commitment to ... systematic and exhaustive analysis'.[14] The situation is now changing with emphasis moving from annotation and analysis – still crucial in the preparation of a corpus – to the development of generic mechanisms and ontologies for the representation of information.[15] The scholarly debate on the current shift in old paradigms is complex and seems unnecessarily divisive. For the sake of simplicity, in this chapter corpus scholarship in the context of the *CRSBI* is defined traditionally: that is, as the process of describing and analysing a complex body of primary evidence in order to facilitate the interpretation of an individual object or phenomenon (be it a piece of sculpture, a site, an artistic school, geological material, etc.). '[A]ny individual example is best seen and understood as one of a series', commented Zarnecki on the typology adopted by the Anglo-Saxon Corpus in 1984.[16] Some twenty years later and with a notable change in language, Fred Orton described the same Corpus as the 'enabling of knowledge in so far as it permitted the visibility of an object to pass into discourse'. Orton was also critical of the way in which 'the process of "seeing and describing" in the *Corpus* is overtly concerned with recognition of similarities', distracting from rather than encouraging the understanding of what he termed 'the insides' of objects.[17] Despite this and other criticism, the 'compare and contrast' approach remains at the core of stylistic, iconographic and many other studies. Until recently museum displays tended to be governed by juxtaposition;[18] it remains common to the casual appreciation of artefacts. After all, 'we see – comparatively' as Emily Dickinson suggests.[19]

---

14 Introductory notes to the journal *Corpus Linguistics and Linguistic Theory*, Mouton de Gruyter, vol. 1, 2005.

15 For an overview see N. Ide, 'Preparation and Analysis of Linguistic Corpora', in S. Schreibman, R. Siemens and J. Unsworth (eds), *A Companion to Digital Humanities* (Oxford: Blackwell Publishing, 2004), pp. 289–305.

16 Cramp (ed.), *Corpus of Anglo-Saxon Stone Sculpture*, vol. 1, *County Durham and Northumberland* (Oxford: Oxford University Press, 1984), p. 7.

17 See Bailey's response to Orton's criticism in C.E. Karkov and F. Orton (eds), *Theorizing Anglo-Saxon Stone Sculpture*, Medieval European Studies IV (Morgantown: West Virginia University Press, 2003), p. 94f.

18 Nicholas Serota identified the recent shift championed by museums of modern art, as a departure from 'the traditional museum disciplines of juxtaposition, analysis and interpretation [that are being] reduced to the minimum; experience [becoming] paramount'. See his *Experience or Interpretation, the Dilemma of Museums of Modern Art* (Thames and Hudson, 1996), p. 17.

19 See the poem '*We see – comparatively*' by Emily Dickinson, <http://www.repeatafterus. com/print.php?i=1104>.

The use of digital tools borrowed from corpus-based linguistics and other disciplines is not without impact on the traditional typologies widely used by mainstream scholarship in the history of art. Art studies relied on classifications even before the academic history of the discipline. Early-modern collecting and connoisseurship may have occasionally been dismissed as part of mere curiosity-cabinet culture, but both pursuits can also be recognized as close to natural history in their reliance on taxonomies, a good example being Cassiano dal Pozzo's seventeenth-century *Museo Cartaceo* or Paper Museum.[20] The visual records of artefacts and natural history specimens commissioned by Pozzo for this ingenious archive predate modern concerns with classification and cataloguing, the keeping and preservation of cultural heritage. With such lineage in archival methods, the history of art has developed a catalogue entry as a standard format of documentation of artefacts. This long-established, structured method of recording and presenting information prepared the discipline well for the advent of databases and remains persistent in online catalogues of art collections; it is also visible in the structure of a *CRSBI* site report. Alongside standard typologies supporting the analysis of artistic forms, traditional classifications of semantic information proved equally helpful in the development of digital research tools.[21] The ICONCLASS system for classification of iconographic subjects, themes and motifs in Western art, is a well-known example of an alpha-numerical information system which was developed in the pre-computer era to support iconological interpretation of figurative art and its meaning through semantic connotations. It was subsequently adapted for automated, computer use.[22]

The appeal of art history as an academic pursuit lies for many in the opposition of the objective validity of the material evidence and the subjectivity of the aesthetical, interpretative judgement. The freedom to interpret art anew has been a driving force in this discipline, but it makes the development of digital tools suitable for conveying the ambiguity of art-historical information notoriously difficult. Electronic information systems created for the use of art history need to accommodate both the absolute (normally primary) and relative (normally secondary) data. The ongoing TTC-ATENEA Project demonstrates the terminological and semantic problems this complex need involves. It seeks to address the issue by developing digital tools for

---

20 *The Paper Museum of Cassiano dal Pozzo: A Catalogue Raisonné* (Royal Collection in association with H. Miller, 2004). See also <http://warburg.sas.ac.uk/pozzo/.html>.

21 For introduction to the art-historical understanding of typology, teleology and other basic classification principles specific to the discipline, see E. Fernie (ed.), *Art History and its Methods: A Critical Anthology* (Phaidon, 1995 and later editions).

22 ICONCLASS was originally developed by Henri van de Waal (d. 1972), completed and edited by L.D. Couprie, E. Tholen et al., *ICONCLASS: An Iconographic Classification System*, 17 vols (North-Holland Publishing Company for Koninklijke Nederlandse Akademie van Wetenschappen, 1973–85). See also <http://www.iconclass.nl>. An ontological version of ICONCLASS, compliant with W3C standards has been developed by the Semantic Computing Group (SeCo) of the Helsinki University of Technology, see <http://www.seco.tkk.fi/ontologies/iconclass/>.

the interpretation of Early Modern art theory within the framework of a linguistic digital corpus.[23]

Digital technologies have in certain respects segmented research processes, as manifested by the structures of data and documentation standards enforced by the use of databases. The descriptive nature of a conventional entry in a *catalogue raisonné* coped well with ambiguity and gaps in historical information, and inconsistency of historic terminology (which tends to vary even between primary sources of the same period). A database, however, can impose prescriptive uniformity of data entry and retrieval. Markup languages allow more flexibility in this respect, thus facilitating more meaningful retrieval of information. Particularly useful in this regard is the XML language, on which is based the syntax being developed for the interchange of information and knowledge on the web within the Resource Description Framework (RDF) and other standards of the World Wide Web Consortium (W3C).[24] The former *CRSBI* project coordinator, Sophie Church saw the encoding as instrumental for the objectivity of the retrieval it offers: 'The *CRSBI* above all provides comprehensive, factual information organised within a logical search mechanism, enhanced by the formulaic and non-interpretative methods used to record the sculpture.'[25] Adhering to this standard also allows the *CRSBI* to take advantage of emerging technologies and digital tools.

The digital *Corpus*

The function of the *Corpus* is primarily to 'describe and illustrate'.[26] The *CRSBI* is doing exactly that: recording sculpture country by country, county by county, site by site, feature by feature, providing historical and topographical information about each site, as well as a body of critical commentary and bibliography. Its electronic format, as opposed to that of a book, transforms the traditional function of a corpus entirely and adds considerably to the many potential uses for the project. However, this may also raise the user's expectations beyond the project's practical ability to deliver.

Besides improving access to the source material, another advantage of the *CRSBI* website is that it allows the seamless incorporation of knowledge, and the exploitation of the many advantages of publishing online: reports may be updated to include the latest research; and unavoidable (yet hopefully rare) errors are easy to correct. Unlike the book corpora referred to earlier, it is unlikely that the online *CRSBI* will require updating through the use of appendices. In practical terms, posting site reports online

---

23 The acronym TTC-ATENEA stands for *Desarrollo de un tesauro terminológico conceptual (TTC) de los discursos teórico-artísticos españoles de la Edad Moderna, complementado con un corpus textual informatizado (ATENEA)*. The project is led by Nuria Rodríguez of the University of Málaga, Spain. It has been presented at a number of conferences but not yet published.

24 See the resources available at the W3C Semantic Web Activity page at <http://www.w3.org/2001/sw/>.

25 Email correspondence of 6 April 2006.

26 See Bailey's response to Orton's criticism in Karkov and Orton (eds), *Theorizing Anglo-Saxon Stone Sculpture*, p. 96.

in small batches, on a case-by-case basis, without waiting for full coverage of the whole county, makes incremental publication possible. This, however, requires additional editorial processes that are specific to electronic media.

When describing sculpture, the *Corpus* fieldworkers are required to follow a strict order (for example, the description of exterior decoration should precede that of interior features: stringcourses before corbel tables; triforium before the clerestory, etc.). The report must be submitted in a prescribed format (instructions are available on the project's intranet) using approved terminology (the glossary is freely available on the project's website). This method, while labour intensive, makes the reports consistent, and therefore easier to format and convert to XML documents. It is occasionally difficult for the *Corpus* data to 'observe' the rigour of the compulsory design of the entry, but generally the XML structure required little modification. Perl scripts are used to convert the original text files into XML; to tag glossary terms; to generate indices; add images; import image captions from the project's database and convert XML documents into web pages.[27]

As a next step, the implementation of a more dynamic XML framework developed by the CCH team for the *CRSBI* and a number of other projects is envisaged. This new framework is called xMod and is compliant with the Text Encoding Initiative (TEI) standards.[28] Its main benefits include a more fluent editorial process enabled via desktop, robust and flexible retrieval of information and enhanced design of the website. It has been argued that the *CRSBI* is similar to a linguistic corpus in its use of markup (using XML tags) of electronic text and images so that different terms (objects) could eventually be studied in a variety of configurations and contexts. The xMod framework offers new possibilities in this respect, opening up the *CRSBI* records to a wide range of interrogation and contextualization.

As is the case with many other electronic resources, the online *Corpus* could benefit greatly from the integration of a variety of new digital methodologies to its material. Primarily, these include digital methods of recording, mapping and surveying. Digital photography has already improved the overall quality of images, making time-consuming digitization redundant, and speeding up editing and archiving.[29]

Panoramic imaging, geo-referencing such as Geographic Information System (GIS), close-range photogrammetry and three-dimensional laser-scanning, among other methods, have already been used in a number of similar projects, including the recording of medieval sculpture.[30] In 2004 the team of specialists from National

---

27 The XML markup and Perl scripts were devised by John Bradley et al. at the Centre for Computing in the Humanities, King's College London.

28 For more information about xMod and the CCH team, see <http://www.cch.kcl.ac.uk/xmod>. A report on the technical development of *CRSBI* is forthcoming at <http://www.crsbi.ac.uk>.

29 The *CRSBI* image archive now holds over 40,000 master images.

30 S. Jeffrey, *Three Dimensional Modelling of Scottish Early Medieval Sculpted Stones*, PhD thesis, University of Glasgow, 2003 <http://ads.ahds.ac.uk/catalogue/collections/blurbs/387.cfm>. The *CRSBI* fieldworker for Ireland, Rachel Moss of the Irish Art Research Centre, Trinity College, University of Dublin, is involved in photogrammetric and 3D work independently of the *CRSBI*. For an introduction to 3D scanning and modelling techniques, and three interesting

Conservation Technologies of National Museums Liverpool, conducted a survey of the Romanesque doorway at Prestbury in Cheshire. The survey involved 3D laser-scanning, photographic documentation and a 3D model created with 3DStudioMax™ software.[31] Information about this 3D survey has been included in the *CRSBI* record of the site. Both resources 'met' in the virtual space when a demonstration of the model, in the form of a short animation, was included in a virtual poster of the *CRSBI* as part of the exhibition of academic research projects staged in Second Life.[32]

Incorporating advanced surveying methods and their products into the *CRSBI* is, however, proving extremely difficult. The application of emerging digital techniques is challenging to a project with such limited resources, as their implementation is demanding of technical expertise, time and labour.[33] Even integrating panoramic views of architecture into the website, a technique that is becoming ubiquitous and inexpensive, is problematic, as it would be costly to apply this kind of visualization consistently to such a large number of sites.

A new challenge for projects like the *CRSBI* is unlocking the enormous potential of 3D digital visualization, a helpful tool for the examination of structural changes over time, and in particular for the interpretation of many sites that have been reduced to ruins. An early example of the digital reconstruction of a site which can

---

study cases, cf. W. Böhler, M.B. Vicent, G. Heinz, A. Marbs and H. Müller, *High Quality Scanning and Modeling of Monuments and Artifacts*, FIG Working Week 2004, Athens, Greece, May 22–27, 2004 <http://www.fig.net/pub/athens/papers/wsa2/WSA2_2_Bohler_et_al.pdf#search='Guido%20Heinz>; G. Heinz, *Comparison of Different Methods for Sculpture Recording* (Institute for Spatial Information and Surveying, Fachhochschule, Mainz, n.d.) <http://www.i3mainz.fh-mainz.de/publicat/isprs_heinz98/comp-recording.html>.

31 See Conservation Technologies, Liverpool, <http://www.conservationcentre.org.uk/technologies>, for examples of 3D laser-scanning and modelling of sculpture. A brief report, *Recording a Norman Doorway, Prestbury Church*, Case Study 2 (2004) is available at <http://www.heritage3d.org/>. See also 'Romanesque Doorway at Prestbury, Cheshire', *3DVisA Index of 3D Projects*, at <http://3dvisa.cch.kcl.ac.uk/project32.html>.

32 The display presents academic research projects affiliated to the Centre for Computing in the Humanities, King's College London. The exhibition was curated by Hugh Denard and developed by Drew Baker of the King's Visualisation Lab, in the virtual space of the Festspielhaus in Hellerau. The launch coincided with the Digital Resources in the Humanities and Arts (DRHA) Conference, Dartington College of Arts, UK, 9–12 September 2007.

33 See, for example, The Michelangelo Project <http://graphics.stanford.edu/projects/mich/>, a major project from Stanford University, California; Max Planck Center for Visual Computing and Communication, Saarbrücken and Stanford; the University of Washington; and a number of commercial imaging companies, supported by the US National Science Foundation. In an attempt at creating an open-access electronic archive of sculptures and architecture of Michelangelo, as well as the marble map of ancient Rome, *Forma Urbis Romae*, a team of 30 university staff and students spent the academic year 1998–9 in Italy. Using laser rangefinder technology, and algorithms developed at Stanford for combining multiple range and colour images, they scanned thousands of objects, including 1,163 fragments of the *Forma Urbis Romae*. The scanning data were subsequently used to create 3D models. The models supported, among other applications, the restoration of the statue of David. See the project website and S. Bracci, F. Falletti, M. Matteini and R. Scopigno (eds), *Exploring David: Diagnostic Tests and State of Conservation* (Florence: Giunti Editore, 2004).

be partially dated to the Romanesque period, Furness Abbey in Cumbria, was carried out in 1985–90 by Lancaster University Archaeological Unit and English Heritage as part of a full archaeological survey of this complex, ruined site.[34]. The digital reconstruction was a major undertaking, which required sophisticated and state-of-the-art software and hardware, specialist skills and much labour. Today the model is most likely neglected if not obsolete, superseded by more advanced visualization methods and better technology, raising questions about the long-term sustainability of such projects. However, the researchers who worked on the virtual Furness Abbey would possibly be the first to admit that the visualization process offered insights into the construction history of the site that would not have been possible by other means. Those who are directly involved in the creation of computer models appreciate how testing modelling processes requires a rigorous application of historical and archaeological knowledge. One's understanding of the subject is greatly enhanced by examining evidence from all possible angles, and by the often difficult decisions that need to be taken to compensate for the gaps in evidence. New knowledge gained through the process of such reconstructive interpretation may outshine the limitations of the imperfect, final product. It is paramount, however, that the chosen solutions are made transparent either through visual means or textual annotations; techniques developed by linguistic corpus scholarship might be imitated here. A concern was addressed at the early stages of the *CRSBI* that, owing to the nature of the *Corpus* entries, 'the distinction between description and judgement (in areas such as the dating of material) might not always be sufficiently clear'.[35] This can be regarded as an expression of general criticism of corpus scholarship, as the risk of blurring the distinctions between description, analysis and interpretation of archaeological evidence. Scholarship will increasingly have to rely on inquiry that resorts to digital methodologies and e-resources, which makes this criticism even more acute: in digital, visual environments distinctions tend to blur even more and ambiguities are difficult to discern. A product of hypothetical digital visualization can easily be confused with historically 'accurate' iconographical evidence. Recent work on 'mapping' interpretative ambiguities on virtual reality models of historic architecture, as well as international initiatives concerned with establishing theoretical frameworks for the transparency of 3D visualization has attempted some systematization of these complex issues and guidance on good practice. Notably, these developments include instruction of students of classics and archaeological computing.[36] Some schools of

---

34 K. Delooze and J. Wood, 'Furness Abbey Survey Project: The Application of Computer Graphics and Data Visualization to Reconstruction Modelling of an Historic Monument', in K. Lockyear and S. Rahtz (eds), *CAA 90: Computer Applications and Quantitative Methods in Archaeology* (Oxford: Oxford Archaeological Reports, 1991), pp. 141–8.

35 The British Academy Corpus of Romanesque Sculpture in the British Isles, *Minutes of the Fifth Meeting of the Committee*, 9 February 1990, p. 2.

36 J. Pollini, L. Swartz, D.K. Kensek and N. Cipolla, 'Problematics of Making Ambiguity Explicit in Virtual Reconstructions: A Case Study of the Mausoleum of Augustus', in *Theory and Practice. Proceedings of the 21st Annual Conference of CHArt*, vol. 8, British Academy, 10–11 November 2005, <http://www.chart.ac.uk/chart2005/papers/index.html>. This paper describes the approach adopted for postgraduate courses in classics and archaeology run by the University of Southern California, Los Angeles. See also the Virtual Pasts projects developed

physical restoration, which apply clear visual distinction between what is original and what is reconstruction, as well as the method of digital archaeosynthesis that was advocated in the 1990s and was based on the same principle, are both useful precedents.[37]

The application of ever more specialist digital methodologies to a project such as the *CRSBI* raises a number of new issues. The *Corpus of Romanesque Sculpture* was originally intended as a strictly academic resource for art historians. Its electronic format and web interface are expanding the original remit in a number of ways, and beyond art history. This puts considerable demand on specialist expertise and the level of funding that is required to fulfil such expectations. Digital methodologies are transforming corpus scholarship in general. Corpora that relied on print have had the benefit of progressing along a well-trodden path and confining their content within hardback covers. Digital environments affect the concept of completeness that is inherent in corpora. Is an online corpus confined to the information contained within its web pages? Opportunities for cross-referencing its material, both internally and externally, are only limited by the number and quality of relevant electronic resources. A disused and forgotten parish church in the English countryside, for example, may now be open to global study because its record containing a National Grid reference has been posted online. Such a site enters, in a literal and virtual sense, on an international stage of mobile, multimedia, interdisciplinary inquiry. The site can be looked at on Google Earth; its stone can be identified and examined in the *Stone in Archaeology* database;[38] its history studied on the *Victoria County History* website[39] – anywhere where the internet is available. A site may be discussed by a group of experts and students in several remote places simultaneously, via Access Grid, inSor or similar technology, each of the participants contributing to the discussion not only viva voce, but also by adding to or editing the same digital resource (for example, a computer model of Shobdon Arches[40]) in real time. Their discussion can be archived

---

by postgraduate students on the MSc in Archaeological Computing at the University of Southampton, <http://www.arch.soton.ac.uk/ACRG/default.asp?D=2&SD=2&SSD=0>. The proposed *London Charter for the Use of 3-dimensional Visualisation in the Research and Communication of Cultural Heritage* <http://www.londoncharter.org> is discussed in ch. 14 (Beacham) above.

37 See, for example, D. Stratford, '"Archaeosynthesis" and Thera Frescoes: Solving the Restoration Dilemma', *Apollo*, 138/377 (1993): 13.

38 K. Knowles, D. Peacock and F. Lewis (2005), *Stone in Archaeology* <http://ads.ahds. ac.uk/catalogue/archive/stones_ahrb_2005/>, an evolving database of stone known to be used in England, developed by Archaeology, School of Humanities, University of Southampton, in collaboration with the Archaeology Data Service. The database enables identification of stone and provides information regarding the location of quarries, distribution and use of the stone throughout various periods of history.

39 *The Victoria County History* <http://www.victoriacountyhistory.ac.uk>, an online resource for English local history, based at the Institute of Historical Research, University of London. The project converts to electronic format, and continues, a series of some 240 volumes which began in 1899.

40 Shobdon Arches, an eighteenth-century architectural folly in Herefordshire, is composed of Romanesque fragments removed from the nearby church of St John the

and disseminated via a number of digital media. Sponsors and editors of a corpus may wonder where to draw the line.

It remains to be seen to what extent the *CRSBI* offers new opportunities for interdisciplinary exploration and re-contextualization of Romanesque stone sculpture. At this time, however, new developments would distract from, and possibly jeopardize, the project's main objective, which has always been the completion of fieldwork. In its early days the Corpus was at the forefront of digital methodology, adopting procedures in anticipation of, rather than following, specific technologies. It would be a shameful paradox if due to the current lack of funding adequate to the requirements of a project of this scale and academic rigour a similar level of innovation could not be maintained.

Evangelist, after it was demolished in 1752. The original appearance of the church and setting of the surviving fragments is open to interpretation, which could be supported by digital visualization.

Chapter 16

Conclusion: Virtual Representations of the Past – New Research Methods, Tools and Communities of Practice

Lorna Hughes

The papers in this volume, and the presentations and discussions at the Expert Seminar that were its inspiration, exemplify the varied uses of ICT methods in history and archaeology. They represent a snapshot of ongoing work in this field, and provide a valuable exemplar to other researchers in the disciplines represented here of the sort of new knowledge that can be created using ICT tools and methods, and fostered by collaborations and conversations with a vibrant, interdisciplinary community of practitioners. What they demonstrate – ably and confidently – is that the field is mature and reflective, and that ICT methods are becoming firmly embedded in historical and archaelogical practice. In fact, the application of such methods to some of the research problems outlined here seems so logical, so similar in analysis and approach to traditional methods, that it is not so much a new methodology or discipline, but an understandable continuum of existing methods – simply a question of using new tools to achieve familiar looking results. Even when the work presented is demonstrably something that would be impossible without ICT methods, it is still recognizable as 'history' or 'archaeology'. Digital sources and methods, therefore, are part of a historical, aesthetic and conceptual continuum, and as such we must use this work to question its legacy and future direction.[1]

One way of developing a synthesis of the disparate work represented in this volume is to approach it as a series of benchmarks for assessing the evidence of the value and impact of ICT methods in the arts and humanities. In this way, we can start to form an understanding of the digital tools that enable analysis, as well as the communities of practice that have emerged around new ICT methods, tools and technologies, and that facilitate interdisciplinary collaboration.

---

1 G. Rockwell, 'Multimedia, is it a Discipline? The Liberal and Servile Arts in Humanities Computing' (Munich, 2002) <http://computerphilologie.uni-muenchen.de/jg02/rockwell. html#fn15>, accessed 21 December 2007.

The evidence of value: ICT methods

Time, space and object can all be represented in digital form, and the starting point for the research described in this volume is digital source materials. Using ICT tools and methods to work with a digital object (a surrogate created from a primary source that has been subject to a process of digitization, or data that were born digital) enables us to recover and challenge the ways in which our senses of time and place are historically and archaeologically understood, something that cannot be effectively communicated through traditional media.

It is particularly important, therefore, to emphasize that all the work in this volume has at its core new ways of engaging with primary source materials – the meat and drink of humanists – in ways previously unimaginable, more fully and intimately. Whether it is the de/re-construction of textual materials via deep markup techniques (Spaeth); mining such materials for previously unseen patterns and combinations (Hitchcock); applying digital imaging to a high-resolution image of a medieval manuscript for forensic analysis in order to identify a scribal hand (Twycross); assessing the administrative documents of assessors, clerks and scribes (Prescott); or examining archaeological data through the lens of geospatial processing tools (Cripps, Gregory, Gaffney), the direct and enhanced engagement with the source material (albeit in digital form) – enables researchers to have a far greater understanding of the original materials. Such understanding would have been simply impossible otherwise – how often do manuscript scholars find access restricted to the sources they need due to conservation concerns? And can we imagine a more impossible scenario than a scholar allowed to apply ultraviolet lighting to a fragile, and possibly priceless, manuscript, as Twycross is able to do with her digital images? This is an important refutation of the argument that digital surrogates distance the scholar from the original sources. They do not. They give the scholar far greater control over the primary evidence, and therefore allow a previously unimaginable empowerment and democratization of source materials.[2]

Advanced ICT research methods in history and archaeology

Advanced ICT research methods involve the use of formal computationally based methods for the capture, investigation, analysis, study, modelling, presentation, dissemination, and publication of arts and humanities materials. Some described in detail in this volume include advanced markup and metadata techniques; keyword searching and text mining; electronic editing; formal methods in the modelling of textual data; manuscript studies; palaeographic techniques; image analysis; modelling of image databases; visualization; image enhancement and virtual reconstruction; multimedia image databases; 3D modelling, mapping and GIS; and structured data techniques including advanced data modelling. Many more exist, and can be applied to humanities data. For a more comprehensive assessment of ICT methods used in the arts and humanities, the reader is directed to the Arts and Humanities Data

---

2 Stanley N. Katz, 'Why Technology Matters: The Humanities in the 21st Century', *Interdisciplinary Science Reviews*, 30/2 (2005): 105–18.

Service's (AHDS) 'Methods Taxonomy for ICT in the Arts and Humanities'. This resource classifies ICT method types by behavioural similarity. The classifications in the taxonomy are the basis for our understanding of ICT methods and have assisted greatly in the development of our understanding of the ways in which ICT is actually used in arts and humanities research, and in scoping the activities in the field. It also provides the knowledge base of the Methods Network and related project websites.[3]

ICT Methods demand rigour and consistency in their application, in order to create findings that can be reproduced and tested. This presupposes an understanding of both the computational methods at their core, and their theoretical underpinning. Understanding how these computational methods can then be applied effectively in the arts and humanities context also involves a clear vision of the arts and humanities research methods that can be 'mapped' onto them. Therefore, although we are examining the application of 'computing' methods to historical and archaeological research, this work is driven by the research questions intrinsic to these humanities disciplines. This process is what we have come to call 'methodologies of use' – the concept that the end uses of ICT for research should be factored into decisions regarding digitization, and decisions about which tools to use for analysis.[4] Thus, methodologies of use are evaluated at the very outset of the digital life cycle. This also has implications for the sustainability and longevity of digital resources, as resources that are used are far more likely to be maintained. As Arnold has explained in this volume, 'a digital representation of an artefact is a representation of certain relevant characteristics of the artefact. It is not the original and complete artefact, nor even a metonymy or *simulacrum* of the complete artefact. It is only a representation of some 'relevant characteristics' (p. 160). However, if methodologies of use are factored into both the creation of the digital image, and the selection of ICT methods for its analysis, then the 'characteristics' that are captured are indeed relevant.

With this concept in mind, there are clear examples in this volume of work that could not have been accomplished without ICT Methods. This is broadly categorized as the ways in which ICT methods are used to create new knowledge in history and archaeology:

1. Enabling research that would otherwise be impossible: addressing research questions that would have been impossible to resolve without the use of ICT tools.
2. Asking new research questions, i.e. questions that are driven by insights that were only achievable through the use of new tools and methods.
3. Facilitating and enhancing existing research, by making research processes easier via the use of computational tools and methods.

---

3 The Methods Taxonomy was originally developed by the AHDS, and has now become part of the broader ICT Guides project: <http://ahds.ac.uk/ictguides/>, accessed 21 December 2007.

4 See M. Jessop, 'Computing or Humanities?' *Ubiquity*, 5/41 (2004).

A postscript to this description is the question of evaluation. While the mechanisms for the evaluation and peer review of the traditional print outputs of scholarly research in the arts and humanities are well established, assessing the value of digital resources and of the scholarly work which leads to their creation has been difficult. The AHRC recently funded an ICT Strategy project to establish a framework for evaluating the quality, sustainability and impact over time of digital resources for the arts and humanities, using history as a case study.[5]

Methods and interdisciplinarity

Methodologies drawn from discipline areas outside the arts and humanities, for example engineering and computer science, were the original impetus to the development of 'historical computing'.[6] However, as Prescott describes, there has been a marginalization of what was once known as 'historical computing', as much of the use of digital technology in history was originally (in the 1980s and 1990s) based around the presentation and preparation of source materials (databases, standards for digital data exchange and encoding, digitization, etc.) rather than using these materials to create new historical knowledge.

However, Prescott argues that different sorts of interdisciplinarity are now having an impact on historical practice. In particular, he illustrates the value of using the methodologies more common to digital scholarship in literary studies, where researchers preparing electronic editions have pioneered the use of high-quality digital images as an essential component to developing an authoritative 'electronic edition' – see, for example, the use of manuscript images and transcription at the Walt Whitman archive, at the University of Nebraska.[7] This illustrates the techniques developed by literary scholars to develop online critical editions, which enable the reader to see every draft of a poem's development, complete with alterations and second thoughts, different-coloured inks and coffee stains, and the development of historical archive records. Digital images can reveal complex layers of historical sources, and help us to understand the iterative ways in which archives are developed, and subject to amendment, bias and outright falsity. Prescott argues persuasively that a melding of both text and image is essential in the development of thematic 'digital archives', as the visual evidence is as important as the textual. Similarly, Bowden demonstrates the application of qualitative research methods to better understand the

---

5 See D. Bates and J. Winter, ' Peer Review and Evaluation of Digital Resources for the Arts and Humanities' (AHRC 2006) <http://www.ahrcict.rdg.ac.uk/activities/strategy_projects/reports/ihr/full%20report.pdf>, accessed 21 December 2007.

6 For a concise history of 'historical computing' see the archives of the conferences of the Association for History and Computing (ACH), available at <http://grid.let.rug.nl/ahc/>, accessed 21 December 2007, and also O. Boonstra, L. Breure, and P. Doorn, 'The Past, Present and Future of Historical Information Science', *Historical Social Research/Historische Sozialforschung*, 29/2 (2004).

7 <http://www.whitmanarchive.org/>, accessed 21 December 2007.

Cecil family history. This sort of research has a long pedigree in the social sciences,[8] so her description of its application to historical sources as a way of framing and managing sources is extremely useful. Cripps's work introduces new ideas about visual patterns associated with landscapes, and shows how a range of technologies can be combined to shed new light on the subject. GIS, for example, is being used to generate novel hypotheses about landscapes, by introducing non-linear narrative into our visualizations.

The next phase of interdisciplinarity is the application of e-Science tools and methods to humanities data. 'e-Science' stands for a specific set of advanced technologies for internet resource sharing and collaboration – so-called grid technologies, and technologies integrated with them, for instance for authentication, data mining and visualization. This has allowed more powerful and innovative research designs in many areas of scientific research, and is capable of transforming the arts and humanities as well. The AHRC ICT Programme established an e-Science programme in 2005 – to support this, JISC funded the Arts and Humanities e-Science Support Centre (<http://www.ahessc.ac.uk>) based at the Centre for e-Research, King's College London.

The use of grid technologies fall into three main categories:

- The tools for large-scale data management and sharing provided by data grid technology facilitate the location, access to and integration of the content of resources that embrace text, still and moving images and sound, are highly distributed, of variable quality, encoded and described using different standards, and often incomplete, fuzzy, and complex.
- The advanced video-conferencing facilities provided by the access grid enable collaborative research, and in particular provide exciting opportunities for sharing performance and creative interaction.
- The sharing of processing power through the computational grid enables shared access to high-performance tools for analysis of resources.

However, e-Science is about much more than the grid: it is a vision of creating integrated research infrastructures. Academic collaborations and initiatives have increasingly come to rely on a robust and ubiquitous networked 'e-Infrastructure', or 'e-Information infrastructure', which allows shared access to large-scale datasets, advanced tools for analysis of this data, and fully integrated systems for representing and publishing the results.[9] In the UK, the term 'e-Infrastructure' has been used increasingly to refer to the concept of this networked, distributed environment, and the technology and organizations, services and researchers that it supports.[10] In the US, this concept is known as the 'Cyberinfrastructure', and the American Council of

---

8 See, e.g., K. Orren and S. Skowronek, *The Search for American Political Development* (Cambridge: Cambridge University Press, 2004).

9 T. Hey, 'Foreword', in Hine, C.M. (ed.), *New Infrastructures for Knowledge Production: Understanding E-science* (Information Science Publishing, 2006), pp. iv–vii.

10 For more information, see: T. Hey, D. De Roure and A.E. Trefethen, 'e-Infrastructure and e-Science', in E. Aarts and J.L. Encarnacao (eds), *True Visions* (Berlin: Springer-Verlag, 2006), pp. 209–28.

The Virtual Representation of the Past

Learned Societies (ACLS) recently commissioned a report on 'Cyberinfrastructure and the Humanities: Our Cultural Commonwealth'[11] to which the reader is directed.

One of the most obvious ways in which the e-Science infrastructure can assist researchers in history and archaeology is by grid-enabling large and complex datasets, so that they can be interoperable, with the potential for re-use and re-purposing for different sorts of analysis.

However, the issue is complex, and requires the use of standard formats and ontologies for the data. Richards and Hardman outline the argument for the use of data standards in the development of online digital resources, to enable cross-searching and analysis of multiple data sources. Historians and archaeologists are well versed in the topic of standards for data exchange. Historians were some of the earliest adopters of the Standard Generalized Markup Language (SGML) for the markup and exchange of historical materials, and their work contributed to the development of the Text Encoding Initiative (TEI[12]) in 1994. Subsequent assessment and implementation of XML markup illustrated the potential for using the semantic web for historical and archaeological sources. The newest, and most exciting, phase of standards development is introduced by Thaller, that of using the ontology-based intellectual framework, the CIDOC-CRM, described here as 'a format for the interchange of information between heterogeneous information architectures'. This may well prove to be the 'wrapping' that enables digital resources to be unlocked via the e-Infrastructure.

Digital tools development and implementation

The development of tools for research in the humanities has been described elsewhere in some detail by, among others, John Unsworth.[13] However, a very broad summary will set the work described here in context. The first uses of digital tools in history and archaeology were, broadly, the attempts to use generic, off-the-shelf software for statistical research or the representation of data (particularly through the use of databases). The inevitable discovery that historical and archaeological data were too varied, complex and fuzzy to 'fit' into a conventional application was frequently followed by a wave of 'humanities computing' software development projects. These have flourished or foundered to varying degrees as researchers recognize that 'bespoke' tools are not necessarily the most suitable but some fundamental principles

---

11 The report of the ACLS Commission on Cyberinfrastructure for the Humanities and Social Sciences, 'Our Cultural Commonwealth: The Report of the American Council of Learned Societies Commission on Cyberinfrastructure for the Humanities & Social Sciences' (2006), <http://www.acls.org/cyberinfrastructure/OurCulturalCommonwealth.pdf>, accessed 21 December 2007.

12 <http://www.tei-c.org/index.xml>, accessed 21 December 2007.

13 J. Unsworth, 'Tool-time, or 'Haven't We Been Here Already?' Ten Years in Humanities Computing', paper presented at Transforming Disciplines: The Humanities and Computer Science', January (2003) <http://www3.isrl.uiuc.edu/~unsworth/carnegie-ninch.03.html>, accessed 21 December 2007.

regarding the implementation and development of ICT tools for humanities research have emerged.

The first is that the use of digital tools should primarily be part of the process of research, and that this should always be the focus, rather than the functionality of a specific technology or product. Second, existing tools may well have limitations that must be recognized at the outset. For example, as Gregory mentions in his paper, tools may be limited to representing just one format – space, time or object – and the integration or amalgamation of suites of tools may be more appropriate. This might involve the combination of different data types and technical methods: for example, some combination of text, database, image, time-based data (video or sound) and GIS. Third, we must be open to the use of tools created for a variety of purposes: those created specifically for the humanities; commercial and business software; and applications created for other research purposes or academic disciplines. Their effective use is contingent on a careful assessment of their functionality against the desired research outcomes.

Several of the chapters in this book illustrate these points by describing their use of existing tools for research. Prescott describes using software that has been specifically created for working with humanities manuscripts: the Edition Production and Presentation Technology (EPPT), a suite of generic innovative editing tools developed from concepts first worked out in the process of editing very badly damaged Old English manuscripts and applicable to use with other documentary materials. Bowden demonstrates how qualitative software tools can facilitate the management and analysis of complex data from a variety of sources. Twycross uses proprietary software and standard imaging techniques to produce extraordinary results in forensic manuscript analysis. This is possible because commercial developers are rapidly adopting new technologies to create more and more powerful image analysis and enhancement software, and new techniques and applications are continually being established. This is not because developers like Adobe have a particularly altruistic concern for the archival scholar, of course, but because there are so many non-academic applications for this type of software (fraud assessment, entertainment, e-publishing, etc). Similarly, Spaeth describes research that is merging tools and methods: encoding and anlaysis is effected via the use of the commercially available tools xQuery and xPath, and analysis languages to interrogate historical data with hierarchical anomalies. Both Spaeth and Twycross describe research that illustrates the truism 'garbage in, garbage out' – the research results of any analysis will not be effective if one attempts to work with poor-quality images (Twycross), or texts that have gone through inaccurate encoding or markup (Spaeth). The preparation of digital materials must anticipate future methodologies of use.

In terms of taking the tools agenda forward, there may be lessons to be drawn from the experience of the e-Science community. In the UK, the National e-Science programme[14] has developed a number of tools for academic research, frequently configured to handle large amounts of complex data. While it is true, as Gaffney states in his paper, that there is less uptake of these tools by the arts and humanities community than by other communities, this is being rectified by a number of

---

14 <http://www.rcuk.ac.uk/escience/default.htm>, accessed 21 December 2007.

initiatives. The tools and methods, and their applicability to the arts and humanities, have been assessed by the AHDS e-Science Scoping Survey.[15] Similar work is being undertaken by the Arts and Humanities eScience Support Centre.[16] It is now necessary for the historical and archaeological communities comprehensively to test these existing tools: we need a methodological approach to evaluating these tools against our research methods.[17] There is also a need to assess which e-Science tools can be integrated (or layered) in order to address different questions: this may be a way to realize the possibility of adding a temporal layer to GIS tools, or even to develop temporal mapping tools, to demonstrate the questions 'who was where, when?' posited here by Gregory and Thaller. On this latter point, a team of computer science researchers at Southampton University are presently exploring such tools for the mSpace musicology project.[18] There is immense potential benefit for scholars if they are able to use a range of 'standard' tools to exploit digital resources, and this is another reason to stress the importance of using open technical standards for the creation of digital data resources with the potential for infinite manipulation and re-use.

Communities of practice

One of the things that has clearly emerged from the work described in this volume is that there exist many active and emerging communities of practitioners which have formed around the various types of work described here – methods, tools or disciplinary areas of study. Methodologies drawn from discipline areas outside the arts and humanities are increasingly important in arts and humanities research where ICT is involved. An increasing number of major research projects depend on bringing together disciplinary and technical specialists to work in collaborative frameworks that are new, especially to the arts and humanities. Increasingly sophisticated and flexible technologies are making possible new kinds of interdisciplinary work and the creation of truly multidisciplinary digital resources. This kind of work has given rise to numerous 'communities of practice' – researchers who may come from disparate backgrounds and areas of interest, but who come together around particular ICT methods and tools. For example, visualization, text encoding and GIS all have extremely active communities of practice.

Since the inception of the Methods Network in April 2005, we have monitored these communities of practice and supported them via sponsored activities and events, and encouraged their interaction via the Methods Network website. In 2007, we formally launched a new initiative, arts-humanities.net (<http://www.arts-

---

15 <http://ahds.ac.uk/e-science/e-science-scoping-study.htm>, accessed 21 December 2007.

16 <http://www.ahessc.ac.uk>, accessed 21 December 2007.

17 See L. Hughes, 'Methodologies of Use: Advanced Arts and Humanities Research Methods and e-Science Communities of Practice', *Digital Humanities Quarterly*, forthcoming.

18 See <http://www.nopain2.org/archives/000089.html>, accessed 21 December 2007, for more information.

humanities.net>), a virtual community of arts and humanities researchers using ICT methods. arts-humanities.net presently exploits web 2.0 technologies to enable users to share and discuss ideas, promote their research, and discover the digital arts and humanities as a whole. The Methods Network has also identified various emerging communities of practice, supported them by documenting their methodologies of use, and worked on building a wider digital arts and humanities community with interdisciplinary links for knowledge transfer. arts-humanities.net will become a virtual 'bridge' connecting the various disciplines and communities, and help to foster a mutually supportive virtual community. It will sustain and expand the Methods Network's current community of researchers and practitioners. As a collaborative endeavour, linking various groups, projects and individuals, arts-humanities.net will be a living directory of activities in the field, far more accessible and effective than static, and disparate, reports and guides. It is based around some of the extensive research undertaken into social networking.[19]

arts-humanities.net will not replace existing community sites and portals, but rather create a meta-community site that serves as exploratory tool, directory and match-making agency, a bridge across communities, and an aggregator of content. As part of a much wider 'community ecosystem', it aggregates content from other websites in order to build a living directory of the digital arts and humanities. Communities will either find their virtual home on arts-humanities.net, have a virtual branch on the site or simply choose to announce specific events or flag issues for discussion. Through the open nature of the site and its aggregation capabilities, this will ideally involve seamless integration: users can move from one site to another or interact with the content of different communities on one site.

It is based around the AHDS 'taxonomy of methods' for classification of 'tools' and 'methods', and so will be a forum that takes this initiative forward. It uses this resource as a folksonomy[20] for the site, which encourages user-developed tags and content. The shared folksonomy developed by the community and informed by the Methods Taxonomy makes content accessible by meaning and not by location. However, the folksonomy is more than a way of organizing content. It also doubles a living directory of methods used in the field and can be developed into a comprehensive guide to methodologies of use. Furthermore, it enables the site editor to identify issues of particular interest to the community and then flag and promote topics of particular interest and discussions of advanced methods. In this way, the site can become 'living' evidence of value, as it concurrently discusses advanced methods and their application and, through user participation, makes it obvious which methods are especially valuable for the communities of practice it supports. We are encouraging broadest uptake by the arts and humanities ICT community,

---

19 See, for example, the work of <http://www.danah.org>, accessed 21 December 2007.

20 'Folksonomy' is a collaboratively generated, open-ended labelling system that enables internet users to categorize content such as web pages, online photographs and Web links. The freely chosen labels – called tags – help to improve search engines' effectiveness because content is categorized using a familiar, accessible and shared vocabulary. The labelling process is called tagging. Two widely cited examples of websites using folksonomic tagging are <http://www.flickr.com> and <http://del.icio.us>.

including the community of arts and humanities data creators and curators up to now supported by the AHDS; learned societies; and professional associations. The Association for History and Computing has been actively using the site since its inception.

The future

No discussion of digital resources and their use for scholarship is complete without questioning the legacy and future of this sort of work. It is crucial to highlight the fact that the sustainability of much of the work described here is fragile and uncertain. As Bentkowska-Kafel illustrates, many projects have to fight for ongoing support: she describes a project that checks all the available boxes of 'evidence of value'. It is collaborative, pushing the boundaries of research, supporting graduate students and also supporting preservation of the original artefacts, yet its existence is fragile and endangered.

In terms of where we go next, we must certainly hope, as Gaffney states in his chapter, that national and international funding agencies will heed the rallying call to build on the enormous potential of the e-Infrastructure, and develop a framework of integrated technologies, grid-enabled digital resources, and virtual network computing, to support distributed research groups. However, this volume is completed in uncertain times. If we examine the background detail of this panoramic 'snapshot' of the use of ICT methods in history and archaeology, the impressive range and depth of the work described allows us to date this work to a point at which there has been considerable public investment in digital resources for the arts and humanities, via initiatives including the AHRC's resource enhancement and research grant schema and a number of national and international digital museum, library and archive initiatives. This has created a 'data deluge' in the arts and humanities – the development of a critical mass of digital resources that is changing the nature of our work. As Thaller points out, digitization initiatives are following the large-scale digitization of printed materials with a move towards the systematic conversion of manuscript collections, such as the project to digitize the entire archive of the Cathedral Library of Cologne. This is an era of mass digitization initiatives, facilitated by the fact that the cost of digitization has decreased significantly in recent years.[21] Hitchcock has outlined ways in which access to digital resources is changing the way people do research, simply because they can now choose to focus on areas where there exist readily accessible digital resources. Anecdotally, we know this to be true – and yet, while on the one hand this may be perceived as shallow and opportunistic on the part of the researcher, the desire to use these (expensive) digital resources is an encouraging endorsement for the investment in their creation. Both the AHDS and the Methods Network were funded to support the community as it engaged with the difficult questions of the creation, management, and use of digital resources in

---

21 For a discussion of the mass digitization of manuscripts, see the report of the Methods Network workshop on 'large scale manuscript digitization': <http://www.methodsnetwork. ac.uk/activities/act4.html>, accessed 21 December 2007.

the arts and humanities, and their sustainability over the long term – which is so crucial, if the investment in their digitization is to pay off.

However, the AHRC ICT Methods Network will come to an end in March 2008, as will the AHDS, which has promoted the digitization, management and preservation of primary source materials, and made them freely available for use by scholars. This loss of centralized ICT support, and a move towards supporting digital scholarship and the technologies and tools that support it via responsive mode funding, has caused us to pause and address questions of sustainability for the sort of work that has been described in this volume. It is hard to see how the agenda can be taken forward – it is, for example, difficult to imagine how a large part of the work described in this volume might have been possible had it not been for the support of the AHDS, which is mentioned in five of the papers here. It is hard to see where centralized support for the use of the standards that will be a core part of adopting the e-Infrastructure will come from. However, it is to be hoped that the virtual community of practitioners will continue to be fostered by arts-humanities. net, and that this community might enable the strategic implications of this work to be addressed in future.

To conclude with an example from Beacham: we can imagine that 'light and motion' is a metaphor for our digital resources, but while these images and visualizations are charming and useful, perhaps we should be more concerned with the grumbles of Ben Jonson – do we have in place our 'paint and boards' to support and sustain these valuable, yet fragile, resources, the structures that underpin the use of ICT in the arts and humanities? What is the future support available for standards (of all sorts), collaborative research models, support and training for researchers and graduate students, the development of tools and the further articulation of ICT methods?

Appendix

Glossary of Acronyms and Terms

ADS	Archaeology Data Service. The ADS supports the deployment of digital technologies and resources in academic research, teaching and learning. It preserves, promotes and disseminates archaeological digital data and promotes good practice in its use. ADS also provides technical advice to the research community. <http://ads.ahds.ac.uk/>.
AJAX	Asynchronous Javascript and XML. AJAX is a group of interrelated web development techniques for creating interactive web applications. <http://www.ajax.org/>.
AOL	America Online. AOL is a global internet service provider and media company. <http://www.aol.com/>.
API	Advanced Programming Interface, or Application Programme Interface. A set of protocols and tools for building software applications.
ARENA	In this volume, ARENA is the Archaeological Records of Europe – Networked Access. The main aims of the ARENA project were to research ways towards a European network for archaeological archives, making selected European archaeological datasets available through the creation of an Internet Portal. <http://ads.ahds.ac.uk/arena/>. It ran from 2001 to 2004 supported by the European Community through the Culture 2000 programme.
CAD	Computer-Aided Design. CAD is a tool which allows the creation of 3D models or 2D drawings.
CAQDAS	Computer Assisted Qualitative Data Analysis Software. CAQDAS is used to search, organize and annotate textual and visual data.
CBA	Council for British Archaeology. The CBA is an UK-based educational charity promoting the appreciation and care of the historic environment. <http://www.britarch.ac.uk/>.
CIDOC-CRM CIDOC (The International Committee for Museum Documentation)	Conceptual Reference Model. CIDOC-CRM provides definitions and a formal structure for describing the concepts and relationships used in cultural heritage documentation. <http://cidoc.ics.forth.gr/>.

COLLATE	Collation software tool developed by Peter Robinson (now at the University of Birmingham, UK) in the 1980s. It is a tool primarily associated with the *Canterbury Tales* electronic editions.
DACO	Digital Autonomous Cultural Object protocol. DACO, a concept developed by Manfred Thaller, builds on the Open Archive Initiative (OAI) and offers access to data without the necessity of reorganizing existing databases.
DCMI	Dublin Core Metadata Initiative. DCMI develops interoperable online metadata standards. <http://dublincore.org/>.
DLF	Digital Library Foundation. The DLF is an international association of libraries and related institutions using electronic and information technologies to extend services. <http://www.diglib.org/>.
DOI	Digital Object Identifier system. DOI is a recognized standard for identifying content objects in the digital environment. <http://www.doi.org/>.
DTD	Document Type Definition. A DTD defines the structure of an XML document.
EDM	Electronic Distance Measuring.
EPPT	Edition Production and Presentation Technology. EPPT facilitates the integration of images and text through XML encoding. <http://www.eppt.org/>.
EPOCH	European Research Network of Excellence in Open Cultural Heritage. EPOCH promotes and supports the use of information and communication technology in the cultural heritage sector. <http://www.epoch-net.org/>.
GIF	Graphics Interchange Format. GIF is an 8 bit per pixel bitmap image format.
GEON	Geosciences Network. GEON is a collaborative project engaged in developing a cyberinfrastructure that supports an environment for integrative geoscience research. <http://www.geongrid.org/>.
GIS	Geographic Information Systems. GIS is a collection of computer hardware, software, and geographic data for capturing, managing, analysing and displaying geographically referenced information. <http://www.gis.com/index.html>.
GPR	Ground Penetration Radar. The GPR method uses radar impulses to survey the subsurface of the earth.
GRID Computing	The deployment of Grid technologies for distributed computing, especially the use of the Data, Computational and Access Grids. Grid computing allows the sharing of information, equipment and network links.
HER	Historic Environment Record. HERs are usually local-authority-based services involved in planning. They were previously known as Sites and Monuments Records or SMRs.

HTTP	Hypertext Transfer Protocol. HTTP is a communication protocol used to convey information on intranets or the World Wide Web.
JPEG	Joint Photographic Experts Group. A method of compression for photographic images, now used as a community-adopted standard format.
LiDAR	Light Detection And Ranging. LiDAR is a remote sensing system used to collect topographic data.
METS	Metadata Encoding and Transmission Standard. The METS schema is a standard for encoding metadata about objects in a digital library. <http://www.loc.gov/standards/mets/>.
MIDAS	The Monument Inventory Data Standard is a framework data standard for monument inventories. Associated with this data standard are a suite of XML schemas which provide a self-documenting structure for holding information from databases conforming to the MIDAS standard for content.
MDA	The Museums Document Association is a UK organization for documentation and information management in museums.
OAI	The Open Archives Initiative promotes standards for content exchange and dissemination, and promotes interoperability and broadest access to digital resources for research and teaching. OAI has close ties to the open access and institutional repositories initiatives. <http://www.openarchives.org/>.
OASIS	In this volume, OASIS refers to the Online Access to the Index of Archaeological Investigations, a project developed by a number of partners and led by the University of York. It has created a standard, web-based, form that can be used to create a single unified index to data gathered by archaeological investigations. <http://ads.ahds.ac.uk/project/oasis/>.
OHCO	The OHCO (Ordered Hierarchy of Content Objects) is an influential thesis behind the way in which much text is structured when marked up. It is a theoretical framework that has influenced the work of, for example, the Text Encoding Initiative (<http://www.TEI-C.org>).
OWL	The Web Ontology Language is machine-readable language recommended by the World Wide Web Consortium (W3C) for representing ontologies.
PCDATA	Parsed Character DATA. A reserved word used in a DTD, used to mean that the element being defined may contain any valid character data. If used on its own the element may not contain any sub-elements.
PDF	Portable Document Format. Established by Adobe as a format to capture and view information, from any application and on any computer system.

RDF	The Resource Description Framework is a suite of World Wide Web Consortium (W3C) specifications for describing resources on the web.
RCAHMS	Royal Commission on the Ancient and Historical Monuments of Scotland.
SIGGRAPH	The annual conference on computer graphics convened by the professional association on computer graphics, ACM-SIGGRAPH. This is the Association for Computing Machinery's Special Interest Group on Computer Graphics (<http://www.siggraph.org>).
SOAP	Originally the acronym for the Simple Object Access Protocol, SOAP is a XML-based protocol to facilitate application exchange information over HTTP.
SPARQL	A recursive acronym that stands for SPARQL Protocol and RDF Query Language, an emerging standard for querying RDF.
SQL	Structured Query Language designed for the retrieval and management of data, specifically for querying relational databases.
SVG	The Scalable Vector Graphics language describes 2D graphics and graphical applications in XML.
TIFF	Tagged Image File Format, a container format for storing images.
TMT	The Thesaurus of Monument Types provides a controlled vocabulary used by archaeological excavation units, museums and local government Sites and Monuments Records.
UKLIGHT	A UK national facility to provide shared infrastructure services to support projects that are developing optical networks and the applications that will use them.
URI	The Uniform Resource Identifier is a string of characters used to identify or name a resource. URLs (Uniform Resource Locators) and URNs (Uniform Resource Names) are both URIs.
UTM	The Universal Transverse Mercator System of Geographical Coordinates is based around 60 geographical zones worldwide, each of which then provides a specific longitude and latitude reference coordinate to a particular location.
VRE	A JISC-funded activity that helps researchers manage the complex range of project tasks by building and deploying Virtual Research Environments based on currently available tools and frameworks. <http://www.jisc.ac.uk/whatwedo/programmes/programme_vre.aspx>.
W3C	The World Wide Web Consortium is an organization that develops interoperable specifications, software, and tools. <http://www.w3.org/>.
WINGENEA	Shareware for Windows that displays and prints family trees.

WSDL	The Web Services Description Language is an XML-based language for describing Web services and how to access them.
XML	The eXtensible Markup Language is a markup language designed for the exchange of structured data over the web.
XPATH	XML Path Language is a Path Language for finding information in an XML document.
XQUERY	The XML Query is designed to query XML data.
XSLT	eXtensible Stylesheet Language Transformations is an XML-based language used to transform XML documents into other formats, like XHTML.

Bibliography

The place of publication is presumed as London, unless otherwise stated.

Abiteboul, S., Buneman, P. and Suciu, D., *Data on the Web: From Relations to Semistructured Data and XML* (San Francisco: Morgan Kaufmann, 2004).

ACLS, 'Our Cultural Commonwealth: The Report of the American Council of Learned Societies Commission on Cyberinfrastructure for the Humanities & Social Sciences' (2006), available online at <http://www.acls.org/cyberinfrastructure/OurCulturalCommonwealth.pdf>.

Addison, A.C., 'Beyond Digital Recording: A Shared Portal to the World's Heritage', paper presented at the International Workshop on Recording, Modeling and Visualization of Cultural Heritage, Ascona, Switzerland, 22–27 May 2005.

Addison, A.C., 'The Vanishing Virtual', in T. Kvan and Y. Kalay (eds), *New Heritage: Beyond Verisimilitude, Conference on Cultural Heritage and New Media* (Hong Kong: Faculty of Architecture, University of Hong Kong, 2006), pp. 36–48.

AHRC, *AHRC Research Funding Guide, 2006/7* <http://www.ahrc.ac.uk>.

Antoniou, G. and Harmelen, F. v. *A Semantic Web Primer* (Cambridge, MA.: MIT Press, 2004).

Arkell, T., Evans, N. and Goose, N. (eds), *When Death Do Us Part* (Oxford: Leopard's Head, 2000).

Austin, A., Pinto, F., Richards, J.D. and Ryan, N., 'Joined-up Writing: an Internet Portal for Research into the Historic Environment', in G. Burenhult (ed.), *CAA 2001: Archaeological Informatics: Pushing the Envelope*, British Archaeological Reports, International Series no. 1016 (Oxford, 2002), pp. 243–51.

Avalle, D'A.S., *Principi di critica testuale* (Padova, Antenore, 1972), p. 33.

Baines, A. and Brophy, 'K., What's Another Word for Thesaurus? Data Standards and Classifying the Past', in P. Daly and T.L. Evans (eds), *Digital Archaeology: Bridging Method and Theory* (Routledge, 2006).

Barnard, D.T. et al., 'Hierarchical Encoding of Text: Technical Problems and SGML Solutions', *Computers and the Humanities*, 29 (1995): 211–31.

Barnard, D.T., Hayter, R., Karababa, M. et al., 'SGML-Based Markup for Literary Texts: Two Problems and Some Solutions', *Computers and the Humanities*, 22 (1988): 265–76.

Barrett, J., 'The Glastonbury Lake Village: Models and Source Criticism', *Archaeological Journal*, 144 (1987): 409–23.

Bates, D. and Winter, J., ' Peer Review and Evaluation of Digital Resources for the Arts and Humanities' (AHRC 2006) <http://www.ahrcict.rdg.ac.uk/activities/strategy_projects/reports/ihr/full%20report.pdf>.

Baudrillard, J., *Simulations* (New York: Semiotext(e), 1983).

Beadle, R. and Meredith, P., *The York Play: A Facsimile of British Library MS Additional 35290, together with a Facsimile of the 'Ordo Paginarum' Section of the A/Y Memorandum Book* (Leeds: University of Leeds School of English, 1983).

Beck, A., 'Intellectual Excavation and Dynamic Management Systems', in G. Lock and K. Brown (eds), *On the Theory and Practice of Archaeological Computing* Oxford University Committee for Archaeology Monographs no. 51 (Oxford: Oxford University Committee for Archaeology, 2000), pp. 73–88.

Bewley, R.H., Crutchley, S.P. and Shell, C.A., 'New Light on an Ancient Landscape: LiDAR Survey in the Stonehenge World Heritage Site', *Antiquity*,79 (2005): 636–47.

Böhler, W., Vicent, M.B., Heinz, G., Marbs, A. and Müller, H., *High Quality Scanning and Modeling of Monuments and Artifacts*, FIG Working Week 2004, Athens, Greece, May 22–27, 2004 <http://www.fig.net/pub/athens/papers/wsa2/WSA2_2_Bohler_et_al.pdf#search='Guido%20Heinz>.

Boonstra, O., Breure, L. and Doorn, P., *Past, Present and Future of Historical Information Science* (Amsterdam: Netherlands Institute for Scientific Information, Royal Netherlands Academy of Arts and Sciences, 2004).

O. Boonstra, L. Breure, and P. Doorn, 'The Past, Present and Future of Historical Information Science', *Historical Social Research/Historische Sozialforschung*, 29/2 (2004).

Bowman, A.K. and Thomas, J.D., *The Vindolanda Writing Tablets Volume III* (British Museum Press, 2003).

Bracci, S., Falletti, F., Matteini, M. and Scopigno, R. (eds), *Exploring David: Diagnostic Tests and State of Conservation* (Florence: Giunti Editore, 2004).

Bremmer, J. and Roodenburg, H. (eds), *A Cultural History of Gesture* (Ithaca and London: Cornell University Press, 1991).

Brundage, M., *XQuery: The XML Query Language* (Boston: Addison-Wesley, 2004).

Buneman, P., 'Semistructured Data', *Proceedings of the Sixteenth ACM SIGACT-SIGMOD-SIGART Symposium on Principles of Database Systems* (New York: ACM, 1997), pp. 117–21.

Burt, J. and James, T.B., 'Source-oriented Data Processing: The Triumph of the Micro over the Macro?', *History and Computing*, 8/3 (1996): 160–68.

Butlin, R.A., *Historical Geography: Through the Gates of Space and Time* (Edward Arnold, 1993).

Butterfield, H., *The Whig Interpretation of History* (George Bell and Sons, 1950).

Caffo, R., 'MICHAEL Project: Towards a Trans-European Portal of Culture', in V. Cappellini and J. Hemsley (eds), *Electronic Imaging & the Visual Arts, EVA 2006 Florence Conference Proceeding* (Bologna: Pitagora Editrice, 2006), pp. 48–50.

Cahn, W. and Seidel, L. (eds), *Romanesque Sculpture in American Collections* (New York: B. Franklin, Turnhout: Brepols, 1979 and c. 1999).

Carver, M., Chapman, H., Cunliffe, B. et al., *Archaeological Publication, Archives and Collections: Towards a National Policy*, prepared for the Society of Antiquaries and the Museums Association, *British Archaeological News* 7/2 (1992) Supplement.

Caton, P., 'Markup's Current Imbalance', *Markup Languages: Theory & Practice*, 3 (2001): 1–13.

Ciravegna, F., Chapman, S., Dingli, A., Wilks, Y., 'Learning to Harvest Information for the Semantic Web', in *Proceedings of the 1st European Semantic Web Symposium* (Heraklion, 2004).

Clarke, A., Fulford, M. and Rains, M., 'Nothing to Hide – Online Database Publication and the Silchester Town Life Project', in M. Doerr and A. Sarris (eds), *CAA2002: The Digital Heritage of Archaeology. Computer Applications and Quantitative Methods in Archaeology, 2002* (Hellenic Ministry of Culture, 2003), pp. 401–10.

Conrad, P. and Reinarz, S., 'Qualitative Computing: Approaches and Issues', *Qualitative Sociology*, 7 (1984): 34–60.

Coren, S., Ward, L.M. and Enns, J.T., *Sensation and Perception*, 6th edn (Hoboken, NJ: Wiley, 2004).

Couprie, L.D., Tholen, E. et al., *ICONCLASS: An Iconographic Classification System*, 17 vols (Amsterdam: North-Holland Publishing Company for Koninklijke Nederlandse Akademie van Wetenschappen, 1973–85).

Cramp, R. (ed.), *The Corpus of Anglo-Saxon Stone Sculpture in England* (British Academy, Oxford University Press, 1984–).

Cripps, P.J., 'Pathways through the Avebury Landscape: A Study of Spatial Relationships Associated with the Beckhampton Avenue, Avebury, Wilts'. Unpublished MSc dissertation, University of Southampton (2001) <http://www.soton.ac.uk/~pjc196/files/CrippsPJ_MSc2001_LoQuality.pdf>.

Cripps, P., Earl, G. and Wheatley, D.W., 'A Dwelling Place in Bits', in V.O. Jorge, J.M. Cardoso, A.M. Vale, G.L. Velho and L.S. Periera (eds), *Journal of Iberian Archaeology*, vol. 8 (Porto: Adecap, 2006).

Cronon, W., *Nature's Metropolis: Chicago and the Great West* (New York: W.W. Norton, 1991).

Crosby, A., *The Measurement of Reality: Quantification and Western Society, 1250–1600* (Cambridge: Cambridge University Press, 1997).

Cunfer, G., 'Causes of the Dust Bowl' in A.K. Knowles (ed.), *Past time, Past Place: GIS for history* (Redlands, CA: ESRI Press, 2002), pp. 93–104.

Cunfer, G., *On the Great Plains: Agriculture and Environment* (College Station TX: A&M University Press, 2005).

Cunliffe, B.W., *The Publication of Archaeological Excavations: Report of a Joint Working Party of the Council for British Archaeology and the Department of the Environment* (Department of the Environment, 1983).

Curtius, L.P. (ed.), *The Historian's Workshop* (New York: Knopf, 1970).

Darwin, Charles, *Narrative of the Surveying Voyages of His Majesty's Ships Adventure and Beagle between the Years 1826 and 1836 . . .* (Henry Colburn, 1839).

Davidson, D., 'A Coherence Theory of Truth and Knowledge', in E. LePore (ed.), *Truth And Interpretation: Perspectives on the Philosophy of Donald Davidson* (Oxford: Blackwell, 1986), pp. 307–19.

Day, M., 'E-print Services and Long-term Access to the Record of Scholarly and Scientific Research', *Ariadne*, 28 (2001) <http://www.ariadne.ac.uk/issue28/metadata/>.

Dekhtyar, A., Iacob, I.E., Jaromczyk, J.W. et al., 'Support for XML Markup of Image-based Electronic Editions', *International Journal on Digital Libraries*, 6 (2006): 55–69.

Delooze, K. and Wood, J., 'Furness Abbey Survey Project: The Application of Computer Graphics and Data Visualization to Reconstruction Modelling of an Historic Monument', in K. Lockyear and S. Rahtz (eds), *CAA 90: Computer Applications and Quantitative Methods in Archaeology* (Oxford Archaeological Reports, 1991), pp. 141–8.

DeRose, S.J., Durand, D.G., Mylonas, E. and Renear, A., 'What is Text, Really?', *Journal of Computing in Higher Education*, 1 (1990): 3–26.

Deswarte, R. and Oostoek, J., 'Clio's Ontology Criteria: The Theory and Experience of Building a History Ontology', paper given at the XVIth International Conference of the Association for History and Computing, Amsterdam, 14–17 September 2005.

Dey, I., *Qualitative Data Analysis. A User-friendly Guide for Social Scientists* (Routledge, 1993).

Diamond, E. and Bodenhamer, D., 'Investigating White-flight in Indianapolis: A GIS Approach', *History and Computing*, 13 (2001): 25–44.

Digges, D., *The Compleat Ambassador: Or Two Treaties of Intended Marriage of Qu. Elizabeth of Glorious Memory; Comprised in Letters of Negotiation of Sir Francis Walsingham, Her Resident in France Together with the Answers of the Lord Burleigh [...]* (Gabriel Bedell and Thomas Collins, 1655).

Dodgson, R.A., *Society in Time and Space: A Geographical Perspective on Change* (Cambridge: Cambridge University Press, 1998).

Doerr, M.and Crofts, N., 'Electronic Esperanto: The Role of the Object-orientated CIDOC Reference Model', in DS. Bearman and J. Trant (eds), *Cultural Heritage Informatics 1999: Selected Papers from ichim99* (1999). Available online at <http://cidoc.ics.forth.gr/docs/doerr_crofts_ichim99_new.pdf>.

Doerr, M., 'The CIDOC CRM: An Ontological Approach to Semantic Interoperability of Metadata', *AI Magazine, 24/3 (2003).*

Dorling, D., Mitchell, R., Shaw, M., Orford, S. and Davey Smith, G., 'The Ghost of Christmas Past: Health Effects of Poverty in London in 1896 and 1991', *British Medical Journal*, 321 (2000): 1547–51.

Eamon, M., 'A "Genuine Relationship with the Actual": New Perspectives on Primary Sources, History and the Internet in the Classroom', *The History Teacher* 39/3 (2006): 32. Available online at <http://www.historycooperative.org/journals/ht/39.3/eamon.html>.

Earl, G.P., 'Texture Viewsheds: Spatial Summaries of Built Archaeological Spaces Derived from Global Light Mapping', *Proceedings of the 11th International Conference on Virtual Systems and Multimedia* (Ghent: VSMM, 2005).

Eiteljorg II, H., Fernie, K., Huggett, J. and Robinson, D., *AHDS CAD Guide to Good Practice* (York: AHDS, 2002). Available online at <http://ads.ahds.ac.uk/project/goodguides/cad/>.

Ekirch, A.R., *At Day's Close: Night in Times Past* (New York: W.W. Norton, 2005).

Elmasr, R. and Navathe, S.B., *Fundamentals of Database Systems*, 4th edn (Boston: Pearson, 2004)

Evans, R.J., *In Defence of History* (Granta, 1997).

Evenden, D.N., *Popular Medicine in Seventeenth Century England* (Bowling Green OH: Bowling Green State University Press, 1988).

Exon, S., Gaffney, V., Yorston, P. and Woodward, A., *Stonehenge Landscapes: Journeys through Real-and-Imagined Worlds* (Oxford: Archaeopress, 2001).

Fairclough, G.J., 'The Long Chain: Archaeology, Historical Landscape Characterization and Time Depth in the Landscape', in H. Palang and G. Fry (eds), *Landscape Interfaces: Cultural Heritage in Changing Landscapes* (Dordrecht: Kluwer Academic Publishers, 2003), pp. 295–318.

Fairclough, G.J., Lambrick, G. and Hopkins, D., 'Historic Landscape Characterisation in England and a Hampshire Case Study', in G.J. Fairclough, S. Rippon and D. Bull (eds), *Europe's Cultural Landscape: Archaeologists and the Management of Change*, Europae Archaeologie Consilium Occasional Paper 2 (Brussels: EAC, 2002).

Fairclough, G.J., Lambrick, G. and McNab, A., *Yesterday's World, Tomorrow's Landscape – The English Heritage Historic Landscape Project 1992–94* (English Heritage, 1999).

Falkingham, G., 'A Whiter Shade of Grey: A New Approach to Archaeological Grey Literature Using the XML Version of the TEI Guidelines', *Internet Archaeology*, 17 (2005) <http://intarch.ac.uk/journal/issue7/falkingham_index.html>.

Fernie, E. (ed.), *Art History and its Methods: A Critical Anthology* (Phaidon, 1995 and later editions).

Fernie, K. and Richards, J. (eds), *Creating and Using Virtual Reality* (Oxford: Oxbow, 2003).

Finn, M., *The Character of Credit: Personal Debt in English Culture, 1740–1914* (Cambridge: Cambridge University Press, 2003).

Fisher, P.F., 'First Experiments in Viewshed Uncertainty: The Accuracy of the Viewshed Area', *Photogrammetric Engineering and Remote Sensing*, 57 (1991): 1321–7.

Fisher, P.F., 'First Experiments in Viewshed Uncertainty: Simulating Fuzzy Viewsheds', *Photogrammetric Engineering and Remote Sensing*, 58 (1992): 345–52.

Flaherty, W., 'The Great Rebellion in Kent of 1381 illustrated from the Public Records', *Archaeologia Cantiana*, 3 (1890): 71–96.

Fleming, A.,'Phenomenology and the Megaliths of Wales: A Dreaming too Far?', *Oxford Journal of Archaeology*, 18/2 (1999): 119–26.

Frere, S.S., *Principles of Publication in Rescue Archaeology: Report by a Working Party of the Ancient Monuments Board for England* (Committee for Rescue Archaeology, 1975)

Fumerton, P., *Unsettled: The Culture of Mobility and the Working Poor in Early Modern England* (Chicago: Chicago University Press, 2006).

Gaffney, V. and Exon, S., 'From Order to Chaos: Publication, Synthesis, and the Dissemination of Data in a Digital Age', *Internet Archaeology* 6 (1999) <http://intarch.ac.uk/journal/issue6/gaffney_index.html>.

Galbraith, V.H., *Introduction to the Study of History* (C.A. Watts, 1964).

Gerchow, J., 'Gilds and Fourteenth-century Bureaucracy: The Case of 1388–9', *Nottingham Medieval Studies*, 40 (1996): 109–48.

Gill, T., 'Building Semantic Bridges between Museums, Libraries and Archives: The CIDOC Conceptual Reference Model', *First Monday* 9/5 (2004) <http://firstmonday.org/issue9_5/gill/index.html>.

Gillings, M., 'Virtual Archaeologies and the Hyperreal: Or, What Does it Mean to Describe Something as Virtually-Real?', in P. Fisher and D. Unwin (eds), *Virtual Reality in Geography* (Taylor and Francis, 2002), pp. 17–34.

Gillings, M. and Goodrick, G.T., 'Sensuous and Reflexive GIS: Exploring Visualisation and VRML', *Internet Archaeology*, 1 (1996) <http://intarch.ac.uk/journal/issue1/gillings_index.html> (accessed February 2006).

Gillings, M. and Wheatley, D.W., 'Seeing is not Believing: Unresolved Issues in Archaeological Visibility Analysis', in B. Slapsak (ed.), *On the Good Use of Geographic Information Systems in Archaeological Landscape Studies* (COST Action G2: European Union: EUR19708, 2001), pp. 25–36.

Goodchild, M.F., 'The Alexandria Digital Library Project: Review, assessment, and prospects', *D-Lib Magazine*, 10/5 (2004) <http://www.dlib.org>.

Gosden, C., *Social Being and Time* (Oxford: Blackwell, 1994).

Gray, J. and Walford, K., 'One Good Site Deserves Another: Electronic Publishing in Field Archaeology', *Internet Archaeology*, 7 (1999) <http://interach.ac.uk/journal/issue7/gray_index.html>.

Green, C., 'An Experiment in the Creation of a Temporal GIS for Archaeology'. Unpublished MSc thesis, Leicester University (2002). Available online at <http://www.zen26819.zen.co.uk>.

Greenstein, D. (ed.), *Modelling Historical Data* (St Katharinen: Scripta Mercaturae Verlag, 1991).

Greenstein, D. and Burnard, L., 'Speaking with One Voice: Encoding Standards and the Prospects for an Integrated Approach to Computing in History', *Computers and the Humanities*, 29 (1995): 137–48.

Gregory, I.N., *A Place in History: A Guide to Using GIS in Historical Research* (Oxford: Oxbow, 2003).

Gregory, I.N. and Ell, P.S., 'Breaking the Boundaries: Integrating 200 Years of the Census Using GIS', *Journal of the Royal Statistical Society*, Series A, 168 (2005): 419–37.

Gregory, I.N. and Ell, P.S., 'Analysing Spatio-temporal Change Using National Historical GISs: Population Change during and after the Great Irish Famine', *Historical Methods*, 38 (2005): 149–67.

Gregory, I.N. and Ell, P.S., *Historical GIS: Technologies, Methodologies and Scholarship* (Cambridge: Cambridge University Press, 2006).

Gregory, I.N., Kemp, K.K. and Mostern, R., 'Geographic Information and Historical Research: Current Progress and Future Directions', *History and Computing*, 13 (2001): 7–21.

Gruber, T.R.A., 'A Translation Approach to Portable Ontology Specification', *Knowledge Acquisition*, 5/2 (1993): 199–220.

Gurvitch, G., *The Spectrum of Social Time*, trans. M. Korenbaum with P. Bosserman (Dordrecht: D. Reidel, 1964).

Habermas, J., *The Structural Transformation of the Public Sphere*, trans. Thomas Burger (Cambridge, MA: MIT Press, 1991).

Hanawalt, B., 'Violent Death in Fourteenth- and Early Fifteenth-century England', *Comparative Studies in Society and History*, 18 (1976): 297–320.

Hanawalt, B., 'The Voices and Audiences of Social History Records', *Social Science History*, 15 (1991): 159–75.

Hardman, C. and Richards, J.D., 'OASIS: Dealing with a Digital Revolution',in M. Doerr and N. Crofts in M. Doerr and A. Sarris (eds), *CAA2002: The Digital Heritage of Archaeology. Computer Applications and Quantitative Methods in Archaeology, 2002* (Hellenic Ministry of Culture, 2003) pp. 325–8.

Harris, T., 'GIS and Archaeology', in A.K. Knowles (ed.), *Past Time, Past Place: GIS for History* (Redlands, CA: ESRI Press, 2002), pp. 131–43.

Harvey, C. and Press, J., *Databases in Historical Research: Theory, Methods and Application* (Houndmills: Macmillan, 1996).

Harvey, C., Green, E.M. and Corfield, P.J., *The Westminster Historical Database: Voters, Social Structure and Electoral Behaviour* (Bristol: Bristol Academic Press, 1998)

Hawkins, T., Cohen, J. and Debevec, P., 'A Photometric Approach to Digitizing Cultural Artifacts', in *2nd International Symposium on Virtual Reality, Archaeology, and Cultural Heritage (VAST)* (Glyfada; 2001) <http://www.debevec.org/Research/LS2/hawkins_debevec_VAST2001.pdf>.

Hazelton, N.W.J., *Integrating Time, Dynamic Modelling and Geographical Information Systems: Development of Four-dimensional GIS* (Melbourne: Melbourne University Press, 1991).

Heinz, G., *Comparison of Different Methods for Sculpture Recording* (Institute for Spatial Information and Surveying, Fachhochschule, Mainz, n.d.). Available online at: <http://www.i3mainz.fh-mainz.de/publicat/isprs_heinz98/comp-recording.html>.

Herbert, S.,'The Red Notebook of Charles Darwin', *Bulletin of the British Museum (Natural History) Historical Series*, 7/24 (1980): 5–19.

Hey, T., 'Foreword', in Hine, C.M. (ed.), *New Infrastructures for Knowledge Production: Understanding E-science* (Information Science Publishing , 2006), pp. iv–vii.

Hey, T., De Roure, D. and Trefethen, A.E., 'e-Infrastructure and e-Science', in E. Aarts and J.L. Encarnacao (eds), *True Visions* (Berlin: Springer, 2006), pp. 209–28.

Higher Education Funding Council for England, *RAE 2008: Panel Criteria and Working Methods. Panel N* (HEFCE, 2006).

Hill, L.L. and Janee, G., 'The Alexandria Digital Library Project: Metadata Development and Use', in D.I. Hillmann and E.L. Westbrooks (eds), *Metadata in Practice* (Chicago: American Library Association, 2004), pp. 117–38.

Hillier, A.E., 'Redlining in Philadelphia', in A.K. Knowles (ed.), *Past Time, Past Place: GIS for History* (Redlands, CA: ESRI Press, 2002), pp. 79–93.

Hillier, A.E., 'Spatial Analysis of Historical Redlining: A Methodological Exploration', *Journal of Housing Research*, 14 (2003): 137–67.

Hitchcock, T., Shoemaker, R. and Tosh, J., 'Skills and the Structure of the History Curriculum', in Alan Booth and Paul Hyland (eds), *The Practice of University History Teaching* (Manchester: Manchester University Press, 2000), pp. 47–59.

Hodder, I., 'Writing Archaeology: Site Reports in Context', *Antiquity* 63 (1989): 268–74.

Holman, J., Ore, C-E. and Eide, O., 'Documenting two Histories at Once: Digging into Archaeology', in K.F. Ausserer, W. Börner, M. Goriany et al. (eds), *CAA 2003. Enter the Past: The E-way into the four Dimensions of Cultural Heritage*, British Archaeological Reports International Series no. 1227 (Oxford: Archaeopress, 2004), pp. 221–4.

Holtorf, C.J., 'Towards a Chronology of Megaliths: "Understanding Monumental Time and Cultural Memory"', *Journal of European Archaeology*, 4 (1996): 119–52.

Hughes, L., 'Methodologies of Use: Advanced Arts and Humanities Research Methods and e-Science Communities of Practice', *Digital Humanities Quarterly*, forthcoming.

Huitfeldt, C., 'Scholarly Text Processing and Future Markup Systems', *Jahrbuch für Computerphilologie*, 5 (2003): 219–36. Available online at <http://www.computerphilologie.uni-muenchen.de/jg03/huitfeldt.html>.

Hunnisett, R.F., *The Medieval Coroner* (Cambridge: Cambridge University Press, 1961).

Hunnisett, R.F.,'The Reliability of Inquisitions as Historical Evidence', in D.A. Bullough and R.L. Storey (eds), *The Study of Medieval Records: Essays in Honour of Kathleen Major* (Oxford: Oxford University Press, 1971), pp. 206–35.

Hunnisett, R.F., *Editing Records for Publication*, Archive and the User, 4 (British Records Association, 1977).

Ide, N., 'Preparation and Analysis of Linguistic Corpora', in S. Schreibman, R. Siemens and J. Unsworth (eds), *A Companion to Digital Humanities* (Malden, MA, Oxford, UK and Carlton, Australia: Blackwell Publishing, 2004), pp. 289–305.

Inman, J.A. et al. (eds), *Electronic Collaboration in the Humanities: Issues and Options* (Mahwah, NJ: Lawrence Erlbaum Associates, 2004)

Jeffrey, S., *Three Dimensional Modelling of Scottish Early Medieval Sculpted Stones*, PhD thesis (University of Glasgow, 2003). Available online at: <http://ads.ahds.ac.uk/catalogue/collections/blurbs/387.cfm>

Jenkins, K., *Re-thinking History* (Routledge, 1991);

Jenkins, K. (ed.), *The Postmodern History Reader* (Routledge, 1997).

Jessop, M., 'Computing or Humanities?' *Ubiquity*, 5/41 (2004): 1.

Johnston, A.F. and Rogerson, M. (eds), *Records of Early English Drama: York*, 2 vols (Toronto: University of Toronto Press, 1979), pp. 48–50.

Jones, A.H., *Wealth of a Nation To Be* (New York: Columbia University Press, 1980).

Jones, S., MacSween, A., Jeffrey, S. et al., 'From the Ground Up. The Publication of Archaeological Reports: A User-needs Survey. A Summary', *Internet Archaeology* 14 (2003). Available online at <http://interarch.ac.uk/journal/issue14/puns_index.html>.

Karkov, C.E. and Orton, F. (eds), *Theorizing Anglo-Saxon Stone Sculpture*, Medieval European Studies IV (Morgantown: West Virginia University Press, 2003).

Katz, S.N., 'Why Technology Matters: The Humanities in the 21st Century', *Interdisciplinary Science Reviews*, 30/2 (2005): 105–18.

Kay, M., *XSLT Programmer's Reference*, 2d edn (Birmingham: Wrox, 2001).

Kelle, U., Prein, G. and Bird, K., *Computer-aided Qualitative Data Analysis: Theory, Methods and Practice* (Sage, 1995).

Kennedy, L. Ell, P.S. Crawford, E.M. and Clarkson, L.A., *Mapping the Great Irish Famine: An Atlas of the Famine Years* (Dublin: Four Courts Press, 1999).

Kenny, J. and Richards, J.D., 'Pathways to a Shared European Information Infrastructure for Cultural Heritage', *Internet Archaeology*, 18 (2005) s 4.2 <http://intarch.ac.uk/journal/issue18/kenny_index.html>, accessed 24 August 2007.

Kiernan, K.S., 'The State of the Beowulf Manuscript 1882–1983', *Anglo-Saxon England*, 13 (1984) 23–42.

Kilbride, W., 'The Danube in Prehistory in the Digital Age: Towards a Common Information Environment for European Archaeology', *Archeologia e Calcolatori*, 15 (2004): 129–44.

Kintigh, K., *The Promise and Challenge of Archaeological Data Integration. Final Report of the Workshop, Santa Barbara, California.* Unpublished report (2005).

Knowles, A.K. (ed.), *Past Time, Past Place: GIS for History* (Redlands, CA: ESRI Press, 2002).

Kurlansky, M., *Cod: A Biography of the Fish That Changed the World* (Vintage, 1999).

Kurlansky, M., *Salt: A World History* (Vintage, 2003).

Langran, G., *Time in Geographic Information Systems* (Taylor and Francis, 1992).

Langton, J., 'Systems Approach to Change in Human Geography', Progress in Geography, 4 (1972: 123–78.

Laqueur, T., 'Bodies, Details, and the Humanitarian Narrative', in L. Hunt (ed.), *The New Cultural History* (Berkeley, CA: University of California Press, 1989), pp. 176–204.

Lee, E., *MIDAS: A Manual and Data Standard for Monument Inventories*, 3rd edn (Swindon: English Heritage, 2003).

Llobera, M., 'Extending GIS-based Visual Analysis: The Concept of Visualscapes', *International Journal of Geographical Information Science*, 17 (2003): 25–48.

Lock, G. (ed.), *Beyond the Map: Archaeology and Spatial Technologies* (Amsterdam: IOS Press, 2000).

McGuinness, D.L. and Noy, N.F., 'Ontology Development 101: A Guide to Creating your First Ontology', in *Stanford Knowledge Systems Laboratory Technical Report KSL-01-05* (Stanford, 2001).

Massey, D., 'Space-time, "Science" and the Relationship between Physical Geography and Human Geography', *Transactions of the Institute of British Geographers* 24 ns (1999): 261–76.

Massey, D., *For Space* (Sage, 2005).

Meckseper, C. and Warwick, C., 'The Publication of Archaeological Excavation Reports Using XML', *Literary and Linguistic Computing*, 18/1 (2003): 63–75.

Meredith, P., 'The *Ordo paginarum* and the Development of the York Tilemakers' Pageant', *Leeds Studies in English*, 11ns (1980): 59–73.

Miles, M.B. and Huberman, M., *Qualitative Data Analysis. An Expanded Sourcebook* (Sage, 1994).

Miller, A.P., 'Metadata for the Masses: What is It, How Can it Help Me, and How Can I Use It?', *Ariadne*, 5 (1996). Available online at <http://www.ukoln.ac.uk/ariadne/issue5/metadata-masses/>.

Miller, A.P., 'The Importance of Metadata in Archaeology', in L. Dingwall, S. Exxon, Gaffney, V., Laflin, S. and Van Leusen, M. (eds), *CAA97: Archaeology in the Age of the Internet: Computer Applications and Quantitative Methods in Archaeology*, British Archaeological Reports, International Series S750 (Oxford: Tempus Reparatum, 1999), p. 136.

Miller, A.P., and Greenstein, D. (eds), *Discovering Online Resources: A Practical Implementation of Dublin Core* (Bath: UKOLN/AHDS, 1997).

Mitakos, T. et al., 'Representing Time-dependent Information in Multidimensional XML', in Kalpic, D. and V.H. Dobric (eds), *Proceedings of the 23rd International Conference on Information Technology Interfaces, Pula, Croatia, June 19-22, 2001* (Heraklion: SKEL Publications, 2001), pp. 111–16.

Neale, K., 'Frederick G. Emmison: Archivist and Scholar', in Kenneth Neale (ed.), *An Essex Tribute: Essays Presented to Frederick G. Emmison as a Tribute to his Life and Work for Essex History and Archives* (Leopard's Head Press, 1987), pp. 1–10.

Newton-Smith, W.H., 'Space, Time and Space-time: A Philosopher's View', in R. Flood and M. Lockwood (eds), *The Nature of Time* (Oxford: Basil Blackwell, 1986): 22–35.

Orren, K. and Skowronek, S., *The Search for American Political Development* (Cambridge: Cambridge University Press, 2004).

Overton, M., 'Computer Analysis of an Inconsistent Data Source: The Case of Probate Inventories', *Journal of Historical Geography*, 3 (1977): 317–26.

Overton, M. et al., *Production and Consumption in English Households, 1600–1750* (Routledge, 2004).

Owen, G.D. (ed.), *Talbot, Dudley & Devereux Papers: 1533–1659*, Calendar of the Mss of the Most Honourable the Marquess of Bath, Preserved at Longleat (HMSO, 1980).

The Paper Museum of Cassiano dal Pozzo: A Catalogue Raisonné (London : Royal Collection in association with H. Miller, 2004).

Parkes, M.B., *English Cursive Book Hands 1250–1500* (Oxford: Clarendon Press, 1969).

Pearson, A.W. and Collier, P., 'The Integration and Analysis of Historical and Environmental Data Using a Geographical Information System: Landownership and Agricultural Productivity in Pembrokeshire c. 1850', Agricultural History Review 46 (1998): 162–76.

Pearson, A.W. and Collier, P., 'Agricultural History with GIS', in A.K. Knowles (ed.), Past Time, Past Place: GIS for History (Redlands, CA: ESRI Press, 2002), pp. 105–16.

Peuquet, D.J., 'It's About Time: A Conceptual Framework for the Representation of Temporal Dynamics in Geographic Information Systems', *Annals of the Association of American Geographers* 84 (1994): 441–61

Peterson, K.A., 'Standards Related to Digital Imagining of Pictorial Materials' (Print and Photography Division of the Library of Congress, 2004). Available online at <http://www.loc.gov/rr/print/tp/DigitizationStandardsPictorial.pdf>.

Petrie, W.M.F., *Methods and Aims in Archaeology* (Macmillan, 1904).

Pitt-Rivers, A.L-F., *Excavations in Cranbourne Chase*, 4 vols (privately printed, 1887–9).

Pollini, J., Swartz, L., Kensek, D.K. and Cipolla, N., 'Problematics of Making Ambiguity Explicit in Virtual Reconstructions: A Case Study of the Mausoleum of Augustus', in *Theory and Practice. Proceedings of the 21st Annual Conference of CHArt*, vol. 8, British Academy, 10–11 November 2005. Available online at: <http://www.chart.ac.uk/chart2005/papers/index.html>

Porter, R., *The Greatest Benefit to Mankind: A Medical History of Humanity* (HarperCollins, 1997), chs 6 and 7.

Potter, S., Kalfoglou, Y., Alani, H. et al., *The Application of Advanced Knowledge Technologies for Emergency Response*, in 4th International Information Systems for Crisis Response and Management (ISCRAM 07) (Delft, 2007).

Prescott, A.J., 'The Judicial Records of the Rising of 1381'. Unpublished Ph.D. thesis, University of London (1984).

Prescott, A.J., 'Writing about Rebellion: Using the Records of the Peasants' Revolt of 1381', *History Workshop Journal*, 45 (1998): 1–27.

Prescott, A.J., '"The Hand of God"': The Suppression of the Peasants' Revolt of 1381', in N. Morgan (ed.), *Prophecy, Apocalypse and the Day of Doom*, Harlaxton Medieval Studies, 12 (Donington: Shaun Tyas, 2004), pp. 317–41.

Putnam, H., *Reason, Truth and History* (Cambridge: Cambridge University Press, 1981).

Raine, Angelo (ed.), *York Civic Records, Vol III*, Yorkshire Archaeological Record Series 106 (1942).

Ray, B.C., 'Teaching the Salem Witchcraft Trials', in A.K. Knowles (ed.), *Past Time, Past Place: GIS for History* (Redlands, CA: ESRI Press, 2002), pp. 19–33.

Reilly, P., 'Towards a Virtual Archaeology', in K. Lockyear and S. Rahtz (eds), *Computer Applications and Quantitative Methods in Archaeology 1990*, BAR International Series 565 (Oxford: Archaeopress, 1991), pp. 133–40.

Reilly, P., 'Three-dimensional Modelling and Primary Archaeological Data', in P. Reilly and S. Rahtz (eds), *Archaeology and the Information Age* (Routledge, 1992).

Renear, A., Mylonas, E., and Durand, D., 'Refining Our Notion of What Text Really Is: The Problem of Overlapping Hierarchies', in S. Hockey and N. Ide (eds), *Research in Humanities Computing*, vol. 4 (Oxford: Clarendon Press, 1996), pp. 263–77.

Richards, J.D., 'Standardising the Record', in M.A. Cooper and J.D. Richards (eds), *Current Issues in Archaeological Computing*, British Archaeological Reports International Series, no. 271 (Oxford, 1985), pp. 93–112.

Richards, J.D., 'Digital Preservation and Access', *European Journal of Archaeology*, 5 (2002): 343–66.

Richards, J.D., 'Archaeology, e-publication and the Semantic Web', *Antiquity* 80 (2006): 970–79.

Richards, J.D., 'Electronic Publication in Archaeology', in P. Daly and T.L. Evans (eds), *Digital Archaeology: Bridging Method and Theory* (Routledge, 2006), pp. 213–25.

Richards, J.D. and Robinson, D.J., *Digital Archives from Excavations and Fieldwork: A Guide to Good Practice* (York: Archaeology Data Service and Oxbow Books, 2000).

Robinson, P., 'Where We Are with Electronic Scholarly Editions, and Where We Want to Be', *Jahrbuch für Computerphilologie*, 5 (2003): 125–46.

Robinson, P., 'Current Issues in Making Digital Editions of Medieval Texts – or, do Electronic Scholarly Editions have a Future?', *Digital Medievalist*, I:I (2005). Available online at <http://www.digitalmedievalist.org/article.cfm?RecID=6>.

Rockwell, G., 'Multimedia, is it a Discipline? The Liberal and Servile Arts in Humanities Computing' (Munich, 2002). Available online at <http://computerphilologie.uni-muenchen.de/jg02/rockwell.html#fn15>.

Ross, S., 'Designing a Tool for Research in Disciplines Using Multimedia Data: The Romanesque Sculpture Processor', in F. Bocchi and P. Denley (eds), *Storia e multimedia*, proceedings of the Seventh International Congress of the Association for History and Computing (Bologna: Manchester University Press, 1994), pp. 629–35.

Ross, S., 'Position Paper', in *Towards a Semantic Web for Heritage Resources*, DigiCULT Thematic 3 (2003), pp. 7–11. Also available at <http://digicult.info/downloads/ti3_high.pdf>.

Sack, R.D., 'A Concept of Physical Space in Geography', *Geographical Analysis*, 5 (1973): 16–34.

Sack, R.D, 'Chronology and Spatial Analysis', *Annals of the Association of American Geographers*, 64 (1974): 439–52.

Schmidt, A., *Geophysical Data in Archaeology: A Guide to Good Practice* (York: Archaelogy Data Service and Oxbow Books, 2002).

Schofield, J. and Tyers, P., 'Towards a Computerised Archaeological Research Archive', in M.A. Cooper and J.D. Richards (eds), *Current Issues in Archaeological Computing*, British Archaeological Reports International Series, no. 271 (Oxford, 1985), pp. 5–16.

Scollar, I., 'Geodetic and Cartographic Problems in Archaeological Data Bases at and within the Boundaries of some Countries', in S. Rahtz and J.D. Richards (eds), *Computer Applications and Quantitative Methods in Archaeology*, British Archaeological Reports, International Series S548 (Oxford, 1989), pp. 251–73.

Segre, C., *Avviamento all'analisi del testo letterario* (Torino, Einaudi, 1985); Engl. edn, *Introduction to the Analysis of the Literary Text*, trans. J. Meddemmen (Bloomington, IN, Indiana University Press, 1988).

Serota, N., *Experience or Interpretation; the Dilemma of Museums of Modern Art* (Thames and Hudson, 1996).

Shadbolt, N.and O'Hara, K., *Advanced Knowledge Technologies: Selected Papers* (Southampton: University of Southampton Department of Electronics and Computer Science, 2004).

Shammas, C., *The Pre-Industrial Consumer in England and America* (Oxford: Clarendon Press, 1990).

Shanks, M. and Tilley, C., *Social Theory and Archaeology* (Oxford: Polity Press, 1987).

Smith, D.M., Crane, G. and Rydberg-Cox, J., 'The Perseus Project: A Digital Library for the Humanities', *Literary and Linguistic Computing*, 15 (2000): 15–25.

Snow, D.R., Gahegan, M., Giles, C.L. et al., 'Cybertools and Archaeology', *Science* 311 (2006): 958–9.

Spaeth, D.A., 'Representing Text as Data: The Analysis of Historical Sources in XML', *Historical Methods*, 37 (2004): 73–85.

Sperberg-McQueen, C.M. and Burnard, L. (eds), *TEI P4: Guidelines for Electronic Text Encoding and Interchange [XML Version]* (Oxford: Text Encoding Initiative Consortium, 2002). Available online at: <http://www.tei-c.org/release/doc/tei-p4-doc/html/>.

Sperberg-McQueen, C.M. and Huitfeldt, C., 'GODDAG: A Data Structure for Overlapping Hierarchies', in P. King and E.V. Munson (eds), *DDEP-PODDP 2000*, Lecture Notes in Computer Science 2023 (Berlin: Springer, 2004), pp. 139–60.

Spicer, D., 'Computer Graphics and the Perception of Archaeological Information: Lies, Damned Statistics and … Graphics!', in C.L.N. Ruggles and S.P.Q. Rahtz (eds), *Computer Applications and Quantitative Methods in Archaeology 1987*, BAR International Series 393 (Oxford: Archaeopress, 1988), pp. 187–200.

Stevens, M. and Dorrell (Rogerson), M., 'The *Ordo Paginarium* [sic] Gathering of the York A/Y Memorandum Book', *Modern Philology*, 72 (1974–5): 45–59.

Stine, J., 'Opening Closets: The Discovery of Household Medicine in Early Modern England'. Unpublished PhD thesis, Stanford University, California (1996).

Stratford, D., '"Archaeosynthesis" and Thera Frescoes: Solving the Restoration Dilemma, *Apollo*, 138/377 (1993), 13

Studer, R., Benjamins, V.R. and Fensel, D., 'Knowledge Engineering: Principles and Methods', in *IEEE Transactions on Data and Knowledge Engineering* 25, 1/2 (1998): 161–97.

Studies in the Public Records (Thomas Nelson, 1948).

Thaller, M., 'A Draft Proposal for the Coding of Machine Readable Sources', *Historical Social Research/Historische Sozialforschung*, 40/3 (1986): 3–46.

Thaller, M., 'The Historical Workstation Project', *Computers and the Humanities*, 25 (1991): 149–62.

Thaller, Manfred, 'Text as a Data Type', paper presented at ALLC-ACH 1996, available at: <http://gandalf.aksis.uib.no/allc-ach96/Panels/Thaller/thaller2.html>.

Thaller, Manfred, 'From Digitized to the Digital Library', *D-Lib Magazine*, 7/2 (February 2001). Available online at <http://www.dlib.org/dlib/february01/thaller/02thaller.html>.

Thomas, J., *Understanding the Neolithic* (Routledge, 1999).

Thompson, E.P., *The Making of the English Working Class* (Gollanz, 1963).

Tosh, J., *The Pursuit of History*, 3rd edn (Longman, 2000).

Toulmin Smith, L., *York Plays: The Plays Performed by the Crafts or Mysteries of York on the Day of Corpus Christi in the 14th, 15th, and 16th Centuries …* (Oxford: Clarendon Press, 1885).

Twycross, M., 'Forget the 4.30 a.m. Start: Recovering a Palimpsest in the York *Ordo paginarum*', *Medieval English Theatre*, 25 (2005 for 2003): 98–152.

Twycross, M., 'The *Ordo paginarum* Revisited, with a Digital Camera', in D. Klausner and K. Sawyer Marsalek (eds), *'Bring furth the pagants': Studies in Early English Drama Presented to Alexandra F. Johnston* (Toronto: University of Toronto Press, 2007), pp. 105–31.

Unsworth, J., 'Tool-time, or "Haven't We Been Here Already?" Ten Years in Humanities Computing', paper presented at Transforming Disciplines: The Humanities and Computer Science', January (2003) <http://www3.isrl.uiuc.edu/~unsworth/carnegie-ninch.03.html>.

W3C, 'XSL Transformations (XSLT) Version 1.0: W3C Recommendation 16 November 1999'.

W3C, 'XML Path Language (XPath) Version 1.0: W3C Recommendation 16 November 1999', <http://www.w3.org/>.

W3C, 'xml:id Version 1.0: W3C Recommendation 9 September 2005', <http://www.w3.org/TR/xml-id/>.

W3C, 'XQuery 1.0: An XML Query Language: W3C Candidate Recommendation 3 November 2005', <http://www.w3.org/>.

W3C, 'XQuery Update Facility, W3C Working Draft, 8 May 2006', <http://www.w3.org/TR/xqupdate/>.

Wachowicz, M., *Object-Orientated Design for Temporal GIS* (Taylor and Francis, 1999).

Weatherill, L., *Consumer Behaviour and Material Culture, 1660–1760* (Routledge, 1988).

Wescott, K.L. and Brandon, R.J. (eds), *Practical Applications of GIS for Archaeologists: A Predictive Modeling Toolkit* (Taylor and Francis, 2000).

Wheatley, D., 'Cumulative Viewshed Analysis: A GIS-based Method for Investigating Intervisibility and Its Archaeological Application', in G. Lock and Z. Stancic (eds), *Archaeology and Geographic Information Systems: A European Perspective* (Taylor and Francis, 1995), pp. 171–86.

Wheatley, D. and Gillings, M., *Spatial Technology and Archaeology: The Archaeological Applications of GIS* (Taylor and Francis, 2002).

Wise, A. and Miller, P., 'Why Metadata Matters in Archaeology', *Internet Archaeology*, 2 (1997): s 8.1. Available online at <http://intarch.ac.uk/journal/issue2/wise_index.html>.

Woods, R.I. and Shelton, N., *An Atlas of Victorian Mortality* (Liverpool: Liverpool University Press, 1997).

Index

DH

907.
2
SEM